Christianity in the Modern World

Also by Ambrose Mong:

Accomodation and Acceptance:
An Exploration of Interfaith Relations (2015)

A Better World is Possible:
An Exploration of Western and Eastern
Utopian Visions (2018)

Dialogue Derailed:
Joseph Ratzinger's War against Pluralist Theology (2017)

Guns and Sospel:
Imperialism and Evangelism in China (2016)

Purification of Memory:
A Study of Modern Orthodox Theologians
from a Catholic Perspective (2015)

Sino-Vatican Relations:
From Denunication to Dialogue (2019)

A Tale of Two Theologians:
Treatment of Third World Theologies (2017)

Christianity in the Modern World

A Study of Religion in a Pluralistic Society

Ambrose Mong

James Clarke & Co

James Clarke & Co

P.O. Box 60
Cambridge
CB1 2NT
United Kingdom

www.jamesclarke.co
publishing@jamesclarke.co

Paperback ISBN: 978 0 227 17762 4
PDF ISBN: 978 0 227 17763 1
ePub ISBN: 978 0 227 17764 8

British Library Cataloguing in Publication Data
A record is available from the British Library

First Published by James Clarke and Co., 2022

Copyright © Ambrose Mong, 2022

All rights reserved. No part of this edition may be reproduced, stored electronically or in any retrieval system, or transmitted in any form or by any means, electronic, mechanical, photocopying, recording, or otherwise, without prior written permission from the Publisher (permissions@jamesclarke.co).

*For Vivencio Gregorio G. Atutubo III,
Gerard Lee How Cheng and Tim Mulroy SSC*

I didn't go to religion to make me happy. I always knew a bottle of Port would do that. If you want a religion to make you feel really comfortable, I certainly don't recommend Christianity.

C.S. Lewis

Contents

Foreword ix

Preface and Acknowledgements xiii

Introduction 1

Chapter 1   Monotheism and Polytheism   7

Chapter 2   Dialectic of Tolerance   29

Chapter 3   Idiosyncrasies of Syncretism   53

Chapter 4   Sociological Perspective   75

Chapter 5   Challenge of Secularism   101

Chapter 6   Challenge of Religious Pluralism   129

Chapter 7   Global Ethic   153

Epilogue   181

Bibliography   185

Index   197

Foreword

I am happy to welcome the book *Christianity in the Modern World* by Ambrose Mong as a contribution to a serious reflection on the experience of being a Christian in the modern world, in which the pluralism of religions is a living experience. The book is obviously written from a Christian perspective, as the title indicates. More particularly, Mong is inspired by a well-known German theologian, Hans Küng, though he is also familiar with all the important authors who have discussed these issues, particularly in Europe. At the same time, it is not a book of Christian theology, but more a social scientific reflection on the author's Christian identity and relationships, while living in a multi-religious society. This book will therefore interest members of other religions in a context of dialogue.

Thanks to migrations, the world today is multi-religious, though one or other religion may dominate in particular regions, like Confucianism and Taoism in China, Buddhism in East Asia, Hinduism in India, Islam in the Middle East and Christianity in Asia, Europe and the Americas. Among the major religions, Buddhism, Christianity and Islam have been missionary, propagating and establishing themselves in many places. Christianity, in particular, has spread across the world, due partly to European colonization. In earlier periods it propagated itself rather aggressively but in recent years, particularly in the post-colonial era, when communities are becoming multi-religious, it is more open to dialogue and living together with other religions. Such an experience throws up many problems and questions, and Mong discusses several of them. His approach is not strictly theological, but rather sociological, exploring questions that arise in such situations like monotheism and polytheism, tolerance, syncretism, secularism, pluralism, globalization, and others. The question is, how does one live in a religiously pluralistic situation? Mong offers us a teaching and a learning tool, with a clear presentation of the themes, giving us questions for discussion at the end of each chapter. A vast amount of careful and critical reading, in the context of his own faith as a Christian, is obviously evident. He must have also worked with groups reflecting on his lectures.

Christianity claims to be strictly monotheist and condemns, for example, the Indian and other tribal and popular religions as polytheist. Yet the Christian God is Trinitarian. We do pray to the Father, the Son (Jesus Christ) and the Holy Spirit. As a matter of fact the author says that the Trinity, in some way, reconciles the one and the many. There are also a vast army of Saints who easily acquire a divine status especially in popular religiosity. In South India, where I come from, Mother Mary and saints like Antony (of Padua) are honoured and prayed to more than God. The author suggests that monotheism tends to become totalitarian. A converse problem in popular religiosity, including Christianity, is syncretism, in which people mix symbols that have similar meanings from various sources. The orthodox believers have a negative view of syncretism, which is seen as an indiscriminate mixing of perspectives and meanings. Our author, however, equates it to what is normally called inculturation. I think that it can be seen more as inter-culturation. Syncretism may be seen as a mixture of cultures in which people live, especially at a moment of cultural interaction and transition, before a new composite culture emerges.

The chapter on 'Sociological Perspective' presents to us the views on religion of European scholars Marx, Engels, Durkheim and Weber. They represent different perspectives, relating sociology and philosophy, being perhaps more philosophical than sociological. In the next chapter, the author brings out the difference between secularization and secularism. While secularization is a philosophical process that empties religion of its transcendence, secularism is a socio-political process that seeks to separate religion from politics in public life. It is not negative towards religion, but rather respects the freedom of religions at their own level, provided they do not become political forces.

It is a fact that Asia has given birth to all the great world religions. Christianity and Islam were born in West Asia, Hinduism and Buddhism in India, Confucianism and Taoism in China. Because of colonialism and migrations the whole world today has an experience of religious pluralism, though one or other religion may be dominant in a particular area. Besides these meta-cosmic religions there are a lot of tribal/popular religions. A society that claims political secularism may not achieve inter-religious harmony at the religious level, though there may be a certain tolerance. While invoking the usual paradigm of 'exclusivism, inclusivism and pluralism' in the study of religions, the author opts for pluralism. But, in practice, religious fundamentalism and communalism are not absent and can be sources of conflict. Fundamentalism is a religious attitude which claims that one's own religion is the only true one. Communalism rather asserts that people who share a particular religion also share the same economic and political interests. It is communalism, rather than fundamentalism, that leads to active social and even political conflicts, but which are given a religious colour to encourage commitment to the struggle. The author indicates that, among the recent Popes, St. John Paul II was more inclusivist, while Pope Benedict XVI was rather exclusivist, as expressed in the document *Dominus Iesus* (the Lord Jesus).

Meanwhile, Pope Francis has shown himself a pluralist. In a document on *Human Fraternity for World Peace and Living Together* signed jointly by him and the Grand Imam Al-Azhar Ahamad al-Tayyib in Abu-Dhabi on 4 February 2019, they say:

> Freedom is a right of every person: each individual enjoys the freedom of belief, thought, expression and action. The pluralism and the diversity of religions, colour, sex, race and language are willed by God in His wisdom, through which He created human beings. This divine wisdom is the source from which the right to freedom of belief and the freedom to be different derives. Therefore, the fact that people are forced to adhere to a certain religion or culture must be rejected, as too the imposition of a cultural way of life that others do not accept.

Pope Francis refers to and reaffirms this perspective in his encyclical *Fratelli Tutti* (Sisters and Brothers All: Nos. 271-284). At the end of this letter, the Pope quotes the appeal that he and the Grand Imam had made in *Human Fraternity*. I shall give here just a few quotes from that appeal.

> In the name of God, who has created all human beings equal in rights, duties and dignity, and who has called them to live together as brothers and sisters, to fill the earth and make known the values of goodness, love and peace

> In the name of the poor, the destitute, the marginalized and those most in need, whom God has commanded us to help as a duty required of all persons …

In the name of *human fraternity,* that embraces all human beings, unites them and renders them equal

In the name of God ... we declare the adoption of a culture of dialogue as the path; mutual cooperation as the code of conduct; reciprocal understanding as the method and standard. (No. 285)

    I am sure that our author would agree with this perspective. In his final chapter, he suggests the possibility of developing a global ethic, following the reflections of Hans Küng.

    I appreciate and congratulate Ambrose Mong for his achievement in giving us a very useful and clear manual for a dialogue between Christianity and the modern world with its many religions. A second volume that explores the resources of other Asian religions like Buddhism, Confucianism, Taoism, Islam and Hinduism for promoting harmony would be welcome, not ignoring the more popular religious traditions also present and active in Asia, so that the dialogue that he suggests could be carried on and prove more practical and fruitful for the peoples of Asia, reaching out to the grass roots. The present book's final sentence states that 'Christianity is here to stay' in Asia, while it may be losing steam in the West. So much the more reason that it should become more and truly Asian!

Michael Amaladoss, S.J.
Institute of Dialogue with
Cultures and Religions,
Loyola College, India.

Preface and Acknowledgements

The demise on 6 April 2021 of Hans Küng, one of the last few surviving *periti* (experts) who attended Vatican II (1962–65), marks the passing of a great theologian who spent decades making Christianity more meaningful and relevant to a broad range of people. In spite of his criticism of the ecclesiastical authorities, Küng loved the Catholic Church and remained a priest of good standing. More than a critic of the Church, he was a person who wanted to renew and reform it. A scholar who was always ready to discuss and debate, Küng knew how to write and communicate religion in a way that was accessible to non-Christians and to those who had left the Church. Above all, he was a pioneer in ecumenism and interreligious dialogue.

Stripped by church authorities in 1979 of his right to teach as a Catholic theologian, Küng understood suffering and rejection, yet he never failed to stand up for his convictions. He was committed as a theologian to communicate the gospel values, not just to Christians alone, but to all people of goodwill. Dialogue about religion to formulate a global ethic was of great concern to Küng. Guided by the spirit of Vatican II, in his theological vision, he envisioned a Church that would be involved with the realities of life and the world as it is.

Bishop Felix Gmür of Basel once said, 'That is why he [Küng] dealt with the Church as it is. He did the same with me, his bishop. He loved, and because he loved, he demanded. That could sometimes also be exhausting. This was experienced by some with whom he did not hold back with criticism, especially the popes.'[1] In spite of his struggles, Küng stood by the papacy because he was a lover of the Church.

[1.] Cindy Wooden, 'Bishops recall Fr. Hans Küng as theologian who loved Catholic Church', *National Catholic Reporter*, https://www.ncronline.org/news/people/bishops-recall-fr-hans-k-ng-theologian-who-loved-catholic-church.

Since the 1980s, I have been reading Hans Küng's writings and following the theological trail he blazed. In this work, I have attempted to incorporate Küng's ideas and his spirit of openness to both the spiritual and secular thoughts of non-Christians and non-believers. Many people have assisted me in the writing of this book. I would like especially to mention Kenzie Lau, an educationist and a humanist, who not only proofread and edited the text, but also suggested the questions at the end of each chapter. Special thanks are offered also to Bro. Patrick Tierney FSC, Sister Mary Gillis CND, Francis Chin, and Ellen McGill for their editorial assistance.

I remain indebted to the following who have encouraged and supported me in my writing endeavours all these years: Lai Pan-Chiu, Peter Phan, Wendy Wu, Denis Chang, George Yeo, Teresa Au, Ronnie Enguillo, May Koon, Garrison Qian, Josephine Chan, William Chan, Charles Chu, Juliana Jie, K.S. Goh, Esther Chu, Philip Lee, John Tan, George Tan, Emmanuel Dispo, Mark Lam, Jolene Otremba, Mindy Tagliente, and Anthony Tan. Thanks to the Parish Priest of St Andrew's Church, Rev. Jacob Kwok and my colleagues, Rev. Mitch Reginio CICM and Rev. Joseph Fung for their friendship and guidance.

Last but not least, I am very grateful to Professor Leo Lefebure for reading the text, pointing out my mistakes and giving suggestions for revisions and improvements.

Special thanks to Adrian Brink, the managing director, Samuel Fitzgerald, the assistant editor, Debora Nicosia, the production editor, and the dedicated staff at James Clarke & Co. for bringing this modest work into print. Any errors that remain are, of course, my own.

Ambrose Mong
St Andrew's Church
Tseung Kwan O, Hong Kong
Trinity Sunday
30 May 2021

Introduction

Influenced by the theory of evolution and organic growth, English theologian and poet John Henry Newman (1801–90) was forced to rethink his concept of the Church and his understanding of history. The result of this reflection was his *Essay on the Development of Christian Doctrine*, a work wherein Newman supports an organic evolutionary theory of doctrinal development. Further, Newman deliberates Christianity's ability to assimilate ideas and practices from other religious traditions without sacrificing pre-existing truths and goodness. He believes that all religious systems possess some universal subject matter, i.e. the human search for truth and enlightenment. Christianity was influenced by the philosophies of the Greek and Roman world, which asked the same questions and advocated many of the same truths. Christianity, because of its continuity and the firmness of its principles, has succeeded in assimilating ideas that other religions find incompatible with their own traditions.

Like many other world religions, Christianity is not static, but subject to continuous change, according to certain forces within human society and the needs of its believers. The Christian religion evolves in progressive stages, manifesting the life of God in humanity. In short, Christianity is an evolutionary faith. The religious life proceeds in sequences, from simple to more complex and higher forms, in its institutions, spiritual life, doctrines, and practices. It manifests God in history and, in the person of Jesus Christ, has made and continues to make a deep and far-reaching impact on the moral life of humanity in the past, the present and the future.

Viewing religion as essentially historical and God as the self-unfolding *absolute spirit* and the object of philosophical inquiry, the German philosopher G.W. Hegel (1770–1831) was able to integrate his transcendental philosophy with the emergence of social, political, and legal institutions. Hegel defined religion as 'the standpoint of the consciousness of the true ... of the universal, of the absolutely self-determining true that has being in and for itself'.[2] He held that the most important element in religion is the doctrine and its concern for the truth, and not any subjective and irrational feeling or experience. The truth of religion depends on how it can change human beings' moral or ethical behaviour for the better. For Hegel, Christianity is closest to the absolute truth. Unfortunately, he had no interest in non-Christian faiths. In spite of this missing piece, his stress on the *Geist*, the Spirit, which develops in the course of history, is insightful and universal. We have witnessed how the spirit of Christianity has transformed the West's social, political and legal institutions.

Another significant contribution of Hegel was his dialectical method, which had a great influence on Karl Marx. Dialectic is a method of philosophical debate which involves presenting contradictory positions between opposites: back-and-forth dialogue. Hegelian dialectic is an interpretive method that relates specific entities to an absolute idea; a thesis is proposed followed by an anti-thesis (contrary position) and reconciled at a higher level of truth known as a synthesis.[3]

Hegel's dialectical method consists of three moments that can be applied to any concept or anything that is true in general. The first moment of this dialectical method is 'understanding' and 'the moment of fixity, in which concepts or forms have a seemingly stable definition or determination'. The second is the moment of 'instability', 'a one-sidedness or restrictedness', which is the antithesis of the first moment, known as the *sublate,* cancelling, negating, and preserving at the same time. The third moment is 'speculative' or 'positively rational'. Once we grasp the unity of the two opposites, i.e. the first and second moment, we arrive at the third moment with a positive result. Hegel's dialectic does not require new ideas to show up. The nature of the earlier determinations drives the movement from one to another and thus 'comes to its own accord'. For Hegel, this movement

---

[2] G.W. Hegel, *Lectures on the Philosophy of Religion, 1: Introduction and the Concept of Religion*, edited by Peter C. Hodgson (Oxford: Clarendon Press, 2007), 205. See also Clement Wayne Hudson, 'The Enlightenment Critique of "Religion",' *Australian E-Journal of Theology* 5, no. 1 (2005): pp. 1–12.

[3] Stanford Encyclopedia of Philosophy, 'Hegel's Dialectics', https://plato.stanford.edu/entries/hegel-dialectics/#HegeDescHisDialMeth.

Introduction

is driven by necessity or 'logic', which is the hallmark of Western thought.[4] It is within this dialectical framework that I have composed the following chapters.

This book was conceived as a textbook or reference for undergraduate students in religious studies, seminarians in preparation for the priesthood, or any reader interested in deeper reflection. Hence I have added questions for discussion at the end of each chapter. Topics such as religious commitment and tolerance, attitude towards other religions, sociological aspects of religion, interreligious dialogue, syncretism, and dual religious citizenship, are examined critically.

This text first deals with the relationship between monotheistic and polytheistic beliefs, identifying their functions and philosophical backgrounds. In the course of exploring the history of the Church, this review also examines the dialectic tension between tolerance and intolerance. Generally speaking, we are more prone to be intolerant when we are the majority. The discourse also attempts to present a more comprehensive view of syncretism from a historical context and its translation into multiple religious traditions in Asian societies. This is followed by a chapter deliberating religion from a sociological perspective, focusing on the works of Marx, Engels, Durkheim, and Weber.

An important topic regarding the future of religion is secularism. Here, we focus on the dialogue between Jürgen Habermas and Joseph Ratzinger in *The Dialectics of Secularization*. Related to secularism is the rise of religious pluralism, where non-Christian religions flourish. In the West, Eastern philosophies such as Confucianism, Taoism, and Buddhism seem to be enjoying a revival while Christianity is retreating.

With the arrival of more immigrants into the United Kingdom and other countries in Europe, we witness the growth of other faiths and the fading of Christianity as the dominant religion. Most of the immigrants that arrive on the shores of Europe come from non-Christian countries, shaping their host societies to become more pluralistic and multicultural, a change that comes together with advantages and disadvantages. Immigrants have contributed much to the economic progress of many Western societies as new arrivals often take up jobs that locals shun. At the same time, Western Europe has moved from a secular to a more pluralistic society.

[4.] Stanford Encyclopedia of Philosophy, 'Hegel's Dialectics', https://plato.stanford.edu/entries/hegel-dialectics/#HegeDescHisDialMeth.

Some of these immigrants hold values concerning sex, marriage, religious beliefs, and customs that are vastly at odds with Western culture and norms, thus creating conflicts and friction. Bigotry is still prevalent in the West where division according to racial, ethnic, and cultural differences has deepened lately. For example, the recent Black Lives Matter protests reached their climax on 6 June 2020, when half a million people turned out all over the United States to protest peacefully and, at times, violently.

Furthermore, since the start of the Covid-19 pandemic, racism against Asians has increased in the United States, Europe, and Australia. Anti-China sentiments have been transformed into bigotry and racial prejudice. Arguably, jealousy and envy of China's rapid economic and technological progress, which is perceived to be threatening the hegemony of the West, have increased rapidly. Chinese communities in different parts of the world have mobilised themselves to raise awareness of these anti-China sentiments.

Unless society addresses these urgent issues and problems, there is a risk of communal violence and suppression of freedom of expression. If and when this happens, it would undermine democracy and threaten our hard-won liberty, solidarity, and equality, as we turn into a society dominated by fear, prejudice, and bigotry.

Western society has been enriched by freedom, democracy, economic prosperity, and scientific and technological advancement. Underpinning this is reason, associated with the rational thinking emphasized by Plato and Aristotle. However, the understanding of reason as an aspect of the divine logos that is generative and creative has been rejected. Instead, many uphold the notion of reason as associated with economic and material progress, while religious faith has been superseded by the 'enlightenment of reason'.[5] Once we separate reason from faith, there are adverse, even dire, consequences. We must return to a basis for our universal values, which our religious tradition has provided in the past. This includes the emphasis on human rights and dignity with its roots in Judeo-Christian tradition, teaching us that human beings are made in the image of God (Genesis 1:27).

The late Swiss Roman Catholic priest and theologian Hans Küng urged Christians and non-Christians to embrace universal humanity as a means to integrate our faith and values; uphold the equal rights,

---

[5]. Mary Frances McKenna, 'A Consideration of Christianity's Role in a Pluralistic Society', *The Way* 55, no. 4 (October 2016), pp. 35–6.

dignity, and value of each person; and at the same time, acknowledge our differences and responsibilities. Our society needs to create a space whereby our differences can be discussed and truth and goodness can be upheld through dialogue. This enables us to move beyond a pluralism that is merely pragmatic and influenced solely by economic expediency. A global ethic, such as the one promoted by Küng, is urgently needed to save our planet and ourselves from self-destruction.

Chapter 1

Monotheism and Polytheism

The practice of worshipping one god, without the distraction of serving other divinities and saints, although not unknown in ancient days, gained widespread acceptance among the elites and the general population in Europe in the sixteenth and seventeenth centuries, leading to the devastating Thirty-Years War (1618–48) between Catholic nations and the Protestant alliance, a conflict that killed a third of Europe's population.

The leaders of the Protestant Reformation, such as Martin Luther and John Calvin, were particularly critical in their attacks on the Roman Church and its rites of worship, which includes devotions to saints. The question of redemption and divine grace was the core question of the Reformation. Later, the terms 'monotheism' and 'polytheism' were introduced by Protestant-inclined preachers and thinkers, to differentiate the one-god worshippers (Protestants who called themselves 'Evangelicals') from the rest of humanity (which *also* included all other Christians such as Catholics, Greek Orthodox, Syrians, Egyptian Coptics and Ethiopians).

'Monotheism' was a cultural and racial expression of superiority used by European whites to justify their 'civilizing' mission in occupying and ruling the Americas, Africa, Asia and the Pacific. So effective was this form of cultural imperialism that it penetrated even into China, which had a long, unbroken history and tradition of religious tolerance of people of all faiths. It was adopted by the Taiping Revolutionary Army in the mid-nineteenth century; they called themselves the God Worshippers as they set out to conquer almost half the empire in their goal to convert their countrymen, who had been praying to both Shangdi (the supreme god and controller of human fate) and lesser divinities.[6] The opposing term, 'polytheism', under which the Protestant preachers and academia lump everyone else, is grossly inadequate to describe the complex and rich intellectual underpinnings of the ancient beliefs of Egypt, India, or China, not to mention those of the ancient Sumerian, Babylonian, Greek, Roman and Germanic-Norse civilizations.[7]

Monotheism and polytheism (with its adjunct reference to pagans, infidels, and heathens) are now seen by contemporary scholars as populist ideas spread by white imperialists since the days of Prince Henry the Navigator (1394–1460), who initiated the European Age of Discovery and Colonization. The terms are ambiguous concepts that frequently led to wars of conquest and the mass enslavement of darker-skinned races.

Adherents of the so-called monotheistic religions, Judaism, Christianity and Islam, all claim to share a common historical reverence of a single god and a legendary spiritual ancestor Abraham. This assertion is more mythical than historical. Some fundamentalist Muslims, for instance, see Christians with their belief in three divine persons as idol-worshippers; Many Jews too view Christians as idolatrous because they worship Jesus not just as the Son of God, but as equal with the Father; not all, but some Protestants despise Catholics for excessive devotion to Mary as the Immaculate Mother of God. These three Abrahamic-based faiths have differences, leading to endless wars and massacres of the innocents.[8]

After the attack of 11 September 2001 on the World Trade Centre in New York, critics of religion are wondering if monotheistic faiths breed fanaticism and fundamentalism. Because of its insistence on one

---

[6.] The Taiping founder Hong Xiuquan (1814–64), a scholar who failed his civil service exams twice, was fired up by reading gospel tracts he received from the missionary Edwin Stevens, and saw himself as the younger brother of Jesus, anointed to cleanse China of idol worshippers as well as other kinds of Christians.

[7.] Excluding of course the Persian Zoroastrians, who also worshipped one god.

[8.] Martin Luther is a well-known example of a powerful religious leader advocating the mass killing of rebels and opponents. Luther wrote the infamous *Against the Murderous, Thieving Hordes of Peasants* (Wider die Mordischen und Reubischen Rotten der Bawren) in 1526 in response to the German Peasants War (1524–26), an uprising against the brutalization of the peasants by the feudal ruling class in Germany.

divinity, monotheism tends to exclude other forms of belief, leading to a 'crusading' spirit that promotes intolerance and violence.[9] Polytheism, on the other hand, has the advantage of being more inclusive and promotes plurality, as long as political stability (which also included worshipping the rulers in Rome and Egypt) is not threatened. Since the singularity of monotheism is historically associated with totalitarianism or dictatorship, polytheistic beliefs seem more human, attractive and advantageous to many thoughtful people.

Polytheism may be more accessible to people who seek favours from various deities, particularly the god of the hearth and the god of municipal affairs (both familiar among the Chinese as the 'kitchen god' and the 'township god'), and those responsible for the seasons, rainfall and a good harvest. According to cultural tradition or government mandate, people may choose to worship a particular god or goddess among the diverse heavenly host. This is considered by some scholars as a kind of 'devotional' monotheism lurking in the background of a polytheistic cult – the exclusive worship of a deity serves to 'relativize a polytheism' because concepts like monotheism and polytheism are hard to define with accuracy.[10]

In this chapter we examine monotheism and polytheism in the context of early religious practices of the Hebrew tribes in Canaan and their transition from the worship of diverse gods to that of a single deity under centralized state-sanctioned worship. Although monotheism was

---

[9.] US president George W. Bush, following the attack on the World Trade Centre, vowed on 16 September 2001, to 'rid the world of evil-doers', then cautioned: 'This crusade, this war on terrorism, is going to take a while'. A commentary by Peter Waldman and Hugh Pope, staff reporters of *The Wall Street Journal*, on 21 September 2001, notes that 'in strict usage, the word [crusade] describes the Christian military expeditions a millennium ago to capture the Holy Land from Muslims. But in much of the Islamic world, where history and religion suffuse daily life in ways unfathomable to most Americans, it is shorthand for something else: a cultural and economic Western invasion that, Muslims fear, could subjugate them and desecrate Islam.' A White House spokesman later said Mr. Bush meant crusade only in 'the traditional English sense of the word, a broad cause'.

[10.] Pierre Gibert, 'Introduction', in *Monotheism: Divinity and Unity Reconsidered*, edited by Erik Borgman, Maria Clara Bingemer, and Andrés Torres Queiruga, *Concilium* (London: SCM Press, 2009), p. 13.

finally established following the era of the biblical Judges,[11] textual traces of polytheism can still be found in the Old Testament. The ruling elites in emerging nations such as the kings and priests of the Hebrew tribal cluster favoured a monotheistic faith because it helps rulers to unify the country and even an empire. The downside is that monotheism was easily manipulated to endorse absolute rule and control.

Besides exploring Jewish history regarding the issues of monotheism and polytheism, this chapter also discusses the thought of Augustine, and the political implications of Jewish monotheism. Finally, we conclude that the attraction of Christianity may be due to its ability to balance polytheistic and monotheistic tendencies by introducing a 'trinitarian' God to sustain unity in diversity in its worship. In the holy trinity (the *concept* is there but the *words* are not present in creeds commonly used in Christian worship) the divine persons exist equally for each other and within each other, and thus satisfy the innate play-safe urge of humans to serve and placate one supreme creator and many smaller deities.

Priority of Polytheism

This play-safe attitude of our ancestors means that the practice of praying to different gods and goddesses with different functions on different occasions was the norm in almost all civilizations. Different deities were said to have various abilities to help people, such as recovering from illness, victory in battle, safe passage in crossing the sea, and success in love, business litigation and exams. Besides scholars and business people, members of different professions also prayed to different deities. Sometimes, a particular god is worshipped in a particular clan or tribe. In Hong Kong, for example, with its motley mix of Chinese and Western cultures, mobile-phone-wielding grannies, teenagers and businessmen flock to the temple of Wong Tai Sin (黃大仙) on his birthday in September

---

[11.] The book of Judges was traditionally thought to be written by the prophet Samuel (1056–04 BC), the last of the judges before the Children of Israel chose Saul as their first king. Samuel, a strong advocate of worshipping one god, had to fight the polytheistic tendencies of his people. The next king, David, was a consistent monotheist but his successor Solomon, endowed with great wisdom by the one god Yahweh, in old age joined his foreign wives to worship many more gods (I Kings 11:4).

to ask the Taoist physician–saint for good health and financial prosperity. Then in December, the same crowd throngs the glittering malls to celebrate the birthday of another divinity, Jesus.

Another interesting feature of polytheism is that these divine figures are autonomous in their spheres of influence, with almost no interference from the paramount deity, whether that deity be the Jade Emperor (the ruler of the heavenly bureaucracy) in East Asia, or Father Odin (in northern Europe before the advent of Christianity). In the minds of the believers, the deities remain dormant most of the time. They come out at a particular period to perform some tasks, according to the cult calendar.

In southern China and across the Chinese diaspora, as well as in Confucian-influenced states like Japan, Korea, Hong Kong, and Singapore, there is the popular Festival of the Dead (盂蘭節) occurring in the seventh month of the Lunar Calendar, usually in August.[12] It is believed that the spirits of the ancestors and recently departed relatives are released from the underworld to mingle with the living during this month. Various rituals and rites take place around the home and the city to appease the spirits. Food, wine, incense and paper-gilded banknotes and paper replicas (these may include iPhones, luxury cars and even condominium apartments) are offered to give comfort to the dead relatives.

Archaeological findings have revealed that the Hebrew supreme deity Yahweh was earlier listed as no. 70 among the heavenly host worshipped by the inhabitants of Canaan. The Hebrews were originally just another undifferentiated cluster of tribes sharing the land with others. For better centralised control, the kings of the Hebrews and their priests ('prophets') evolved a monotheistic religion that centred on Yahweh, although this was frequently opposed by the peasants. During the Exile in Babylon, the Yahweh religion became firmly established; the official dogma was promulgated by the exile leader Ezra that the suffering of the nation was the result of worshipping rival gods and not Yahweh.

The emergence of Yahweh as the sole god of the Israelites was due to the process of 'convergence' and 'differentiation'.[13] This means Yahweh was able to absorb and reject the supernatural attributes and cultic practices of several deities. However, it was the process of differentiation

---

[12.] In Japan, this is known as the Bon (盆) Festival.

[13.] Robert Karl Gnuse, *No Other Gods: Emergent Monotheism in Israel* (London: Bloomsbury Publishing, 1997), 226.

that transformed a polytheistic cult into a monotheistic faith. This involves rejecting practices that were regarded as disruptive to the smooth functioning of society, such as human sacrifice, adultery, rowdy neighbourly behaviour, cheating in business and theft.

Platonists and Augustine

Monotheism existed independently of Judaism, the religion of the Jews in the Roman Empire. The belief in one supreme creator was popular in Europe and the Middle East among the educated elites influenced by Greek thought. During Late Antiquity, Platonist philosophers generally agreed about the unity of God – that the divine is singular. The vast majority of the ancient Greek philosophers believed in a god who is the first principle that governs all things in the universe.

The most comprehensive definition of God in the West was given by the Roman Stoic philosopher Seneca (c. 1 BC-65 AD), whose *Letters* formed a major influence on European religious thinking. Seneca defines God as everything one sees and everything one does not see. Nothing greater than God is conceivable. God is completely soul (*animus*) and reason (*ratio*) or 'reason in action' (*ratio faciens*). God can be referred to by many names: fate, the cause of all causes (*causa causarum*), providence, nature and the cosmos. God is corporeal. God is a part of the world (*pars mundi*), and he is always beneficial towards humans.[14]

An early Church Father who was responsible for setting Christian doctrines in concrete, St Augustine of Hippo (345–430 AD) was aware that non-Christian philosophers believed in one God and that the positions held regarding monotheism by Platonists and Christians converged. Platonists classified angels as gods and accepted a hierarchy of gods, to reconcile their conviction in the unity of God. Augustine wrote:

> If the Platonists prefer to call these angels gods rather than demons and to number them among the gods who, according to Plato, their founder and master, were created by the Supreme God, they are welcome to do so, and I shall not bother them with a battle over words. And if they admit that, though blessed, they are so not intrinsically but only by their

---

[14.] Stanford Encyclopedia of Philosophy, *Seneca*, https://plato.stanford.edu/entries/seneca/, 5.3.

union with God by whom they were created, then they are saying what we say, whatever the name they may give to the angels.[15]

For Augustine, it does not matter if the Platonists call angels 'gods' as long as they understand that these deities are different from the Creator God, that they derive their immortality and other good attributes from him. As long as the Platonists understand that these minor spirits have their being from the one true God, it is irrelevant what labels they are given.

Augustine discovered that the difference between Christians and Platonists is not in their idea of God but in their rituals of worship. In other words, they have the right concept of God but the wrong idea of cult – they worship many gods. According to Augustine, 'some of them went so far as to think that the divine honours of rites and sacrifices should be offered to demons'.[16] As a result, Augustine considered their religion false because it contradicted the idea of one true God. In the ancient world, Christians' concern was the practice of worshipping one God, not the question of how many gods might exist.[17]

The One and Many

Intellectually, monotheism is perceived as the highest form of religious belief because philosophically, the absolute has to be one and only. Friedrich Hegel (1770–1831), the highly influential German imagist–philosopher, wrote about the gradual development of consciousness from natural religion to revealed religion. Dismissing images and concepts, Hegel perceives God as 'spiritual essence', 'a philosophical

---

[15] Saint Augustine, *The City of God*, Books VIII–XVI, The Fathers of the Church: A New Translation (Washington, DC: Catholic University of America Press, 2008), p. 111.

[16] Saint Augustine, *The City of God*, 116.

[17] See Alfons Fürst, 'Monotheism between Cult and Politics: The Themes of the Ancient Debate between Pagan and Christian Monotheism', in *One God: Pagan Monotheism in the Roman Empire*, edited by Stephen Mitchell and Peter Van Nuffelen (Cambridge: Cambridge University Press, 2010), pp. 83–8.

cognition' – God 'Is'.[18] The 'One' in Judaism has not attained completion and perfection in the form of the spirit. Christianity thus fulfils Judaism and completes it as the absolute religion. According to Hegel, 'God as spirit contains in himself the phase of subjectivity and singularity; his phenomenal appearance can, therefore, be but a single one, and it can occur but once'.[19]

Hegel attempts to incorporate Judaism and all other religious beliefs into a single whole or process, culminating in Protestant Christianity. In fact, Hegel seeks to mediate all absolute distinctions, including those between divine and human, true and false gods, as One; thus, no diversity is allowed. In Hegel's philosophy of religion, we see a gradual transition from polytheism to monotheism in a dialectical movement. The Christian polemist C.S. Lewis (1898–1963) also viewed monotheism and polytheism as a continuum:

> Monotheism should not be regarded as the rival of polytheism, but rather as its maturity. Where you find polytheism, combined with any speculative power and any leisure for speculation, monotheism will sooner or later arise as a natural development. The principle, I understand, is well illustrated in the history of Indian religion. Behind the gods arises the One, and the gods as well as the men are only his dreams. That is one way of disposing of the many. ... The gods are to be aspects, manifestations, temporary or partial embodiments of the single power.[20]

As societies become more pluralistic and sophisticated, they tend to worship 'fewer Gods of greater scope'.[21] An omnipotent God is better than many deities fighting each other. Absolute or pure monotheism, however, is rare. In Christianity, we find the presence of rebellious angels,

---

[18]. Georg Wilhelm Friedrich Hegel, *Philosophy of Religion*, Part III, 'The Absolute Religion', translated from the German by Louis F. Soldan, in Louis F. Soldan, 'God as the Eternally Begotten Son', *The Journal of Speculative Philosophy* 16, no. 2 (1882): pp. 173–4.

[19]. Soldan, 'God as the Eternally Begotten Son', p. 176.

[20]. Quoted in Jan Assmann, *Of God and Gods: Egypt, Israel, and the Rise of Monotheism*, George L. Mosse Series in Modern European Cultural and Intellectual History (Madison, WI: University of Wisconsin Press, 2008), p. 53.

[21]. Rodney Stark, *One True God: Historical Consequences of Monotheism* (Princeton, NJ: Princeton University Press, 2001), p. 23.

one of them even trying to set himself higher than his creator.[22] In the current monotheistic religions, we are presented with an omnipotent God surrounded by lesser spiritual beings, both good and evil. Thus, it is not an absolute monotheism but a restricted one which acknowledges the presence of other spiritual beings, known as monolatry.

Monotheistic faiths – Judaism, Christianity, and Islam, as well as Zoroastrianism in ancient Persia – all believe there is a supreme being and a corps of lesser spirits. These religions are labelled dualistic monotheisms. Here 'dualism posits two opposite powers of good and evil, attributing evil to the will of a malign spirit'.[23] While acknowledging the existence of inferior spiritual beings, it is the almighty God who underwrites the moral order, ensuring that good will triumph over evil. Jürgen Moltmann writes, 'The God of the Exodus and of the Covenant is at one and the same time transcendent and immanent with regard to the world. He has nothing to do with the metaphysical one that stands in opposition to the physical many ... he dwells among the people he has chosen'.[24] The one God in Abrahamic religions is not just a spiritual essence but a personal being in history.

Jewish Monotheism

Monotheism was promoted in Israel during the reign of Josiah (641–09 BC). The cultic code contained in a 622 BC scroll demanded the worship of Yahweh only and the abolition of the other cults of divinities; it overthrew all previous codes. King Josiah made this the law of the state. Polytheism existed in Israel, but Judah was to worship its national God.[25]

---

[22] Isaiah 14:12–17 'How you have fallen from heaven, morning star, son of the dawn! You have been cast down to the earth, you who once laid low the nations! You said in your heart, "I will ascend to the heavens; I will raise my throne above the stars of God; I will sit enthroned on the mount of assembly, on the utmost heights of Mount Zaphon".'

[23] Stark, *One True God*, p. 25.

[24] Jürgen Moltmann, 'The Inviting Unity of the Triune God'" in *Monotheism*, edited by Claude Geffré and Jean Pierre Jossua, *Concilium: Religion in the Eighties*, 177 (Edinburgh: T. & T. Clark, 1985), p. 52.

[25] Bernhard Lang, 'No God but Yahweh! The Origin and Character of Biblical Monotheism', in *Monotheism*, edited by Claude Geffré and Jean Pierre

In the ninth century, in the northern kingdom of Israel, there took place a battle between the Yahweh-alone movement and the worshippers of Baal. King Ahab (874–53 BC), whose wife, Jezebel, was a Phoenician princess from Sidon, supported the Baal worshippers but the prophets Elijah and Hosea opposed them. In the southern kingdom of Judah, King Hezekiah of Judah (728–699) destroyed pagan temples and advanced the Yahweh-alone movement.

The prophet Hosea, who lived around 750 BC in the northern kingdom, claiming to be Yahweh's mouthpiece, said, 'Yet I have been the Lord your God ever since the land of Egypt; you know no God but me, and besides me there is no saviour' (Hosea 13:4). Nonetheless, the people kept on 'sacrificing to the Baals, and offering incense to idols' (Hosea 11:2). The conflict between Baal worshippers and the Yahweh-alone movement continued. Perhaps Baal shrines were not even that popular, but the memory of the original conflict in the ninth century between Yahweh supporters and Sidonian Baal supporters became embedded in the Israelites' collective consciousness. Perhaps new shrines of Baal attracted many people, causing the older temples that worshipped only Yahweh to lose out financially, and hence conflict ensued. All other gods were denounced as 'Baals', enemies of Yahweh or 'alleged competitors'.[26]

The Yahweh-alone idea can first be traced in the southern kingdom of Judah under the reign of Hezekiah. This idea was brought to Jerusalem with the support of Hezekiah and gained many supporters. A sacred tree (asherah) and a bronze serpent were removed from the temple by the King, which resulted in an 'imageless Yahweh cult' – the start of icon-less worship which was part of the iconoclast programme of the Yahweh-alone movement. The movement had followers because people needed protection from Assyrian military assault.[27]

The death of King Josiah in 609 resulted in the collapse of the Jewish monarchy and the resurgence of Baal and other gods. However, the Yahweh-alone movement was well established with prominent prophets such as Jeremiah and Ezekiel, born of priestly families. This idea of a monolatrous religion was also brought into the Babylonian exile. Jeremiah proclaims Yahweh as the creator of the word: 'It is I who by my great power and my outstretched arm have made the earth, with the people and animals that are on the earth, and I give it to whomever I please' (Jeremiah 27:5). This

---

Jossua, *Concilium: Religion in the Eighties*; 177. (Edinburgh: T. & T. Clark, 1985), pp. 41–2.

[26.] Lang, "No God but Yahweh!" p. 43.

[27.] Lang, "No God but Yahweh!" p. 44.

image of God as creator resonates with the image of the Babylonian god Marduk. It seems that the God of Israel had given sovereignty to King Nebuchadnezzar of Babylon and Yahweh had been elevated to be God of the universe.[28] Monotheism began to take root, especially in the writings of Deutero-Isaiah, who sees Yahweh as the one and only God.

Eventually, the monotheistic doctrine became the rule for the formation of the biblical canon. This means that most of the polytheistic ideas or images found in Israel were revised or omitted. Thus, few testimonies of the old polytheistic belief are left in the Old Testament. God became Yahweh-Elohim. In the beginning, the creator god Elohim was distinct from Yahweh, but soon they merged as one. 'Lady Wisdom', a poetic image in the book of Proverbs (Chapters 1–9), appears to have been an independent deity. 'Shaddai', a guardian god of homes and individuals, has also been merged with Yahweh, the protector God.[29] Deutero-Isaiah and the book of Deuteronomy established firmly the doctrine of monotheism, which Christianity inherited.

The Israelites were not the first people to embrace monotheism. Monotheistic beliefs began in Egypt about one thousand years before the birth of Christ when Pharaoh Akhenaten (Amenophis IV) proclaimed Aten to be the sole God, the creator of the world who is all-powerful and is present in the lives of the people. An ancient monotheistic belief in Persia also influenced Jewish prophets – the Zoroastrian religion, which emphasizes God's omnipotence and omniscience.

It is generally agreed that adherents of Zoroastrianism believe in one supreme God, Ahura Mazdā, creator of the world. Present in the lives of the people, Ahura Mazdā is also a healer and protector, responsible for the land's prosperity and fertility. Intelligent and wise, all-seeing and all-knowing, he has the authority to rule the world. Ahura Mazdā overcomes evil not by virtue of his power but by his intelligence. Everything that comes from Ahura Mazdā, both the material and spiritual worlds, is worthy of worship. This means that other deities are incorporated into the Zoroastrian pantheon but subordinated to Ahura Mazdā. In Roman Catholicism, the cult of the Virgin Mary and veneration of saints is popular. In both religions, the Zoroastrian Yazatas and Catholic angels are not cultic competitors but support the worship of one God.[30] As mentioned already, strict monotheism is rare.

[28.] Lang, "No God but Yahweh!" p. 44.
[29.] Lang, 'No God but Yahweh!' p. 45.
[30.] See Almut Hintze, 'Monotheism the Zoroastrian Way', *Journal of the Royal Asiatic Society* 24, no. 2 (2014): pp. 225–49.

Traces of Polytheism

In spite of its monotheistic outlook, there are still traces of polytheism in the Old Testament. God tells Moses, 'You shall have no other gods before me' (Exodus 20:3). He does not mean there are no other gods; he wanted Moses to worship only him, not other divine figures. Yahweh acknowledges the existence of other deities, but he will not tolerate his people worshipping them. Ironically, it is the existence of other gods that forms the basis of Jewish monotheism. Israel is set apart from other nations because the Jewish people worship the 'true' God, which implies the existence of other gods which are false.

Jephthah, the judge who presided over Israel for six years, says to the King of the Ammonites, 'Should you not possess what your god Chemosh gives you to possess? And should we not be the ones to possess everything that the Lord our God has conquered for our benefit?' (Judges 11:24). In Psalm 82, Yahweh is seen presiding over the assembly of gods and admonishing them:

> *God has taken his place in the divine council;*
> *in the midst of the gods he holds judgment:*
> *"How long will you judge unjustly*
> *and show partiality to the wicked?*

In the above psalm, we are presented with a polytheistic scenario, where the God of Israel pronounces judgment among the gods who not only failed to protect the weak but actually favoured the wicked. For their punishment, they shall lose eternal life and die like human beings. Those powers that favour the wicked and fail to uphold justice are no gods at all. Be that as it may, acknowledging the existence of other divinities reveals a certain level of religious pluralism and tolerance in the region.

We will now examine the meteoric rise of Yahweh from a storm god in Palestine to the Supreme God of the universe.

A God without Genealogy

Polytheistic cults were able to coexist with monotheistic beliefs in the Mediterranean basin. Countries have their own national gods and Yahweh, worshipped by the Davidic household in Jerusalem and great prophets of Israel, was held in great esteem. As a God without relations,

Yahweh has the advantage of not being entangled in a network of kinship with its attendant struggles and conflicts. Therefore, it was natural for the Israelites to choose Yahweh, a God with no pedigree. As a deity without genealogy, Yahweh attains the status of sole God in Israel, although polytheism was common in the neighbouring countries. When the state of Judah was conquered by Babylon, the Israelites believed that only a powerful God who ruled the universe could save them. It was a belief based not only on dogma but on hope – there is no God but Yahweh who is their saviour (Isaiah 45:21).[31]

God is their only hope to liberate them from bondage: 'I am the Lord your God, who brought you out of the land of Egypt, out of the house of slavery; you shall have no other gods before me' (Deuteronomy 5:6–7). He also warns the people against believing other oppressive powers to be gods. The only true God is the one who liberates. However, this command to worship Yahweh as the only God was not practiced universally. There were instances where Yahweh was worshipped together with female gods like Asherah in the royal temple (2 Kings 21:1–7). A cult of female divinity in some households existed at that time.[32] Monotheism was not practised universally in Israel in the early stages.

The command to be loyal to Yahweh was not just a religious observance, but a political concern, for the God of Israel would deliver his people from foreign domination and slavery. To be liberated, the people of Israel had to obey Yahweh wholeheartedly in accordance with his dictates. This worship of Yahweh by the Israelites in relation to how they were saved from political oppression has been described as a 'soteriological monolatry'.[33] The worship of one God in Israel guaranteed them freedom from slavery as promised in the Decalogue. Israel would no longer be a vassal state of Assyria. The irony is that they would now be subjected to a spiritual despot, Yahweh, who demands unquestionable obedience and punishes severely those who go against his will. Moses and the other prophets would be proclaiming the lordship of Yahweh with great passion, with no room for polytheistic practices.

[31.] Lang, 'No God but Yahweh!' p. 48.
[32.] Marie-Theres Wacker, 'Biblical Monotheism between Dispute and Re-vision: Christian and Old Testament Viewpoints', in *Monotheism: Divinity and Unity Reconsidered*, edited by Erik Borgman, Maria Clara Bingemer, and Andrés Torres Queiruga, *Concilium* (London: SCM Press, 2009), p. 24.
[33.] Wacker, 'Biblical Monotheism between Dispute and Re-vision', p. 23.

The zeal for the One and Holy is expressed in ruthless brutality in the Book of Exodus:

> He said to them, 'Thus says the Lord, the God of Israel, "Put your sword on your side, each of you! Go back and forth from gate to gate throughout the camp, and each of you kill your brother, your friend, and your neighbour."' The sons of Levi did as Moses commanded, and about three thousand of the people fell on that day. Moses said, 'Today you have ordained yourselves for the service of the Lord, each one at the cost of a son or a brother, and so have brought a blessing on yourselves this day' (Exodus 32:27-9).

Those who committed idolatry were slaughtered. Moses felt God commissioned him to perform this severe punishment, which included executing one's relatives. The dancing and shouting, which was witnessed at the foot of Mount Sinai, could not be the worship of Yahweh; it was idolatrous. Such drastic acts, including the angel of death passing over the Jewish doorways marked with the blood of the lamb (*pessach*, 'pass over') while entering the Egyptian households and murdering their firstborn sons, are deeply embedded in the Jewish collective memory.

The Babylonian Captivity (586-38 BC) marks another critical event when monotheism was developed – the clash between the God of the Israelites and the imperial gods of Babylon was politically dramatized. The God of the enslaved people was granted absolute superiority, concealed in the meantime, but asserted symbolically over the deities of the captors. Here we witness the separation of spirit and power – the power lies with the despotic rulers, the spirit of truth is found in the Israelites. In spite of the harsh realities, hope was instilled in the Israelites, who believed their God would triumph. Monotheism arose from such a protest situation, representing the religion of the oppressed and resistance against foreign domination.

The breakthrough of monotheism is found in Isaiah:

> *Declare and present your case;*
>   *let them take counsel together!*
> *Who told this long ago?*
>   *Who declared it of old?*
> *Was it not I, the Lord?*
>   *There is no other god besides me. (Isaiah 45:21)*

The God of Israel is now the King of the whole universe, encompassing heaven and earth, who alone has the power to save and to uphold justice. This command to worship only Yahweh is addressed not only to Israel but also to the rest of the world. The monotheistic thrust in these Deutero-Isaiah texts focuses on the power of God in history; other gods are impotent and thus non-existent. The saving power of a just God appeals not just to the Israelites but to all people in the world.

Monotheism and Monarchy

We have thus observed how Yahweh has been elevated to be the God of Israel. Its power and prestige grew through its connection with the city of Jerusalem and its temple in the early period of Israelite monarchy. King Solomon and King David did not suppress the worship of minor divinities in Jerusalem but integrated their functions and features into Yahweh. This was especially true of the traits of the sun god, whose function was the implementation of law and justice. Through transformation and integration, Yahweh became a monarch surrounded by a heavenly council: the development of 'monarchical monotheism'.[34] The sons of God mentioned in the scene in Chapter 1 of Job have been demoted to angels. Yahweh is now commander-in-chief surrounded by his heavenly court of angels. The movement towards monotheism in the Old Testament provides a good pretext for monarchs to monopolize their rule on earth.

In the ancient world, political unification provided a religious foundation for the numerous deities to be merged as one under different names. The mystery cult in the ancient Hellenistic and Roman worlds developed the idea of divine transcendence in a polytheistic context of divine representations. This concept of one sovereign God was not mere speculation by theologians but a religious devotion practised throughout the ancient Mediterranean world. This universal fatherhood of God also led to the idea that God created the world – the link between monotheism and creation is forged during this Greco-Roman era. Thus, when the gospel was spread to the Mediterranean basin, it encountered a political-religious ideology personified in conquerors such as Cyrus, Alexander, and Caesar, who were divinized. Christian apologists

---

[34.] Wacker, 'Biblical Monotheism between Dispute and Re-vision', 28.

taught that '[a] plurality of leaders is not a good thing. Let there be only one!'[35] Philo of Alexandria (15–10 BC–45–50 AD) utilized Hellenistic philosophy and Persian symbolism to interpret Jewish monotheism. Thus, the pagan Celsius warned of the great harm such monotheism could do to an empire underpinned by polytheism.

The political need to unify the Roman Empire paved the way for the spread of Christianity. This unification was further strengthened when Constantine solidified imperial power with the monotheistic faith of Christianity and monarchical rule when he was elected as Imperator (commander-in-chief, one who holds the imperium or army command). The Augustan Court theologian Eusebius (265–339 AD), in his *De laudibus Constantini* written in 335, advanced this connection between monotheism and the merger of the Empire.[36] Eusebius argued that the belief in one God aids the unification of the empire and spreads the gospel to new subjects. The belief in one God justifies the existence of a sovereign monarch: one ruler on earth corresponds to one God in heaven. The marriage of the throne and altar facilitates the effective proclamation of the gospel. A united Roman Empire lessens the risks of conflict, promotes peace throughout the land, and creates an 'eschatological peace' as foretold by the prophets.[37] Eusebius expounded that the father has no relationship with his creatures except through the Logos or the Word (John 1:1). The Logos that proceeds from the father is also his image. This Logos creates an earthly empire, which is a reflection of the heavenly kingdom. The Christian emperor must imitate the 'Logos-Christ-king', proclaiming like Jesus that the Kingdom of God is at hand.[38] Thus there can only be one emperor, as there can be only one father.

---

[35]. Yves Congar, 'Classical Political Monotheism and the Trinity', in *God as Father?*, edited by Johannes Baptist Metz, Edward Schillebeeckx and Marcus Lefébure, *Concilium*, 143 (Edinburgh: T. & T. Clark; New York: Seabury Press, 1981), p. 32.

[36]. Congar, 'Classical Political Monotheism and the Trinity', p. 32.

[37]. Giuseppe Ruggieri, 'God and Power: A Political Function of Monotheism?' in *Monotheism*, edited by Claude Geffré and Jean Pierre Jossua, *Concilium: Religion in the Eighties*, 177 (Edinburgh: T. & T. Clark, 1985), p. 17.

[38]. Congar, 'Classical Political Monotheism and the Trinity', p. 33.

Religious Imperialism

The evolution from polytheism to monotheism in the Roman Empire was a revolution that greatly affected the society's social and political structures at that time. In fact, the rise of monotheism marks the dividing line between the modern world and classical antiquity: the polytheism of the Greco-Roman world stands in contrast to the monotheism of Abrahamic religions.[39] Our perception of polytheism is conditioned by the teachings of monotheistic faiths. Monotheism continues to influence, directly or indirectly, our present discourse on culture and politics.

Colonial and Western imperialist discourse have been evolving from monotheism since late antiquity.[40] People who worship the only God see themselves as more civilised and superior to others. This philosophical development, which regards monotheism as superior to polytheism, has been called into question. The labelling of other religions with polytheistic and animistic features as 'pagan' in contrast to the unique Judaeo-Christian monotheism has been criticized. Religious systems are highly complex and do not easily fit into this dualistic labelling. A better understanding of the major religions from the East and of Christianity itself would help us to be less contemptuous of the nature of polytheism.

Polytheism is often projected as paganistic, primitive, and pantheistic, and contrasted with a more rational monotheistic faith. Jürgen Moltmann regards this development as nothing more than 'religious imperialism' intended to subordinate people from developing countries and destroy their native beliefs.[41] Monotheistic and theocratic religions have assisted conquerors to dominate other nations. On the other hand, disdain for monotheism has led people to become atheists.

The English biologist Richard Dawkins is convinced that the Judeo-Christian God does not exist: 'The oldest of the three Abrahamic religions, and the clear ancestor of the other two, is Judaism: originally a tribal cult of a single fiercely unpleasant God, morbidly

---

[39.] Stephen Mitchell and Peter van Nuffelen, eds., *One God: Pagan Monotheism in the Roman Empire* (Cambridge: Cambridge University Press, 2010), p. 1.

[40.] Garth Fowden, *Empire to Commonwealth: Consequences of Monotheism in Late Antiquity* (Princeton, NJ: Princeton University Press, 1993), p. 17.

[41.] Moltmann, 'The Inviting Unity of the Triune God', p. 51.

obsessed with sexual restrictions, with the smell of charred flesh, with his own superiority over rival gods and with the exclusiveness of his chosen desert tribe'.[42] Clearly this hostility towards worshipping gods comes from both his experience of monotheism and his scientific background. Atheism, however, guarantees intellectual freedom from an oppressive God.

Polytheism is actually a complex *and complicated* system of belief that seeks to balance natural and supernatural elements. The old religions of China and India, such as Hinduism, possess 'ecological wisdom' and are steeped in 'cosmic mysticism'.[43] Monotheism, with its history of domination of nature and discrimination against women, can hardly be regarded as superior to these so-called 'primitive religions'.

Nonetheless, I would argue that monotheism can also promote pluralism and a diversity of views by uniting people of different nations, such as at the event at Pentecost: 'All of them were filled with the Holy Spirit and began to speak in other languages, as the Spirit gave them ability' (Acts 2:4). Here we witness an opposite effect, belief in one God is accompanied by a plurality of creation. The Bible speaks of one God in order to protect the diversity of the world. Belief in one God in heaven ensures that creation is not raised to the level of divinity by maintaining its plurality. Besides, God wants people to be happy: 'It is not good that the man should be alone' (Genesis 2:18).

If we examine the biblical confession of faith, the unity of God is trinitarian – the relationship between the Father, Son and Holy Spirit. This relationship within the Triune God is open to all: Jews, pagans, Greeks or barbarians, lords and slaves, women and men: 'There is no longer Jew or Greek, there is no longer slave or free, there is no longer male and female; for all of you are one in Christ Jesus', writes Paul, the tireless evangelist of the new faith (Galatians 3:28). The trinitarian life of God which focuses on the loving relationship between the Father, Son and Holy Spirit, helps to overcome patriarchal privileges, oppression of women and destruction of nature.[44]

---

[42]. Richard Dawkins, *The God Delusion* (New York, NY: Houghton, Mifflin, Harcourt, 2006), p. 35.
[43]. Moltmann, 'The Inviting Unity of the Triune God', p. 51.
[44]. Moltmann, 'The Inviting Unity of the Triune God', p. 57.

Trinity: Unity in Diversity

The first commandment of the Israelites is that there is only one *single* divine personhood that they ought to worship. There are different ways of worshiping, such as the offering of sacrifices and incense. In the Old Testament, we witness the willingness of Jews to accept martyrdom rather than to offer sacrifice to other gods. They would not even bow down to another human being: 'When Haman saw that Mordecai did not bow down or do obeisance to him, Haman was infuriated' (Esther 3:5). In this aspect, Christians parted ways from Judaism, moving away to a different sort of monotheism; they incorporated the worship of Jesus Christ, resulting in the formulation of a trinitarian God.[45] Christians began to distinguish themselves from Judaism by moving away from strict monotheism, incorporating diversity in their worship while maintaining unity.

The trinitarian God can be an antidote to political dictatorship, patriarchal domination, and discrimination against women. Emphasis on the trinity would lead to a less absolute or monarchical Church, but a communion in the true sense. In monotheism, there is the danger of subordination and dependence on the One, thus undermining perfect communion. In polytheism, the plurality of divinities will destroy any sense of unity. According to Brazilian theologian Leonardo Boff, the experience of the Mystery can be a unity in diversity, faith in the trinity, where God is revealed as Father, Son and Holy Spirit in 'eternal correlation, interpenetration, love and communion'.[46] In the triune God, we can experience unity in diversity.

Strict monotheism, however, serves to justify totalitarianism and the concentration of power in one person, resulting in dictatorship and authoritarian rule. This is how Christian emperors, such as Constantine, justified their absolute rule. This ideology leads to excessive concentration of power and subordination of others, hindering democracy and increasing the oppression of the people in Latin America, according to

---

[45] James F. McGrath, *The Only True God: Early Christian Monotheism in Its Jewish Context* (Baltimore, MD: University of Illinois Press, 2009), 7. See also L.W. Hurtado, 'First-Century Jewish Monotheism', *Journal for the Study of the New Testament* 21, no. 71 (1999): pp. 3–26.

[46] Leonardo Boff, *Trinity and Society*, Theology and Liberation Series (Maryknoll, NY: Orbis Books, 1988), 4.

Boff. However, dictators and tyrants cannot justify or legitimize their absolute rule from a trinitarian God because this oneness of a single divinity is a unity of three persons, a communion.[47]

The Romanisation of Christianity occurred when the power of the father (*patria potestas*) was transferred to God, who now was seen as holding the power of life and death (*potestas vitae necisque*). This resulted in the male domination of the family, the state and the Church, legitimized by a monarchical image of God. Thus, we no longer recognised the merciful and loving Abba that Jesus addressed. To correct this historical distortion, we must focus on God not in the monotheistic sense but in a trinitarian manner.[48] Strict monotheism also leads to a rigid concept of church unity or uniformity and a concentration of sacred power. The function of the pope was understood in monarchical terms with one Church, one pope, one God. Thus, the pope was seen as the representative of God on earth – *Deus terrenus*. This also led to the abuse of power in the Church. Indirectly, monotheism can also lead to 'patriarchalism' and 'paternalism', resulting in the subordination of women.[49] In the trinity, three persons in one God, however, means there is inclusion rather than exclusion. Set in perfect communion, they embrace differences and avoid confrontation.

A trinitarian God can oppose the distortion and deformation wreaked by pure monotheism, which results in the domination and subjection of people. A trinitarian image of God can increase communion within the Church as well as decentralization of power within the community. In the trinity, the divine persons exist for each other and within each other, thus maintaining unity. If we return to the original biblical confession of faith, we have a Christianity that is able to hold the tension between pluralism and exclusivism, between pluralism and monotheism, found in the trinity.

Finally, the trinity, grounded in the relationship between the Father, the Son, and the Holy Spirit, can be a basis for interfaith dialogues. The Father, the absolute one, has different names in other religious traditions, such as Brahman in Hinduism and *Dao* in Daoism. The Son, manifested in the Christ, can be the *Logos* that is also present in other faiths. He is the mediator between the temporal and the divine orders. The Spirit 'blows where he wills' (John 3:8) and is present in all

---

[47.] Boff, *Trinity and Society*, p. 22.
[48.] Moltmann, 'The Inviting Unity of the Triune God', p. 55.
[49.] Boff, *Trinity and Society*, p. 21.

human hearts for we are the temple of the Holy Spirit (1 Corinthians 3:8). The trinity can be a hermeneutic key to unlock the treasures in non-Christian traditions.

Topics for discussion and reflection

- How do you assess the impact of religion today when faith intersects with modern-day monarchy?
- The deliberation between monotheism and polytheism has been going on for a long time, with trends indicating that modern, sophisticated societies seem to be attracted to 'fewer gods of greater scope' (Rodney Stark). Do you think this is the case? What does your observation say about the lens you use to interpret religion?
- The development of different faiths and their associated practices have clear traces of human influences – be they philosophers, religious leaders, politicians, or your average Jack and Jane. What are the influences that bring inclusion, embrace differences, and avoid confrontation, just like the divine persons in the trinity, existing for each other and within each other, and maintaining unity?

Chapter 2

Dialectic of Tolerance

The roots of intolerance lie beneath institutional safeguards for unity and defence against dissenters. Viewed through the lens of Hegelian dialectic, Christianity, a religion of love and forgiveness, degenerated into an intolerant and repressive belief when it became the dominant faith. This was exemplified by the Inquisition and the Catholic-Protestant divide. It then eventually swung back and developed into the spirit of modern toleration found in the teaching of the Second Vatican Council (Vatican II) and its effort to establish interreligious dialogue. Policies of the state and its relationship with the Church also significantly influenced attitudes, interpretations, and behaviours. Indeed, the dialectic of tolerance is always played out in a socio-political context in which power is a constant factor.

As we have observed in Chapter 1, there is tolerance of polytheism in the Old Testament. For example, in the book of Judges, the Israelites acknowledge the existence of other ethnic deities. Native religions were allowed to exist, and the close relationship between the people and their gods was respected.

Likewise, the Greeks were open-minded regarding the existence of other gods. They incorporated foreign deities and religious practices in their worship in a process known as syncretism. However, they would not allow criticism of their state gods that guaranteed the unity of the nation. Socrates was obliged to drink a cup of poison because he undermined the unity of the state. He was accused of failing to acknowledge the Pantheon of Athens, of impiety and corrupting the youth. Plato wrote, 'No one shall have private religious rites; and if a man or woman who has not been previously noted for any impiety offend in this way, let them be admonished to remove their rites to a public temple; but if the offender be one of the obstinate sort, he shall be brought to trial before the guardians, and if he be found guilty, let him die.'[50] Perhaps Plato was concerned that private religious belief would disrupt society.

Briefly exploring the history of the Church, this chapter discusses the dialectic between religious tolerance and intolerance. When Christianity was a minority religion in the Roman Empire, it pleaded for tolerance, but when it became the state religion, it became authoritarian and repressive. During the Reformation, Protestants living in Catholic countries pleaded for tolerance; as did Catholics who lived in Protestant regions.

Religious Tolerance

To tolerate[51] means to accept, endure or bear something which one would normally reject. It is to accept something grudgingly or reluctantly or to put up with it. Thus, tolerance involves a negative attitude underlying that acceptance. In every act of tolerance, we wish things were different or better.

There is a difference between tolerating a person's religious *belief* and tolerating the *person* who holds that belief. Religious tolerance is not so much about enduring someone's belief as it is about respecting the person's right to hold a belief that we think is inferior or even false.[52] Thus tolerating a religious belief is primarily a matter of accepting people of different faiths and secondarily a matter of judging what they believe.

In the context of religious tolerance, it is important to differentiate between formal and intrinsic tolerance. *Formal* tolerance is simply non-interference with another faith and is usually associated with religious liberty. Thus, different religions are allowed to exist side by side, and the state does not interfere with their practice. *Intrinsic* tolerance relates to the content of the faith. In this case, there is more than non-interference;

---

[50]. Plato, *Laws*, trans. Benjamin Jowett (N.p.: Xist Publishing, 2016). ProQuest Ebook Central, http://ebookcentral.proquest.com/lib/cuhk-ebooks/detail.action?docID=4504666.

[51]. Originally the meaning of tolerance was related to religious tolerance, but now it covers all kinds of behaviour. It is now applied to ethnic minorities, people with different sexual orientations, and immigrants.

[52]. Jay Newman, *Foundations of Religious Tolerance* (Toronto: University of Toronto Press, 1982), pp. 9–10.

Dialectic of Tolerance

there is an acknowledgment that other religions are also legitimate sources of spiritual consolation for others.[53] This intrinsic tolerance implies empathy with the religious beliefs of others, but it does not mean that we have to surrender our own religious convictions.

Nevertheless, it does imply that we respect the rights of the person in holding those beliefs different from our own. Since Vatican II, the Catholic Church maintains both formal and intrinsic tolerance of non-Christian religions. Before the Council, it had adopted a policy of intolerance throughout most of its history.

Intolerance can be interpreted as prejudice or pre-judgment – thinking ill of others without sufficient reason or evidence. Thus, it is usually based on ignorance or unfounded judgment. Great religions in their teachings stress compassion, forgiveness, solidarity and universal brotherhood. Unfortunately, in the practice of faith, believers are usually divisive and intolerant of other creeds. Monotheism in particular has been criticized as intolerant and dictatorial. William James writes, 'And the bigotries are most of them in their turn chargeable to religion's wicked intellectual partner, the spirit of dogmatic dominion, the passion for laying down the law in the form of an absolutely closed-in theoretic system'.[54] Conflicts and wars among the three Abrahamic religions are well documented, and they are still taking place today. Religious issues are often used as a cover-up for political agendas. Further, religion is more than faith; it represents cultural identity or ethnicity. James asserts, 'Piety is the mask, the inner force is tribal instinct'.[55] Thus piety is a convenient cover for prejudices that have nothing to do with the faith.

Why should we put up with something we disapprove of? This is the central paradox of tolerance. The other paradox is that if one is too tolerant of the intolerant, we end up being intolerant. In pushing it to the limit, tolerance or intolerance disappears. Karl Popper warned us that if a society is tolerant without limit, tolerance will disappear, having been taken over by the intolerants. To avoid this conundrum we need to find a middle way. There is also a danger that too much tolerance may be harmful to those being tolerated. Christianity flourished during

---

[53]. Gustav Mensching, *Tolerance and Truth in Religion* (Tuscaloosa, AL: University of Alabama Press, 1971), p. 12.
[54]. William James, *The Varieties of Religious Experience* (N.p.: Philosophical Library/Open Road, 2015), 480–1.
[55]. James, *The Varieties of Religious Experience*, p. 481.

times of persecution. T.S. Eliot wrote that 'the most intolerable thing for a Christian is to be tolerated'.[56] Christians tend to be lax when they are not challenged or persecuted.

Prophets and Pharisees

The ancient Israelites acknowledged the existence of foreign gods and territorial claims of others. But during the age of the prophets, a few charismatic preachers condemned polytheism with passion, and Israel became increasingly intolerant. Declaring the falsity or the non-existence of other gods, the Old Testament prophets denounced the sin of apostasy from Yahweh: 'Has a nation changed its gods, even though they are no gods? But my people have changed their glory for something that does not profit' (Jeremiah 2:11); 'Their land is filled with idols; they bow down to the work of their hands, to what their own fingers have made' (Isaiah 2:8). In the name of God, Moses commands the Israelites to kill worshippers of other gods in the promised land (Deuteronomy 20:17–18).

Besides apostasy and worshipping of idols, the prophets also gave reasons for their intolerance: 'Because these people draw near with their mouths and honor me with their lips, while their hearts are far from me, and their worship of me is a human commandment learned by rote' (Isaiah 29:13). Although the prophets proclaimed an absolute truth, monotheism in the Old Testament was not a static belief system but developed in stages against the backdrop of social and political changes. The intolerance of the prophets can be contrasted with the tolerance found in the book of Jonah.

The tale of Jonah is a lesson on religious tolerance and conversion. On his way to Tarshish, Jonah was caught in a terrible storm, and the ship threatened to break up. The crew on board prayed to Jonah's God and threw their cargo into the sea to lighten the boat, but it was in vain. While Jonah was sleeping below the deck, the captain came to him and said, 'What are you doing sound asleep? Get up, call on your god! Perhaps the god will spare us a thought so that we do not perish.'

[56.] John Christian Laursen and María José Villaverde, 'Introduction', in *Paradoxes of Religious Toleration in Early Modern Political Thought*, edited by John Christian Laursen and Maria Jose Villaverde (Lanham, MD: Lexington Books, 2012), p. 10.

Trapped by lot, Jonah admitted, 'I am a Hebrew and I worship the Lord, the God of heaven, who made the sea and the dry land' (Jonah 1:9). Terrified, the men tried to reach the shore by rowing hard and begging Yahweh to spare their lives. Surprisingly, the men regarded Jonah as an innocent person even though he had admitted his guilt in running away from God. They also acknowledged that it was Jonah's God that caused the storm. A 'near-catastrophic' event, Jonah's story is a tale of enlightenment revealed by different people willing to acknowledge a religious truth during a crisis.[57] The experience of Jonah foreshadows that of Jesus in many ways.

The Jewish religion during the time of Jesus was rather intolerant towards individuals of certain professions, such as tax-collectors and prostitutes, who were considered ritually and morally impure. However, this attitude of the community did not prevent Jesus from turning towards the ostracized and thus arousing the wrath and indignation of the Scribes and Pharisees, who adhered rigorously to the Mosaic Law. They grumbled, 'This fellow welcomes sinners and eats with them' (Luke 15:2). The compassion of Jesus went beyond the restrictions imposed by organised religion regarding professions or dietary laws. Although this attitude of Jesus is not, strictly speaking, religious tolerance, it reveals how the Son of Man was opposed to the hypocrisy and prejudiced attitude of the Scribes and Pharisees.

Religious tolerance is revealed when Jesus rebuked his disciples who wanted to call down fire from heaven on the Samaritans who rejected him (Luke 9:55). In the accounts of the Samaritan woman (John 4: 7–42) and the healing of the official's son at Capernaum (John 4:46–54), Jesus emphasized the necessity of faith, trust and openness to God in gaining salvation. In other words, membership in a community, religion, or ethnic group is not the most important requirement. In fact, it can be a stumbling block because it breeds complacency and even a false sense of security. Here Jesus sees religion as personal conviction.

When the Samaritan woman asked Jesus about the right place to worship God, Jesus replied, 'Woman, believe me, the hour is coming when you will worship the Father neither on this mountain nor in Jerusalem ... But the hour is coming, and is now here, when the true worshipers will worship the Father in spirit and truth, for the Father seeks such as these

---

[57.] Baruch A. Levine, 'Tolerance in Ancient Israelite Monotheism', in *Religious Tolerance in World Religions*, edited by Jacob Neusner and Bruce Chilton (West Conshohocken, PA: Templeton Press, 2009), p. 25.

to worship him. God is spirit, and those who worship him must worship in spirit and truth' (John 4:21–4). This means that location, rules, and regulations are peripheral; it is the sincerity and simplicity of the person that counts. Seeing beyond geographical and ethnic differences in our relationship with God reveals the intrinsic religious tolerance of Jesus. In the parable of the Good Samaritan, Jesus shows us that neighbourly love goes beyond one's own physical and religious territories.

In the cleansing of the temple (Matthew 21:12–17), Jesus appears to be violent and intolerant. Defiling the temple with commercial activities cannot be tolerated because it goes against his sense of righteousness and religiousness, which is passionate and prophetic. There cannot be a compromise in this case when the House of God is turned into a House of Mammon: 'No slave can serve two masters; for a slave will either hate the one and love the other, or be devoted to the one and despise the other. You cannot serve God and wealth' (Luke 16:13). There are limits to religious tolerance, as we can observe in the treatment of Christians in the classical world.

Persecution of Christians

When Christians were perceived to be disrupting the unity of the Roman Empire by their refusal to worship the emperor and his gods, persecution began, first by Nero (37–68). This struggle between Christians and the Roman authorities continued with intensity reaching its peak with Decius (249–51) and Diocletian (283–305). To preserve the unity of the empire, Decius imposed the state religion and killed those Christians who refused to comply with his command to offer sacrifices to Roman gods. Diocletian issued an edict in 303 to have all the churches destroyed, the Scriptures burned, and Christians holding high official positions removed. The decree initiated a bloody persecution, which continued under Diocletian's successor. But this does not mean that Christians were persecuted all the time in an organised genocide.

The persecution of Christians occurred throughout the imperial period in a sporadic and isolated way. It was by no means a systematic and coordinated strategy led by central authorities. In fact, there were government officials sympathetic towards the Christians and their religion. If they were persecuted, it was not for simply being 'Christians' per se, but because they had broken some laws, like refusing to venerate the gods of the state. In other words, Christians were punished because they were unwilling to recognize other divinities and refused to participate in public ceremonies associated with the Roman imperial cults. Thus, Christianity was regarded by the Romans as atheistic because the members refused to 'pay cult to the gods'.[58]

This monotheistic conviction of Christians was considered dangerous because it disrupted the functioning of society by breaking with tradition, not to mention their open disobedience towards authority. In fact, Christians did much to provoke the authorities by their ardent desire for martyrdom and thus brought persecution upon themselves.

Like the Greeks, religion for the Romans in the classical world was more a civil affair than a spiritual exercise. The citizen was expected to adhere to the official religion as a civic duty to promote the common good and the smooth running of business. Since religion was tied to a political identity, submission to the imperial power did not require foreigners to switch to the deities of the state. The people in conquered territories were allowed to keep their own native religious practices, with the condition that they must also offer sacrifices to the state-approved deities. The Jews were even allowed to keep their religion provided they prayed to their own God for the well-being of the emperor.[59]

That the Romans pursued a policy of religious tolerance does not mean they were theologically open-minded. The motive for accepting and assimilating foreign deities was to have better control over the people. This policy of tolerance was calculated to serve as a strategy to maintain peace and harmony within the boundaries of the empire. Granted to different groups in different degrees according to their dispositions towards imperial rule, this policy could be revoked at any time. Because of their open hostility and refusal to take part in the cult of the Emperor, Christians were classified as dangerous and thus could not be tolerated.

Peace and Privilege

Persecution ended with the Edict of Milan, a letter issued by Licinius to the governors of the Eastern Roman Empire in Nicomedia in 313, which allowed Christians as well as others the freedom to follow their

---

[58.] Cary J. Nederman, 'Introduction: Discourses and Contexts of Tolerance in Medieval Europe', in *Beyond the Persecuting Society: Religious Toleration Before the Enlightenment*, edited by John Christian Laursen and Cary J. Nederman (Philadelphia: University of Pennsylvania Press, 1997), p. 16.

[59.] Nederman, 'Introduction', p. 15.

own religion. This proclamation allowed Christians the freedom to worship in the spirit of ancient Rome. Unfortunately, this favour soon became a privilege, which led to exclusivity and intolerance. Constantine considered Christianity as a means to unify the empire. Once Christianity was accepted as the official religion, adherents of other faiths were discriminated against and oppressed. No work was allowed on Sunday, and even the simplest sacrifice to a household god was forbidden. Although the law was harsh towards those who practised magic and held superstitious beliefs, there seems to have been no widespread violence. Christian teaching on love, mercy and forgiveness mitigated the harsh policy of monotheism.[60]

Julian (331–63) became emperor in 361. Rejecting the Christian faith in which he had been brought up, Julian promoted Neoplatonic Hellenism and mystery religions. Julian the Apostate, as he was called, wanted to restore polytheism in his domain by observing 'formal tolerance' in the worship of one universal God with ethnic deities under his control.[61] This tolerant policy became intolerant when he excluded Christians from certain offices because they would not submit to his theocratic policy. Called an apostate by Christians, which was understandable, Julian actually had high ideals and was tolerant towards other faiths.

Julian's successors re-established Christianity as the official religion, but they refrained from persecuting other religions. However, this tolerant policy came to an end with Emperor Theodosius and Emperor Gratian (359–83). Theodosius in his Edict of 380 ordered all people under his rule to embrace Christianity under pain of punishment for those who refused. The Theodosian Code (438) consists of a collection of laws promulgated against heretics and pagans. The notorious practice of Inquisition could be traced to this development: the persecutions of heretics. For example, Nestor, the Bishop of Constantinople, urged Theodosius, 'Give me, my prince, the earth purged of heretics, and I will give you heaven as recompense. Assist me in destroying the heretics and I will assist you in vanquishing the Persians'.[62] This marked the beginning of the cooperation between the Church and the state, which led to dire consequences.

---

[60] Searle M. Bates and International Missionary Council, *Religious Liberty: An Inquiry* (New York, NY and London: International Missionary Council; International Missionary Council, 1945), p. 134.
[61] Mensching, *Tolerance and Truth in Religion*, p. 145.
[62] Quoted in Bates, *Religious Liberty*, p. 134.

Treatment of Jews

Once Christianity was established in the empire, Judaism was discriminated against, and Jews were persecuted. Judaism was characterized in the Theodosian Code as 'abominable superstition' and the gatherings of Jews were labelled as 'sacrilegious assemblies'.[63] Christians who visited synagogues were considered treasonous against the sovereign power and were subjected to harsh punishment. From 423 onwards, no new synagogue could be built without the permission of the Church. In the fifth century, Jews who converted others to Judaism faced capital punishment. During the seventh century, they also faced expulsion from Spain, Italy and France if they refused to be converted to Catholicism.

St Isidore of Seville (560–636) called for the persecution of Jews and encouraged the monarch, Sisebut, to impose conversion to Catholicism upon them. The Church did not officially endorse these measures. But the Church was determined to punish Jewish Christians, who had been forced into conversion in the first place but who now were suspected of returning to Judaism. The Church believed that even if the conversion was forced upon them, the sacrament of baptism was an indelible sign that could not be erased. The Council of Toledo (694) decreed Jews and their posterity to be in perpetual servitude subjected to the monarch's will. The ill-treatment of Jews in Europe was caused by social, economic and religious factors: Jews were accused as the killers of Christ and they remained the only non-Christian group in Christendom. Interestingly, this cruelty towards the Jews was mitigated when the Arab Muslims arrived in Spain in 711. The zeal of the Muslim invaders was nothing compared with the savage cruelty of the Christian clergy.[64] This violence and abuse of power continued in a more systematic manner and was endorsed by the Church when it established the so-called 'Holy Office'.

The Inquisition

One disastrous consequence of a close relationship between the Church and the state was the enactment of heresy laws, which later formed the legal basis for the establishment of the Inquisition – an institution intent on persecuting and burning heretics. Heresy became an ecclesiastical

---

[63] Bates, *Religious Liberty*, p. 136.
[64] Bates, *Religious Liberty*, p. 137.

offence as well as a public crime, condemned by both sacred and secular authorities because it threatened the public order. The persecution of heretics by the Inquisition was perhaps the most extreme form of intolerance practiced by the Catholic Church in medieval times.

The Fourth Lateran Council, which took place during the papacy of Pope Innocent III (1198–1216), established laws and regulations concerning the treatment of heretics and the Inquisition. Supported by secular authorities with material resources, Innocent sent about twelve hundred Cistercian monks to combat the Albigensian heresy in southern France. This was the start of the Inquisition, which was later named as the Holy Office (*Sanctum Officium*) and today is known as the Congregation for the Doctrine of the Faith (CDF).

Death by burning at the stake was the usual form of punishment for heretics around 1200. Innocent IV in the Bull *Ad Extirpanda* (1252) allowed the use of moderate torture to extract confessions from the heretics. In spite of the Church's desire to uphold the principle of *ecclesia non sitit sanguinem* (the Church does not shed blood), at least formally, dispensation and absolution were given to priests to use torture during the Inquisition in order to preserve order and unity in Christendom.[65]

During the papacies of Innocent IV (1243–54) and Alexander IV (1254–61), hundreds of heresy bulls and decrees were issued ordering the persecution and expulsion of dissenters. Even Thomas Aquinas wrote against the heretics: 'Wherefore if forgers of money and other evil-doers are forthwith condemned to death by the secular authority, much more reason is there for heretics, as soon as they are convicted of heresy, to be not only excommunicated but even put to death' (*Summa Theologiae*, II. II. Question 11, Article 3).[66] For Aquinas, counterfeiting God's truth is worse than counterfeiting the prince's coin, for which death was the penalty. The sin of heresy separates a man from God, which is the worst sin. Thus Aquinas approved of the handing over of heretics by the Church to secular courts for trial and punishment.

The Inquisition was legalized by the state. Civil authorities were more than willing to cooperate with the Church to persecute heretics because they had a share in the properties confiscated from the condemned. To put it bluntly, it was good business for the secular rulers. This accounts

---

[65]. Mensching, *Tolerance and Truth in Religion*, p. 49.
[66]. Thomas Aquinas, *Summa Theologiae*, https://www.newadvent.org/summa/3011.htm#article3.

for its persistence and extension to many parts of Europe. The Law of Ravenna (1232) demanded every Christian report heretics known to him to ecclesiastical authorities. Unable to defend himself, the heretic was convicted when he confessed or when two witnesses accused him in a statement.

At times, the Church requested the civil authorities to be merciful and to spare the heretics. It could be an example of sheer hypocrisy displayed by the Church. The main aim of the Inquisition was to impress the masses with fear – they must keep the faith and be united with the Church. The execution of the heretic was carried out in public with pomp, and thus the sinfulness and wickedness of the accused were made known to all. The burning of heretics was a great occasion for the Church to display its power and to uphold the truth of its teaching.[67]

For those who repented, the penitents had to wear a cross or have the sign stitched to their clothes so that everyone could see that they were repented heretics. For penance and punishment, they had to fast, give alms or go on pilgrimages. If a penitent continued to adhere to heretical beliefs, he or she would be brought to trial and executed, usually by burning at the stake. Naturally, the Church would not give a Christian burial. Further, the properties of the executed heretic were appropriated, and a heretic's children and relatives could not hold public office unless they were specially reformed. Church Fathers such as Justine Martyr, Tertullian, Hilary of Poitiers and Chrysostom had adopted tolerant attitudes towards heresy. But as the coercive power of the Church grew, it became less compassionate: 'It began with the principle of absolute toleration; it ended with the stake.'[68] How could a church founded on the principles of love and forgiveness carry out such horrific treatment of its dissenters?

Lactantius, an early Christian writer and adviser to Constantine, taught that we must defend our religion, not by cruelty but by patience. Lactantius maintained that forced sacrifice is not a genuine sacrifice at all. Compulsion is useless in religious matters because worship of God must be based on free will.[69] The Church Fathers warned against shedding blood and slaughtering those who rejected the Christian faith.

---

[67]. Mensching, *Tolerance and Truth in Religion*, p. 50.
[68]. Quoted in Bates, *Religious Liberty*, p. 144.
[69]. Rainer Forst, *Toleration in Conflict: Past and Present*, Ideas in Context (Cambridge: Cambridge University Press, 2013), p. 43.

Compulsion enforced by the Church was not in keeping with Christ's command to turn the other cheek in response to one's enemies. St Augustine was hesitant to suppress the Donatist heresy with violence. He believed heresy could be combatted by pastors with sound study and good preaching. In fact, Augustine believed persecution is the work of evil people who do not understand the nature of faith. It was as a last resort that St Augustine decided to suppress heresy because Donatism was spreading rapidly and destroying the souls of the faithful.

In the final analysis, Augustine believed it was better to force dissidents from their error by fear and punishment than that they lose their salvation. Influenced by Augustine, the classic argument is: 'When error prevails, it is right to invoke liberty of conscience; but when, on the contrary, the truth predominates, it is just to use coercion.'[70] In other words, *error non habet ius* (error has no rights). Unfortunately, this Catholic principle has been misused to suppress dissenters. Warnings against the persecution of heretics were ignored and totally discarded by the end of the twelfth century with the establishment of the Inquisition, a prime example of the Church's extreme intolerance.

The Church's obsessive fear of heresy in medieval times was not only due to theological errors of heretics that might cause the damnation of their followers, but due to the fear of schism, of a divided church, and of discord in society. The institution's determination to preserve unity at all costs is the root cause of such extreme intolerance. But opposition was inevitable when the Catholic Church was transformed into a monolithic institution, which was oppressive, intolerant, and corrupt. There were, however, a few tolerant voices among prominent churchmen and statesmen before the advent of the Reformation. They were part of the drive that sought to revive authentic Christian living within the context of the Renaissance.

Christian Humanism

During the fourteenth century, an intellectual movement flourished in European culture known as Christian humanism, which aimed at revitalizing Christian life. Originating in Italy, it was also a cultural movement to revive the study of classical languages, literature, history, philosophy, grammar, and rhetoric. The humanists who dedicated

---

[70.] Quoted in Bates, *Religious Liberty*, p. 139.

their lives to such studies were scholars, teachers, churchmen, and civil servants, who devoted their time to reading the works of ancient Greek and Roman writers. Critical of the Church's teaching, this so-called 'new learning' was different from the dry and abstract scholastic philosophy and theology taught at medieval universities, which seemed to have nothing to do with the gospel.[71] This Christian humanism eventually spread from Italy to the rest of Europe.

There were humanist scholars who attempted to promote a Christianity that was peaceful and open to other religious traditions. In other words, they preached tolerance among people with different religious viewpoints. One of them was Cardinal Nicholas of Cusa (1401–64), who in his work *The Peace of Faith* imagined a conference where representatives of world religions, united by a common belief in a supreme God, whom they worship according to their own rites and rituals, could come together to engage in dialogue and seek common ground.[72] Desiderius Erasmus of Rotterdam (1466–1536) and the Englishman Sir Thomas More (1478–1535) were two great Christian humanists who wrote works that dealt with the issue of tolerance.

Critical of superstitious beliefs, Erasmus wanted Christians to cultivate a personal relationship with Christ. With humour and critical observations, in his writings he offered a moral guide that emphasized Christian living. *The Praise of Folly* (1511), a work dedicated to Thomas More, is a witty satire in which Erasmus observes the absurdity and stupidity of people from all walks of life, including the clergy. Characterizing the gospel teaching as the philosophy of Christ, Erasmus emphasized love as the heart of religion, followed by kindness, tenderness, humility and simplicity, a teaching which is accessible to all regardless of age and gender. One of his greatest achievements as a Christian humanist was the publication of the Greek text of the New Testament in 1516, with annotations, which he dedicated to Pope Leo X. Erasmus also favoured the translation of the Bible into vernacular languages so that common people everywhere could read it.

Opposed to violence and fanaticism, Erasmus encouraged conversation rather than confrontation. Sceptical of scholastic philosophy and dogmatism, he maintained that we just need a few truths found in scriptures that are necessary for salvation. This involves distinguishing

---

[71.] Perez Zagorin, *How the Idea of Religious Toleration Came to the West* (Princeton, NJ: Princeton University Press, 2005), p. 51.

[72.] Zagorin, *How the Idea of Religious Toleration Came to the West*, p. 50.

essential doctrines from non-essential doctrines. Although the writings of Erasmus revealed a certain tolerant attitude towards diverse religious views, his stance towards the reformation started by Martin Luther was not encouraging. The anarchy sparked off by Luther's revolt affected Erasmus, who was against violence and persecution.

At the time when theological debates and controversies were raging in Europe, Erasmus held that it was absurd and dangerous to persecute heretics. A heretic is one who has diverged from the gospels and the articles of faith. Erasmus lamented that in his time, anyone who deviated from the teachings of Aquinas was considered heretical. Erasmus did not consider Luther a heretic. Like Erasmus, Luther criticized the sale of indulgences and papal abuse of power. Nonetheless, Erasmus was careful not to be identified with Luther and his revolt but advised both sides of the dispute to use moderation and to tolerate different interpretations of scriptures. Although Erasmus was keen to reform the Church, he was against the Reformation because it was contrary to the ideal of the 'concordia of Christians and a unified Church'.[73] Central to Erasmus' justification of tolerance are love, peace and freedom of conscience.

Erasmus' friend, Thomas More, however, dealt directly with the issue of tolerance in his work *Utopia*, published in 1516. In the first part of *Utopia*, Thomas More denounces the many injustices, exploitation of the poor, and partiality of criminal law in England. In the second part, More describes the commonwealth of Utopia where neither private property nor an official church exist. The citizens of this imaginary nation are free to follow their own religion. To convert others, they must rely on persuasion and not on compulsion. Those who resort to abuse and violence in proselytizing are punished with exile or imprisonment. There are many religions and forms of worship in Utopia, all united by a common belief in one Supreme Being.

Utopus, the king who founded Utopia, believed that God wanted a variety of religions so that people could hold different views. Convinced that it was wrong to force conversion, Utopus believed that if there were one true religion, it would be known by all eventually. In Utopia, no one should suffer for his religious belief. If converts to Christianity preached aggressively against other faiths, they would be sent into exile for inciting disorder in society. The idea of heresy did not exist. For the sake of the

---

[73.] Forst, *Toleration in Conflict*, p. 105.

common good, people would enjoy freedom of worship.[74] The tolerance and religious freedom on this imaginary island stood in sharp contrast to the bigotry and persecution that took place in Christian Europe.

Thomas More's attitude towards tolerance was quite similar to that of Erasmus: both were critical of scholasticism and were open to different religious viewpoints. Although different religions exist in Utopia, they share the same fundamental belief in the worship of one supreme God conceived in diverse ways: different roads leading to the same destination. Pagan belief based on natural religion can be seen as a preparation for the coming of Christianity. The anti-materialistic and egalitarian values found in Utopia resemble the teaching of Christ.[75] From a political perspective, the policy of tolerance strengthened the state because religious intolerance led to conflict and violence. Hence those who disparage the beliefs of others are punished severely. Atheists, however, are not tolerated, as they are not prevented by the fear of God from committing crimes against the state. More was against Luther, and, ironically within a few years of the publication of this ideal society, became a persecutor of heretics when the Protestant revolt took place.

The Reformation

The Protestant Reformation of the sixteenth century, which split Christianity into two main branches, was a momentous event in Western history. Started by Martin Luther in Germany in 1517, it was a religious upheaval that affected the lives of many. By challenging the Catholic Church, the reformers shattered the unity of Western Christianity, and created new churches and new forms of religious life. It also led to civil and religious war, and profound cultural and political changes in society. The immediate effects were the disunity of Christian churches and the problem of religious intolerance.

Aware of the extreme intolerance of the Catholic Church, the early Protestants vowed to be advocates of tolerance and religious liberty. The tragic fact is that the rise of Protestantism was accompanied by an outburst of intolerance, cruelty and violence in which both Protestants and Catholics took part. In spite of its emphasis on spiritual and personal decisions regarding the faith, Protestantism eventually became an

---

[74.] Zagorin, *How the Idea of Religious Toleration Came to the West*, p. 57.
[75.] Forst, *Toleration in Conflict*, p. 110.

organization with an ecclesiastical structure quite similar to the Catholic Church. The formation of the Lutheran Church as based on *Formula concordiae* of 1577 also became coercive.[76] The notions of concord and tolerance appear to be synonymous, but in the legal sense, this is not so. In fact, the notion of concord is antithetical to that of tolerance.

In the early period of the Protestant revolt, some conciliatory churchmen, both Catholic and Protestant, organized interconfessional colloquies, for example, those of Leipzig (1534, 1539), Haguenau (1540), Ratisbonne (1541, 1546), Augsburg (1548), Worms (1557) and others, with the aim of uniting the two churches. A Concord means each party attempts to convert the other to its own vision of the faith. To tolerate another religion is to break the Concord. Catholics desired to reconstitute the one Holy, Catholic, and Apostolic Church, while the Reformers wanted to convert the whole kingdom to Protestantism. Thus, the notion of tolerance goes against the aim of Concord.[77]

Calvin, an important reformer, published his *Institutes of the Christian Religion* (*Institutio religionis Christiani*) in 1536; it contained fundamental principles of Calvinist Protestantism and other reformed churches. One of its main doctrines was predestination, which means that, according to God's will, from the beginning of creation only some human beings are selected for eternal salvation and the rest for consigned to eternal perdition. By virtue of his intellectual powers, theological learning, and polemical skills, Calvin attracted a number of followers.

Defending its unity, integrity and righteousness with strict principles and policies, Protestantism became as intolerant as Catholicism. In fact, 'the genuine early Protestantism of Lutheranism and Calvinism is, as an organic whole, in spite of its anti-Catholic doctrine of salvation entirely a church civilization like that of the Middle Ages'.[78] As a result, the repressiveness of the medieval Church continued during the Reformation era and persecutions became even more savage.

The Council of Trent begun in 1545 by Pope Paul III, far from seeking compromise and reconciliation with Protestantism, intensified the division between Catholicism and the Reformed churches. To combat

---

[76.] Mensching, *Tolerance and Truth in Religion*, p. 111.

[77.] Mario Turchetti, 'Religious Concord and Political Tolerance in Sixteenth- and Seventeenth- Century France', *The Sixteenth Century Journal* 22, no. 1 (1991), pp. 16–17.

[78.] Quoted in Bates, *Religious Liberty*, p. 151.

Protestant teaching, Pope Paul III established the Roman Inquisition (Congregation of the Holy Office) in 1542 and Pope Paul IV created the Roman Index of Prohibited Books in 1559 to censor Protestant writings and publications that contradicted the Catholic faith. Persecution of Protestant heresy in the sixteenth century resulted in thousands of deaths. Protestants reacted with equal ferocity, resulting in savageries committed by both sides. The intolerance was mutual.[79]

John Robinson, famous pastor of the Pilgrims, summed up the dialectic of tolerance neatly: 'Protestants living in the countries of papists commonly plead for toleration of religions; so do papists that live where Protestants bear sway: though few of others of either, especially of the clergy ... would have the other tolerated, where the world goes on their side'.[80]

Cuius regio, eius religio

Emperor Charles V and the Lutheran princes signed the Peace of Augsburg Agreement (1555), to implement the principle *cuius regio eius religio*, 'whose region, his religion'.[81] This means the ruler of the state determines the religion of his subjects. The shortcoming was that some people were compelled to adopt the religion of their Protestant princes without any understanding of the teachings of the Reformation. Nonetheless, a unified state with a unified religion was achieved. There were around three hundred states in the Germanic region at that time and each state could choose its own religion. People could emigrate to escape religious persecution.[82] Charles V desired a peaceful reunion of both parties through dialogue and compromise. His aim for a united church that would help to support a united empire was political. Be that as it may, the Peace of Augsburg represents a step forward towards religious liberty and tolerance.

---

[79] Zagorin, *How the Idea of Religious Toleration Came to the West*, p. 80.

[80] Quoted in Bates, *Religious Liberty*, p. 155.

[81] 'It was agreed that the Lutheran religion should be legalized within the Empire, and that all Lutheran princes should have full security for the practice of their faith ... the Protestants demanded toleration for all Lutherans living within the territories of Romanist princes.' Theodore Hoyer, 'Religious Peace of Augsburg', *Concordia Theological Monthly* 26, no. 11 (November 1955), p. 824.

[82] Bates, *Religious Liberty*, p. 151.

The term 'tolerance' was used to designate a policy permitting freedom of worship for Protestants in an edict issued by Charles IX in January 1562, marking the official recognition of the Reformed Church in France.[83] Unfortunately, this edict did not stop the fighting between Catholics and Protestants. The majority of Catholics were opposed to this policy of tolerance. The Huguenots or French Protestants were also against this policy because of the limitations it prescribed. In 1598, Henry IV issued the Edict of Nantes, which tolerated Protestants under certain restrictions. This arrangement was a product of political manoeuvring and was revoked in 1685.

Martin Luther seemed to uphold the principle of religious liberty in the early years of the Reformation when he wrote: 'Belief is a free thing which cannot be enforced' and 'heresy is a spiritual thing which no iron can hew down, no fire burn, no water drown'.[84] But Luther was totally intolerant towards his opponents: Roman Catholics as well as those Christians who were against his ideas. The anarchy in Germany confused him, and he reacted with harsh repressiveness. Those who disagreed with him were punished first with banishment, then imprisonment, and finally death. Luther considered an absence from the Church a 'blasphemy'. He told the Duke of Saxony to exercise both political and religious compulsions: no Catholics were allowed in the land of Luther: *cuius regio, eius religio*.[85] Obviously, Catholic worship was forbidden in the Lutheran stronghold.

If Calvin ever wrote anything about religious liberty, it was a 'typographic error', a Reformation scholar wrote. To be absent from a sermon in Calvin's so-called Christian state was a crime, and to miss the sacrament was punished with one year in exile. Making fun of or cracking jokes about Calvin was a serious offence to be punished with severity. Living in Calvin's theocratic state, Geneva, was no laughing matter. Criticizing Calvin's clergy was considered blasphemy – violent language was reserved for his clergy. Absolutely intolerant, Calvin and his close associates were unmerciful towards those who did not share their philosophical and theological outlooks.[86]

---

[83]. Zagorin, *How the Idea of Religious Toleration Came to the West*, p. 81.
[84]. Quoted in Bates, *Religious Liberty*, p. 151.
[85]. Quoted in Bates, *Religious Liberty*, p. 156.
[86]. Bates, *Religious Liberty*, p. 156–7.

The intolerance of Calvinism has its roots in his belief that the elect of God were called to direct the world towards the Kingdom of God. Those who are damned cannot be converted, but they must not offend the godly. The damned must be forced to worship God in the Church and to be instructed in the scriptures in the hope that they would not blaspheme the name of God and his majesty. This is perhaps the most intolerant religious philosophy ever invented by humans.[87] No positive contributions regarding religious tolerance can be expected from Puritans.

Calvinism and the independent churches that it inspired continued to flourish in many places. Outside Geneva, they were a minority, and they pleaded for tolerance and fought for their right to exist with greater conviction. It was this difficult situation that urged people to fight for freedom, a condition that gave rise to an 'autonomous society based on self-help, self-administration, self-government' which was based on the liberal principle of *Dieu et mon droit*, 'my God, my right'. The equality of members in society gave them an incentive to discuss and to criticize. The clergy or ministers of religion were chosen not by ecclesiastical authority or the government, but from below, by the people. This was the seed that was planted for the flowering of a democratic state. Calvin and his followers were dreaming of a theocratic state, which eventually turned out to be an earthly state united by 'the cohesive force of individuals'.[88]

Thus, indirectly, the Reformation eventually led to the development of modern democracy, religious liberty, and tolerance. It abolished an exclusive and infallible organization, which compelled nations to accept a single vision of Christianity. The Reformation gave men and women freedom in their quest for salvation. In England, thoughtful Protestants, such as John Locke, were attracted to the principles of the Enlightenment and began to be identified with the cause of political liberalism and religious tolerance.

Locke's Letters of Tolerance

The English philosopher John Locke (1632–1704), one of the great pioneers of the Enlightenment movement, contributed significantly to the development of liberalism with his treatises on tolerance. In his *Letters on Toleration* (1689), John Locke holds that the Christian Church

---

[87] Bates, *Religious Liberty*, p. 157.
[88] Quoted in Bates, *Religious Liberty*, p. 158.

has no right to persecute those who do not share in its beliefs. He reminds his readers that true disciples of Christ expect persecution, but they cannot persecute or compel others to embrace the faith. Christianity is not like a worldly kingdom. The Lord Jesus came to serve and not to be served. Furthermore, the Church, says Locke, is a "free and voluntary society" and thus nobody is forced to enter it.[89] People join the Church because they believe they have found the true religion. However, if they find anything wrong with the Church's doctrine or worship, they are free to leave.

Locke maintains that civil authorities have no mandate for the care of souls; this mandate comes from God alone. Nowhere did God grant men the authority to compel others to adopt their own religion. Nor can such authority be given to a ruler by men. For Locke, salvation occurs through the 'inward conviction of the mind'.[90] Without this conviction, there is no value in believing in a particular religion. Thus, for Locke, tolerance is the distinguishing mark of a true Christian Church. Intolerance is contrary to the Christian practice of charity. He also insists on the separation of state and Church.

The limit to Locke's tolerance is atheism. Those who deny the existence of God cannot be tolerated at all. The atheist cannot be trusted. Once God is denied, Locke believes, the bonds of society will collapse. An atheist cannot demand tolerance in the name of religion because he has no religion to back his claim. Catholics are also excluded from Locke's tolerance because he believed that, as subjects of the Pope, they held political and moral positions that threatened society.

Further, the Church is not obliged to tolerate members who consistently break its laws, but may excommunicate them. However, no individual or particular church can invoke civil rights against a person professing a different religion. The clergy must abstain from persecuting non-believers and teach their followers to be tolerant. Against collusion between state and Church, Locke insists that civil authorities must not impose rules and regulations on rites and ceremonies. A person's salvation is his private concern and, therefore, if he worships wrongly, it does not affect the community. But the state cannot tolerate doctrines that go against the

---

[89] Richard Vernon, 'Locke: A Letter Concerning Toleration', in *Locke on Toleration*, edited by Richard Vernon, 3–46, Cambridge Texts in the History of Philosophy (Cambridge: Cambridge University Press, 2010), p.9.

[90] Vernon, 'Locke: A Letter Concerning Toleration', p. 8.

moral good necessary for the preservation of society. Nor can the churches form alliances with foreign powers. Here again, any threat against the unity and order of society is to be avoided at all costs.

The Church in Modern Times

There is no lack of evidence regarding intolerance in the Catholic Church in modern times. In 1832, Pope Gregory XVI, in his encyclical *Mirari vos*, condemned indifferentism, freedom of conscience, and freedom to publish. Indifferentism refers to the 'perverse opinion ... spread on all sides by the fraud of the wicked who claim that it is possible to obtain the eternal salvation of the soul by the profession of any kind of religion, as long as morality is maintained ... This shameful font of indifferentism gives rise to that absurd and erroneous proposition which claims that liberty of conscience must be maintained for everyone.' The Church also taught that 'we must include that harmful and never sufficiently denounced freedom to publish any writings whatever and disseminate them to the people, which some dare to demand and promote with so great a clamour'.[91] In the *Syllabus* of 1864, Pius IX denounced the errors of liberalism and denounced indifferentism, which is tolerance of other faiths.

It was only during Vatican II that the Church began to teach tolerance as seen in *Dignitatis Humanae*: Declaration on Religious Freedom (1965) and *Nostra Aetate*: Declaration on the Relation of the Church to Non-Christian Religions (1965). Regarding religious freedom, the Council maintained that though the true religion subsists in the Catholic Church, it advocates that every person has the right to religious liberty. In other words, people must be free from individual and community constraints in choosing their religion. No one should be compelled to act against his conscience regarding religious matters. This right to religious freedom is based on the dignity of the human person. The denial of freedom of worship is considered by the Church to be an injustice against human beings and society.[92] The Church teaches a kind of formal tolerance where people are required to respect the rights and freedom of others for the sake of public order and the common good.

[91.] Gregory XVI, *Mirari vos*, https://www.papalencyclicals.net/greg16/g16mirar.htm, nos. 13, 14, 15.

[92.] Paul VI, *Declaration of Religious Freedom: Dignitatis Humanae*, http://www.vatican.va/archive/hist_councils/ii_vatican_council/documents/vat-ii_decl_19651207_dignitatis-humanae_en.html, nos. 2 and 3.

In the 'Declaration on Religious Freedom', the Church adopts a tolerant attitude that is intrinsic in that it acknowledges the elements of truth and holiness in other religious traditions: 'The Catholic Church rejects nothing of what is true and holy in these religions. It has a high regard for the manner of life and conduct, the precepts and doctrines which, although differing in many ways from its own teaching, nevertheless often reflect a ray of that truth which enlightens all men and women'.[93] The Declaration expresses appreciation of Hinduism, highlighting the search of its adherents for the mystery of the divine in myths and philosophical undertakings. In Buddhism, the Declaration recognizes its teaching regarding liberation and enlightenment, and in Islam, it acknowledges their worship of one God and submitting themselves completely to his will. Regarding the Jewish religion, the Church is aware of its common bond, which goes back to Moses and the prophets. There is thus a common spiritual heritage uniting Christians and Jews. Rejecting the idea that Jews are condemned by God, the Church denounces anti-Semitism.

Joseph Ratzinger, the former Prefect of the Congregation for the Doctrine of the Faith, Pope Emeritus Benedict XVI, thinks that the principle of tolerance promoted by Vatican II is wrongly interpreted as acceptance of other religions as on par with the Christian faith. Ratzinger was concerned with the question of truth in other religious traditions. If truth is not taken into consideration, Ratzinger believed that it is no longer possible to distinguish between genuine faith and superstition. The true value in religion lies in the truth that it proclaims.[94]

Be that as it may, we have observed a recurring dialectical movement of tolerance and intolerance played out between religious institutions and its detractors. The established institution, zealous in protecting its unity, would not tolerate any dissidents. Thus, in the scriptures, we witness the clash between priests and prophets, between the Pharisees and Jesus. Eventually prophetic voices were domesticated, incorporated, and institutionalized; and intolerance triumphed over tolerance. The history of the world is the history of intolerance. Our tribal instinct remains intact no matter how civilized we claim to be. We call it group

---

[93]. *Nostra Aetate*, 'Declaration on the Church and the Non-Christian Religions', Second Vatican Council, https://www.bc.edu/content/dam/files/research_sites/cjl/texts/cjrelations/resources/documents/catholic/Nostra_Aetate.htm, no/ 2.

[94]. Joseph Ratzinger, *Pilgrim Fellowship of Faith* (San Francisco, CA: Ignatius Press, 2005), 212–13.

solidarity, a trait that has been intrinsic to the survival of communities. Christianity, the inheritor of the Hebraic heritage, was exclusive and not open to the idea of religious freedom. Supported by rigid dogmas, Christianity was inspired by the idea of a universal mission to convert the world. The Church was held to be an indispensable mediator between God and humanity.

Fortunately, the teaching of love and respect for others, a basic tenet in Christianity, continues to mitigate the exclusiveness of Christianity. Thus, we witness some measures of religious tolerance in its history. Theologians and clerics generally agree that compulsion achieved nothing in matters of faith. The Catholic Church can be tolerant regarding popular piety and superstitious beliefs, provided such beliefs and practices do not threaten its unity and the integrity of its teachings. In fact, some non-Christian practices have been assimilated into the faith in a process called syncretism, a topic we will discuss in the following chapter.

Topics for discussion and reflection

- What are the factors contributing to the phenomena of religious tolerance and intolerance in different eras? Do you see any of these factors in today's world?
- One of the theses in this chapter postulates that 'intolerance can be interpreted as prejudice or prejudgment – thinking ill of others without sufficient reason or evidence'. Do you agree? Does religious tolerance always lead to peace, and to freedom from persecution and discrimination?
- Among the philosophers and scholars referenced in this chapter, such as Thomas More, Erasmus, Martin Luther, John Locke, etc., whose view resonates most with your own, and how?

Chapter 3

Idiosyncrasies of Syncretism

Christianity, in its initial stage, was tolerant of and open to Greco-Roman philosophical thought in formulating its own theological and legal framework. As it was initially a minority faith gaining converts from all walks of life, syncretism – borrowing and mixing other religious and cultural elements – took place naturally. When Christianity became the official religion of the Roman Empire, the Church, as the sole authority of authentication of doctrines and practices, decided whether borrowing was legitimate or illegitimate. The syncretistic strategy was also used by Roman emperors to appropriate the religious beliefs of those they conquered. Syncretism, whether in its positive or negative sense, is a typical feature in religion. The different interpretations of the term reflect the changing historical contexts and political agendas. The bottom line is that syncretism refers to a politics of difference and identity, where the possession of power allows one to dictate which a doctrine or practice is true or false.

Over time, syncretism became a contentious term that is often, but not always, associated with inauthenticity, adulteration or infiltration of a pure tradition. In the writings of Christian missionaries and Church officials, it often has a critical connotation. Theologically, syncretism has a pejorative sense, but in anthropological research, syncretic practices are considered as a natural development of religion and its ritual. Viewed with optimism in anthropology, syncretism has a neutral or even positive overtone. Scholars have generally agreed that different religious traditions have borrowed from each other in the past through a process of amalgamation.

Due to conflicts that occurred during the Protestant Reformation, syncretism acquired value-laden connotations. Some scholars believe syncretism has now become a useless and ambiguous term. Nonetheless, it continues to be used in a negative or positive sense. Given the vagueness, elusiveness, and shifting semantics of this important term, this chapter attempts to present a more comprehensive view of religious syncretism by examining how it has been historically constituted and reconstituted, especially analyzing the practice of multiple religious adherents in the Asian context.

Syncretism and Salvation

From an anthropological point of view, Christianity is a syncretic religion made up of a combination of Judaism and the teachings of Jesus. Judaism, too, is a syncretic religion influenced by the beliefs of surrounding regions, adopting practices such as circumcision and spring sacrifice, which later became the paschal sacrifice. The cultural debt includes the adoption of creation stories, agricultural feasts such as the unleavened bread, art, wisdom literature, Phoenician craftsmanship and liturgy. Furthermore, the Jewish legal and political systems were borrowed from outside. In fact, Israel was syncretic.[95] This means that God's plan for the salvation of his people is achieved when cultures encounter each other in a fruitful exchange of ideas and customs.

In fact, 'the "fertile crescent" of the Middle East was a veritable crossroads of cultures from the earliest times. The Jewish people and their traditions were, humanly speaking, the product of this remarkably varied cultural interaction, and contributed to the on-going intercultural process.'[96] Originally, Yahweh was a pagan deity while Baal was the most powerful god in the Levant. In Biblical times, Baal was the god of fertility and harvest. Yahweh was invoked during war but Baal was worshipped for success in agriculture.[97] The prophets in the Old

---

[95] Luzbetak, *The Church and Culture: New Perspectives in Missiological Anthropology*, American Society of Missiology Series; No. 12 (Maryknoll, NY: Orbis Books, 1988), p. 360. See also Aylward Shorter, *Toward a Theology of Inculturation* (Maryknoll, NY: Orbis Books, 1988), pp. 109–11, 115.

[96] Aylward Shorter, *Toward a Theology of Inculturation* (Maryknoll, N.Y.: Orbis Books, 1988), p. 106.

[97] Luzbetak, *The Church and Culture*, p. 368.

Testament proclaimed Yahweh as absolute Lord of all because the God of history (Exodus) was more important than the God of agriculture for the Israelites. Yahweh could also be tolerant and forgiving. Jonah accepts a syncretic view of Yahweh by acknowledging the existence of other gods. In spite of his pagan belief, God forgives and accepts Jonah.

Early Usage

The earliest usage of the term 'syncretism' appeared in the writing of Plutarch (AD 45–120), *Moralia*, in the chapter 'On Brotherly Love', where he said it was necessary to be friendly with the friends of a brother and likewise to be hostile to his enemies. He was referring to the Cretans who, he felt, instead of constantly fighting against each other, should put aside their differences and be united against the enemies from outside. This coming together of the Cretans in a united front is 'syncretism'. Thus, from its earliest usage, the word 'syncretism' suggests the setting aside of differences in a political context. Erasmus (1469–1536) also viewed syncretism in a positive light when he supported the idea that Christianity is enriched by classical thought. His preference for early church writings exposed him to Platonic and NeoPlatonic thought.[98]

Syncretism is also related to the idea of naturalistic religion, a belief in a supreme being among humankind, highlighted by Lord Herbert of Cherbury (1583–1648) in his study of comparative religion. Herbert maintained that the great truths of religion are universal. Related to natural religion, genuine faith was open to reason and not tied to a specific historical event of revelation. It was this emphasis on one's uniqueness that led to so much conflict.[99] This idea challenged the teaching of the Catholic Church that there is only one absolute truth authorized by the Church and deviations from this truth were heresies.

The basic disposition of natural religion is syncretic and pragmatic. It is a positive development because natural religion fulfils basic human needs for a good life, for communion with God, for an experience of love, enlightenment and final liberation. Manifested in different forms, natural religions arose to satisfy humanity's longing for a more fulfilling

---

[98] M.A. Screech, *Ecstasy and the Praise of Folly* (London: Duckworth, 1980), p. 21.
[99] Peter van der Veer, 'Syncretism, Multiculturalism, and the Discourse of Tolerance', p. 197.

and meaningful life. Natural religion is thus relativistic and subjective when it comes to the question of truth: its emphasis is on *experience* rather than *truth*. In fact, the standard to measure the value of a religion is the experience. The Dutch missionary scholar Henrick Kraemer wrote, 'Why should one pose the question of truth? ... Religion as manifest in different systems and ways, all belonging to the relative sphere of this phenomenal world, stands by the nature of the case outside the question of absolute truth.'[100] This may explain why pentecostal Christianity is the fastest-growing church in Latin America: people want to experience the Holy Spirit's power rather than to understand the truth of liberation theology. Pragmatic psychology has overshadowed the question of truth and ultimate reality.

Religion deals with the juxtaposition of the illusory world, empirical existence, and the real world of pure essence. The idea of *absolute truth* belongs exclusively to this sphere of pure essence, which is unattainable for human beings living in the relative sphere of this phenomenal world. At best, a religion may have 'accommodated truth'. Doctrines are established to convey relative truth: 'From the standpoint of Pure Essence all is sameness; from the standpoint of accommodated truth all is difference. Monism and pluralism, polytheism and monotheism can equally be true, while equally false, and they have therefore the right to coexist.'[101] In its emphasis on experience rather than on doctrinal purity, we witness the openness and tolerance of naturalistic religion, which also includes Asian religious traditions.

In the seventeenth century, George Calixtus (1586–1656), a German Lutheran theologian, attempted to reunite his church with Roman Catholicism, but his contemporaries were more concerned with the problems of dissent. Like Erasmus, Calixtus saw the rational proof of truth in Christianity in classical Greek, which he believed would unite all Christians. Supporting the Reformation, Calixtus wanted to return to the Church of antiquity, which he believed had been corrupted by the powers of the papacy. He worked hard to bridge the differences but was criticised by both Lutherans and Catholics.

---

[100] Hendrik Kraemer, 'Syncretism', in *Syncretism in Religion: A Reader*, edited by Anita Maria Leopold and Jeppe Sinding Jensen (Sheffield: Taylor & Francis Group, 2004), p. 42.

[101] Kraemer, 'Syncretism', p. 45.

Standing between the two sides, Reformed and Roman, Calixtus' effort to reconcile theological differences sparked the so-called Syncretic Controversy.[102]

Calixtus wanted to use syncretism as a strategy to contain conflict and promote dialogue. But his critics condemned it as 'an illicit contamination' of the true faith, a 'betrayal of principles, or as an attempt to secure unity at the expense of truth'.[103] Since then, this negative meaning of syncretism, suggesting a confused mixing of religions, has become the dominant understanding in modern discourse. Christian literature has been critical of syncretism sometimes for the wrong reasons because of its myopic vision of faith.

Clash of Civilizations

It is natural for religion to avoid syncretism, especially when it claims it possesses the truth. Syncretism, narrowly defined, occurs when two religious beliefs or messages are merged in such a way that the core of each or both is completely transformed into something else. Syncretism naturally poses a threat to the survival of the religion when its original form has been completely modified. The Church has the responsibility of preserving the integrity of the gospel message. Anything that threatens Christian teachings and the structure of the Church is vehemently opposed. The problem arises when the Church believes it has the monopoly on truth and regards other religious traditions as inferior or false. Racial superiority, a colonial mentality deeply engrained in the Western culture from which Christianity grew became a stumbling block to acknowledging the presence of the divine in other religions.

Originating in the Middle East and institutionalized in the West, Christianity is itself shot through with pagan ideas. The global influence of Europeans as a result of aggressive imperialism led to the vision of the Christian faith becoming the norm: 'This habitude of self-consecration made the Western Church prone to view the displacement of other

---

[102] Christian Thorsten Callisen, 'Georg Calixtus, Isaac Casaubon, and the Consensus of Antiquity', *Journal of the History of Ideas* 73, no. 1 (2012), pp. 1–23.

[103] van der Veer, 'Syncretism, Multiculturalism, and the Discourse of Tolerance', p. 197.

religions and culture as the only admissible resultant of its encounter with them and correspondingly to classify *any other* outcome of such encounter as *ipso facto* syncretic.'[104] In other words, syncretism in itself is not an issue, but the pride and prejudice of Western Christianity are stumbling blocks inhibiting the incarnation of the word.

Looking at the rise of Spanish, Portuguese, British and Dutch colonialism, which resulted in Latin Christianity becoming dominant, normative Christianity became conditioned by political power and not biblical truth.[105] Thus, the scholar of religion Paul Hedges contends that the Vincentian canon about the universality of the Church is doubtful. Although we must not give up all traditions, he thinks they are very much related to power struggles. Tradition, therefore, must not be taken as 'normative in the absolute sense'.[106] In other words, Hedges stresses that, like most systems, Christianity as a religion is tied to its cultural context, and there is no such thing as universal truth coming down directly from God. Consequently, Hedges believes that we must allow different expressions of Christianity to exist, and this implies that the normative pattern of Western theology must be challenged.[107] This includes the issue of syncretism and raises the question: how do we draw the line between illicit syncretism and the licit syncretism (inculturation) promoted by the Church?

The point made by Hedges and particularly by Robert J. Schreiter is that all theology is 'contextual'.[108] As taught by the Magisterium, we cannot assume that Latin Christianity is normative, while the Asian

---

[104] Jerald D. Gort, 'Syncretism and Dialogue: Christian Historical and Earlier Ecumenical Perceptions', in *Dialogue and Syncretism: An Interdisciplinary Approach*, edited by Jerald D. Gort, Hendrik M. Vroom, Rein Fernhout, and Anton Wessels (Grand Rapids, MI: William B. Eerdmans Publishing Company, 1989), p. 38.

[105] Paul Hedges, *Controversies in Interreligious Dialogue and the Theology of Religions* (London: SCM Press, 2010), pp. 38-9.

[106] Hedges, *Controversies in Interreligious Dialogue and the Theology of Religions*, p. 42.

[107] Hedges, *Controversies in Interreligious Dialogue and the Theology of Religions*, p. 45.

[108] Hedges, *Controversies in Interreligious Dialogue and the Theology of Religions*, p. 48. See also Kathryn Tanner, *Theories of Cultures* (Minneapolis, MN: Fortress Press, 1997), p. 66.

approach, for example, is contextual in relation to Rome. Schreiter, in fact, argues that plurality is normative: 'The universal theologies ... were in fact *universalizing* theologies; that is to say, they extended the results of their own reflections beyond their own contexts to other settings, usually without an awareness of the rootedness of their theologies within their own contexts.'[109] This point is also highlighted by the Document of the Office of Theological Concerns of the Federation of the Asian Bishops' Conference (FABC) which states: 'The impressive unity in the theological enterprise could only be achieved at the expense of theological pluralism. It is striking how Eurocentric, and even parochial, this theology now appears. The claim of being *the* universal way of doing theology is negated by the obvious limitation that it really is restricted to the particular context in which it originated.'[110]

In other words, we cannot favour one theological style such as the so-called normative, orthodox Christianity, over and above others. Schrieter insists that all theologies must be in relation to other cultural contexts so that we can attend to local needs, while at the same time, developing a theology that is ecumenical.[111] In the religiously pluralistic societies of Asia where Christianity is a minority religion, there should be room for more adaptation and accommodation in the liturgy as well as in theological formulations. Unfortunately, the early missionaries from the West were often driven by an excessive fear of syncretism which was rooted in their sense of superiority and self-righteousness.

During the seventeenth century, the encounter with Asian cultures and religions raised new challenges for foreign missionaries regarding syncretism. In fact, the ancient civilizations of India, China and Japan raised questions about Christian identity and its place in the continent – was there room for Christ in Asia?[112] The Rites Controversy about whether Catholics could take part in ceremonies honouring Confucius

---

[109] Robert J. Schrieter, *The New Catholicity: Theology between the Global and the Local* (Maryknoll, NY: Orbis Books, 1997), p. 2. See also Peter C. Phan, 'Doing Theology in the Context of Cultural and Religious Pluralism: An Asian Perspective', *Louvain Studies* 27 (2002): pp. 53–4.

[110] Quoted in Phan, 'Doing Theology in the Context of Cultural and Religious Pluralism', footnote no. 42.

[111] Schrieter, *The New Catholicity*, p. 49.

[112] Ambrose Ih-Ren Mong, 'Is There Room for Christ in Asia?' *Toronto Journal of Theology* 31, no. 2 (Fall 2015): pp. 223–37.

and family ancestors foregrounds the question of syncretism. Approved initially as a method of accommodation, the Chinese rites were later forbidden by the Vatican in the early eighteenth century because of excessive fear of religious syncretism.

With the publication of *Ad Gentes* by the Vatican, the Catholic Church attempted to restore Matteo Ricci's method of evangelization, bridging the gulf between culture and religion. The Catholic Church now encourages the development of local theologies, which again raises the question of syncretism. In other words, to what extent should a local church be contextualized? What are the limits? One of the challenges facing the Church regarding syncretism is the practice of double religious affiliation where people follow the teachings of two distinct faiths, for example, a Christian who is utilizing Buddhist meditation techniques. The adherent of double religious affiliation does not mix the two religions but keeps them discretely apart. Such practices are popular in Japan, Taiwan, and parts of Asia with Chinese populations. People in these regions wish to experience all channels of divine mediation.

Affiliation with Multiple Religions

The Japanese religion Ryōbu Shintō (Dual Aspect Shintō), also called Shingon Shintō, is a syncretic school that combined Shintō with the teachings of the Shingon sect of Buddhism. Developed between the eighth and fourteenth centuries, this syncretic faith teaches that the Shintō deities are manifestations of Buddhist divinities.[113] In this syncretic faith, there is a mixture of Buddhism and Shintō-based natural kinship. Worshipping in Buddhist temples and Shinto shrines, the adherent is neither a pure Buddhist nor a pure Shintoist. The person participates in Shintō festivals as well as funeral rites performed by Buddhist monks. Japanese religion, which is nation-centred, serves as a means to satisfy the needs of the people either as individuals or collectively.[114] Syncretism is normal and to be expected in Eastern religious traditions; it is in their fundamental structure and practice.

[113.] 'Ryōbu Shintō', *Encyclopedia Britannica*, 19 July 2017. https://www.britannica.com/topic/Ryobu-Shinto.

[114.] Kraemer, "Syncretism," p. 40.

The Chinese approach to religion is pragmatic and universal in the sense that the three dominant religions, Confucianism, Taoism and Buddhism, are treated as one.[115] Their religious allegiance is not to a particular creed but involves participation in the rites and rituals of the three religions. This practice of belonging to several religions simultaneously is a challenge to the Abrahamic faiths that claim exclusivity. Belonging to multiple religions occurs as a result of trying to focus on the ultimate spiritual experience that forms the core of all religious traditions rather than on a given religion itself. It also means remaining faithful to the 'symbolic framework' of one's own religious belief while adopting the 'hermeneutical framework' of another faith. For example, the Mahayana Buddhist tradition has been used to reinterpret Christian theology.[116] There is actually a lot of borrowing between religions: 'religious ideas are fluid and flow into different religions, at times consciously and at times unconsciously, rendering the notion of religious property almost vacuous ... Since all religious borrowing presupposes a certain affinity to particular teachings or practices, it is often difficult to determine where one religion begins and the other ends.'[117]

Increased awareness of religious pluralism in today's world has given people the ability to choose which religions they want to belong to and how many. This practice of belonging to more than one religious tradition appears to be a recent phenomenon in the West. However, in Asia, belonging to more than one religion is very much a part of the history of China, Japan, India, and Nepal. In the East and elsewhere in the ancient world, belonging to multiple religions may have been the norm rather than the exception. Membership in several religions means

---

[115] Leo Lefebure has pointed out to me that 'Chinese history has seen many different stages and differing views of religious diversity, and not all have been open and welcoming to all three traditions. I have heard Buddhists who collectively remember the times when they were persecuted in China.' (E-mail correspondence on June 14, 2021).

[116] Catherine Cornille, 'Introduction', in *Many Mansions?*, edited by Catherine Cornille (Maryknoll, NY: Orbis Books, 2002), 5. The material in this section is taken from Ambrose Mong, *Are Non-Christian Saved?: Joseph Ratzinger's Thoughts on Religious Pluralism*(London: Oneworld Publications, 2015), pp. 228–9.

[117] Catherine Cornille, 'Introduction: On Hermeneutics in Dialogue', in *Interreligious Hermaneutics*, edited by Catherine Cornille and Christopher Conway (Eugene, OR: Cascade Books, 2010), p. xviii.

accepting the theory and practice of other religions and incorporating them into Christianity in a modified form. It involves adopting and living out the beliefs, moral rules and rituals of various religious traditions in the midst of the community of the faithful of yet another religion.

In contrast to the Western context, where belonging to more than one religion implies membership in two or more religious belief systems, in Asia, religions have specialized functions, each responding to different needs and circumstances in a person's life. Asians go to temples, churches, shrines and pagodas to pray and worship, and the basis for their choice, at any given time, depends on their needs and on what a particular deity or spirit is reputed to be able to grant. In this case, it is not religious syncretism in the pejorative sense but a pragmatic approach to the practice of religion.

If non-Christian religions contain 'elements of truth and of grace', belonging to multiple religions is not only desirable, but is also acceptable to many people. The teachings of non-Christian beliefs can be considered a means of salvation from whose traditions and practices Christians can learn and benefit through dialogue. Hence, there should not be any objection or censure if a Christian wishes to follow some doctrinal teachings and religious practices of Buddhism, Confucianism or Hinduism, as long as they are not contrary to or incompatible with Christian faith and morals.[118] One of the most prominent religious scholars who practiced multiple religious belonging was Raimon Panikkar.

Raimon Panikkar

Born in 1918 in Barcelona, Spain, Raimon Panikkar's father was a South Indian of Hindu faith, and his mother a Catalan Catholic. Thus, at an early age, he cultivated two traditions, in which he felt very much at home. Ordained as a Roman Catholic priest in 1946, he became a theologian and sought to integrate Hinduism and Buddhism with his Christian faith. He obtained a PhD in philosophy and a PhD in chemistry from the University of Madrid in 1946 and 1958 respectively, and a PhD in theology from the Lateran University in Rome in 1961. In 1954, he made his first trip to India and studied Hinduism at the University of Mysore and Banaras Hindu University. Regarding his spiritual journey

---

[118.] Peter C. Phan, 'Multiple Religious Belonging: Opportunities and Challenges for Theology and Church', *Theological Studies* 64, no. 3 (2003): p. 504.

Idiosyncrasies of Syncretism 63

on earth, he writes, 'I "left" as a Christian, I "found" myself a Hindu, and I "return" a Buddhist, without having ceased to be a Christian.'[119] His book on Christianity and Hinduism entitled *The Unknown Christ of Hinduism*, first published in 1964 and subsequently revised in 1981, was a groundbreaking work in modern interfaith dialogue.

The letter to the Hebrews tells us that in times past, God had spoken to our ancestors in many ways through the prophets and in these days he has spoken to us through his Son (1:1–2). From this statement, Panikkar concluded that the son had inspired not only the prophets of Israel, but also the Hindu sages. In other words, God has been present through all the works of humankind. He believed the *Logos* itself is speaking in Hinduism, a religion which has been inspiring people for tens of thousands of years.

Since Christ is the Alpha and the Omega, he is also present at the beginning and at the end in Hinduism for 'his grace is the guiding, though hidden, force impelling Hinduism towards its full flowering'. Though the *Logos* is called by many names, his presence and work remain the same. For Panikkar, 'the encounter is not an ideological one, but takes place in the deepest recess of reality – in what Christian tradition calls the Mystery'.[120]

Acknowledging the failure of Christianity and Hinduism to meet at various levels, Panikkar suggested 'interpenetration, mutual fecundation – and a mutation in the self-interpretation of these self-same religious traditions'.[121] Such an encounter, however, required sincerity

---

[119] Raimon Panikkar, *The Intrareligious Dialogue* (New York: Paulist Press, 1999), 42. I was informed that Panikkar was sent to India in 1954 by the founder of Opus Dei to work for them in India, which he then did not do, and he later left the organization. The material on Raimon Pannikar is taken from Ambrose Ih-Ren Mong, *Accommodation and Acceptance: An Exploration in Interfaith Relations* (Cambridge: James Clarke & Co., 2015), pp. 102, 111–13.

[120] Raimon Panikkar, *The Unknown Christ in Hinduism* (London: Darton, Longman & Todd, 1981), p. 3.

[121] Panikkar, *The Unknown Christ in Hinduism*, 35. See also Jyri Komulainen, 'Raimon Panikkar's Cosmotheandrism: Theologizing at the Meeting Point of Hinduism and Christianity', *Exchange* 35, no. 3 (2006), pp. 278–303.

in searching for the truth, ridding oneself of one's prejudices, and affirming a commitment towards one's own religion. This is syncretism in the most positive sense.

Dialogue between religions is becoming more important and imminent today because we are acutely aware that we are dependent on one another: 'The religion of my brother becomes a personal religious concern for me also.'[122] Thoughtful religionists from various traditions realize their need for mutual enlightenment because of conflicts between established religions. There is also an intellectual curiosity to know the other. Panikkar, however, believed true encounters between two living faiths can occur only at the 'existential' or 'ontic-intentional' level.[123] Christianity claims to have special knowledge, a 'gnoseological intentionality', which means the knowledge of God as trinitarian and that our union with him is in Christ. Panikkar believed this 'ontic-intentionality' corresponds to a belief in Hinduism in the 'self-same oneness with the Absolute'.[124] Simply put, both Christians and Hindus seek to be united with God or the absolute at the end of their earthly existence.

This ontic-intentionality may be expressed as 'oneness with the Absolute', 'pure isolation' (*kaivalya*) or *nirvāṇa*, as the Buddhist calls it. Others may even deny the existence of an absolute that one can be united with. Nonetheless, Panikkar maintained that this 'ontic-intentionality' is one and the same: it is this goal or final stage, which all faiths are aiming towards from various perspectives. As such, Christianity and Hinduism have the same beginning and also the same ontic-intentionality. Panikkar also claimed that there is a 'single *terminus a quo* and one *terminus ad quem* in the ontic order'.[125] In other words, they have similar starting and finishing points in spite of differing interpretations regarding them.

[122.] Panikkar, *The Unknown Christ in Hinduism*, p. 35.

[123.] Panikkar, *The Unknown Christ in Hinduism*, 36. Perhaps worth noting in all this is that, as Panikkar insisted, religions do not dialogue, people do! Also, he was not speaking of a philosophical or theological symposium, nor the meeting of religious officials to come to some level of common agreement on a particular point (whether theological or political). Instead, he meant the mystical meeting of religious persons for whom the meeting is a religious event. See Raimon Panikkar, *The Intrareligious Dialogue* (New York, NY: Paulist Press, 1999).

[124.] Panikkar, *The Unknown Christ in Hinduism*, p. 37.

[125.] Panikkar, *The Unknown Christ in Hinduism*, p. 37.

Hesitation of Hindus

Hinduism as a religion prefers peaceful coexistence with other religions to interaction. Besides, some forms of Hinduism are not very concerned with social, economic and political problems. Thus, Christians are often obliged to take the initial step to meet Hindus. Panikkar suggested, 'Christianity and Hinduism meet each other in a reality which partakes of both the Divine and the Human.'[126] In other words, Christ is an ideal point of encounter. Why Christ? Panikkar claimed that in Hinduism, there is no adequate symbol that is mutually acceptable. Besides, Hinduism is not really a religion but a collection of religious traditions.[127]

In other words, Hinduism has no unifying symbol but a plurality of symbols. Furthermore, these symbols do not have the 'same pluralistic polyvalence' which the symbol of Christ possesses.[128] Panikkar admitted that Rama, the Hindu deity, may be a good option because he is both human and the divine, material and spiritual, temporal and eternal. Nonetheless, Panikkar preferred Christ because Jesus is well known globally. There is also the functional similarity that he claimed in relation to *Isvara* in Hindu tradition and Christ in Christian tradition. Further, given its theology of the cross, the importance of suffering and dying, Christ can become a potential key-symbol for other traditions. This is the position that Panikkar holds in *The Unknown Christ of Hinduism*.

Syncretism and the Sign System

As we have seen, Christianity, in its initial development, borrowed and absorbed Greek, Roman, Germanic, Syrian and other cultural and religious elements. In our attempt to understand the nature of syncretism, it is important to ask who determines what is acceptable borrowing and what is not acceptable. This question is related to the relationship between the older churches and the younger churches in mission countries. 'One cannot ask questions about evangelization,

---

[126.] Panikkar, *The Unknown Christ in Hinduism*, p. 37.

[127.] Panikkar, *The Unknown Christ in Hinduism*, p. 38.

[128.] Panikkar, *The Unknown Christ in Hinduism*, 38. See also Daniel P. Sheridan, "Faith in Jesus Christ in the Presence of Hindu Theism," in *The Intercultural Challenge of Raimon Panikkar*, edited by Joseph Prabhu (Maryknoll, NY: Orbis, 1996), pp. 145–61.

conversion, religion, and the like without calling into question the nature and quality of the identity of the existent Christian community.'[129] Are the older churches aware of their own cultural biases? Are they ready to admit their own complicity with colonialism?

Following European expansion in the nineteenth century, Western Christianity invaded local cultures. 'One more Christian, one less Chinese' has long been a popular cliché in the Middle Kingdom. This form of evangelization was considered ideal by missionaries, but it left a negative impression on the collective consciousness of the Chinese, as we have witnessed in the Rites Controversy. Christianity does not seem to be able to accommodate other venerable religious traditions because of its exclusive nature. However, effective evangelization occurs when there is a cultural change: 'If the message of the gospel is genuinely heard in the local culture, that message must find a place among the most fundamental messages of that culture, with a concomitant change in codes, signs, and the entire sign system.' Syncretism is not about doctrines or theology but is about a 'religious sign system' which enables the believers to access the benefits they receive from their faith.[130] A religious sign system is more adaptable to changing conditions. Religion, after all, is a way of life and not merely a particular vision of life based on teachings and traditions.

Syncretism has a power dimension to it: 'In its negative subjective forms, it presupposes an asymmetrical relationship.'[131] The issue of truth is highlighted when there is an accusation of syncretism. Exclusive claims by clergy or religious authorities, believing that only they have the truth, lead to much effort being spent on eliminating contradictions or what they believe to be impure elements that threaten the faith. André Droogers asserts that 'an almost decisive factor determining the reaction of a religion to syncretism (in the objective sense), is the concept of truth prevailing in the religion. In situations of contact, exclusivist claims will give rise to accusations of syncretism (in the negative subjective sense)

---

[129] Robert J. Schreiter, *Constructing Local Theologies*, 30th anniversary edition (Maryknoll, NY: Orbis, 2015), p. 115.

[130] Schreiter, *Constructing Local Theologies*, p. 119.

[131] André Droogers, 'Syncretism: The Problem of Definition, the Definition of the Problem', in *Dialogue and Syncretism: An Interdisciplinary Approach*, edited by Jerald D. Gort, Hendrik M. Vroom, Rein Fernhout, and Anton Wessels (Grand Rapids, MI: William B. Eerdmans Publishing Company, 1989), p. 16.

as their necessary complement.' He writes: 'the exclusive claims are often maintained by a class of religious specialists who monopolize ... the definition of truth, and spend a lot of time eliminating possible contradictions and oppositions.'[132] In the name of truth, the clergy will attempt to maintain unity and control. They will use the full force of their authority to impose their own vision of faith, sometimes with the help of secular powers. Used in a derogatory sense by the religious elite, syncretism is regarded as unauthorized teachings and practices.

However, as we have discussed earlier, for many people, the criterion to judge a religion is a phenomenal experience, not truth in the abstract sense. Besides, the idea of absolute truth is far-fetched and unreachable. As such, popular piety, with its emphasis on experience, is able to exist side-by-side with the official religion depending on how the power struggle is being played out, between laity and clergy or between native culture and colonialism. A good example of this phenomenon is the devotion to the Child Jesus in the Philippines.

Santo Niño de Cebu

The symbols used in syncretism may represent the people's protest, that is, the struggle of the oppressed against secular and sacred authorities. The sufferings that Filipinos endured through the centuries have made them not only more resilient in the face of tragedies and setbacks but also very persistent and faithful in their religious belief, which is woven into the fabric of their culture. One of the most popular devotions in Filipino folk Catholicism is the veneration of the image of Santo Niño or the Infant Jesus. 'Take away the image (Santo Niño) and the Philippines loses the diadem of her Christianity.'[133]

Devotion to Santo Niño is perhaps the start of the foundation of the Catholic faith in the Philippines. The image of the Holy Infant was a gift given to Juana, the local queen, by Magellan at her baptism in 1521. This led to many conversions from paganism to Catholicism. Such peaceful

---

[132] Droogers, 'Syncretism', p. 16.
[133] Luna Dingayan, 'Popular Religion and Evangelization: A Philippine Experience', *International Review of Mission* 82, no. 327 (1993), p. 356. The material in this section on Santo Niño is taken from Ambrose Mong, *Power of Popular Piety: A Critical Examination* (Eugene, OR: Cascade Books, 2019), pp. 50–3.

transition from one belief to another is characterized as 'the irreversible mystical process of proto conversion and proto-evangelization'.[134] In this case, it involved the miraculous power of the Child Jesus substituting for the magical power of *anito*, the local deity. This is a classic example of the acculturation of Christianity into a folk culture – a gradual shift from a pagan to a Christian belief system. This kind of folk Catholicism still retains vestiges of pagan beliefs.

When formal evangelization took place with the Legazpi expedition in 1565, the native people embraced the Christian faith without much difficulty. Indigenous belief was absorbed into the structure of Roman Catholicism. Local practices such as the *sinulug* or 'ritual dance' blended smoothly with Catholic symbolism and practices, thus contributing to the development of a Filipino Christian culture. After 44 years, from 1521 (arrival of Magellan) to 1565 (Legazpi expedition), the Cebuanos claimed Santo Niño as their very own: 'This cognitive paradigm shift is a synchronism which started the largely successful and spontaneous overthrow of pagan religion and its replacement, at the same place and period in time by what is seen here as Christian mysticism.'[135]

In other words, there was already a well-defined system of mystical beliefs and practices when Magellan arrived in Cebu. Evangelization by Spanish friars resulted in the superimposition on the indigenous culture of a more established religious structure, Iberian Catholicism, in which the veneration of the Infant Jesus played an important role.

In this popular piety, Catholic practices include the following: veneration of the original image of Santo Niño at the Basilica, novenas, prayers, petitioning, thanksgiving, the lighting of candles, and the changing the image's clothes before the fiesta. Local folk practices include fulfilling vows, offering of gifts, wiping of the image with a handkerchief, and the traditional *sinulug* ritual dance. There are also civil practices such as the *sinulug* parades and other festive entertainment.

Catholic pious practices and devotions took root in Filipino soil due to the fact that the Spanish friars' brand of folk Catholicism had some similarities with the religious practices of the natives, such as trust in a supreme being presiding over the spirits of the universe, belief in the existence of angels, and veneration of saints. Of course, this is a

---

[134.] Astrid Sala-Boza, 'Towards Filipino Christian Culture: Mysticism and Folk Catholicism in the Señor Sto. Niño de Cebu', *Philippine Quarterly of Culture and Society* 36, no. 4 (2008), p. 281.

[135.] Sala-Boza, 'Towards Filipino Christian Culture', p. 284.

generalization. Some of the early missionaries from Spain were scholars and theologians. Later, however, there were also many friars from the convents in Spain who were simple peasants without higher education; they brought with them religious practices and ways of relating to God to which the ways of worship of the native people could be adapted.[136]

Unlike Protestantism, folk Catholicism accommodates and tolerates some forms of polytheism. Roman Catholicism remains strong in the Philippines in spite of fierce proselytization by American evangelicals since the early twentieth century and the Filipinos' fondness for American culture in contrast to their resentment against the Spanish friars in the past.

The cult of Santo Niño is essentially a syncretism of Catholic indigenous practices and civil activities. This devotion is immensely popular even during the twentieth and twenty-first centuries, partly because it serves as a tourist attraction and also partly because of the flexibility with which the Catholic Church incorporates images taken from the local culture.

Luna Dingayan, a pastor of the United Church of Christ in the Philippines, believes the image of Santo Niño was brought by the Spanish colonizers to pacify the natives. In Spain, devotion to Santo Niño can be understood in relation to their 800 years of suffering and oppression under the Moors, which has resulted in Spanish Christianity being characterized by a profound sense of tragedy and death. Ironically, or perhaps naturally, it seems that the Spaniards treated the Filipinos the way they had been treated by the Moors.

Popular expressions of piety such as devotion to Santo Niño could work in both directions: first, it could be a good expression of repentance and renewal after being liberated from bondage; second, such religious practice could also be encouraged so that people remain passive and simply accept the unjust situation. For example, during the time of the dictatorship under President Marcos, propagation of this kind of popular piety was used to enhance the interests of his family and cronies.[137] However, as we shall see, the image of Santo Niño was also incorporated into Filipino nationalism as a symbol of protest against Spanish domination.

---

[136] Charles J-H. Macdonald, 'Folk Catholicism and Pre-Spanish Religions in the Philippines', *Philippine Studies* 52, no. 1 (2004), pp. 87–8.

[137] Dingayan, 'Popular Religion and Evangelization', p. 357.

Poverty is a complex problem that cannot be alleviated by simply offering prayers to Santo Niño. Such devotion could be alienating, promoting 'a culture of passivity, fatalism, and superstition'.[138] In other words, adherence to the image of the Infant Jesus could consciously or unconsciously perpetuate the situation of poverty and injustice. It could be seen as the opium of the people. However, images can also be liberating if they symbolize the realities of the living conditions and the expectations and hopes of the people. In fact, in the history of the Philippines, Santo Niño had been assimilated as a symbol of protest against Spanish rule.

Anti-Colonial Icon

At the end of the nineteenth century, Santo Niño was utilized by some political activists in Cebu as an anti-colonial symbol. This icon, crafted in Spain, was used as a symbol of nationalism against Spanish domination: 'The national "awakening" inscribed in anti-colonial revolution frames this as a specifically subversive loyalty in which, through the Santo Niño, Cebuano revolutionaries imagined a future autonomous from the designs of the Spanish empire.'[139] In Santo Niño, Cebuanos found a figure that could foster hope and anticipation of being freed from oppression, and could also help to facilitate social and political change in the city. The locals reappropriated this Western icon in a 'Filipinized' form signified by dressing the figure in local attire and thus making it an emblem of anti-colonial revolution.[140]

On 3 April 1898, a group of professionals and gentry clashed with Spanish soldiers at Veleriano Weyler Street (later renamed Tres de Abril Street) in Cebu. Inspired by anti-Spanish sentiments in Manila, the revolutionaries, led by Pantaleon Villegas (Leon Kilat), in collaboration with a secret society known as Katipunan, decided to overthrow the Spanish armed forces in Cebu. They were able to force the colonial troops into the Spanish headquarters, Fort San Pedro. As the Spanish

---

[138] Dingayan, 'Popular Religion and Evangelization', p. 358.
[139] Julius Bautista, 'The Rebellion and the Icon: Holy Revolutions in the Philippines', *Asian Journal of Social Science* 34, no. 2 (2006), p. 294.
[140] Bautista, 'The Rebellion and the Icon', p. 295.

soldiers withdrew, crying 'Viva España!', the revolutionaries shouted triumphantly, 'Mabuhi ang Katipunan! Mabuhi ang Santo Niño!' (Long live the Katipunan! Long live the Santo Niño!).[141]

Unfortunately, the success of this event, now known as the *Tres de Abril* uprising, was short-lived. Spanish warships arrived, reprisal was quick and violent, and many Cebuanos were killed, including the leader Leon Kilat. The Spanish regained control of the city. Nevertheless, the brief victory of the *Tres de Abril* uprising was of great significance compared to the dismal failure of other anti-Spanish campaigns in Manila. As far as the Cebuanos were concerned, the victory was brought about by the Santo Niño icon, which means the uprising had divine support, even if it was for a short duration. It also represents the victory of folk Catholicism, assisted by Santo Niño in no small measure, against its official proponent. An icon of revolution, Santo Niño symbolizes 'syncretistic or "folk" modes of Catholic faith'.[142] Furthermore, there is also a biblical understanding of this *Tres de Abril* uprising. It represents the child Jesus wandering away from his parents during the Festival of the Passover. Jesus was later found in the temple talking to the teachers. The independence of the twelve-year-old Jesus was not lost on the Cebuanos who were seeking independence from the mother country.

Critical Reflection

Syncretism is actually a natural human response towards the absolute mystery, for it satisfies our desire for security and assurance by encircling our faith with diverse spiritual elements. The distinguished missiologist Louis Luzbetak speaks of the relationship between local tradition, Church tradition and the gospel: it is a 'dialectic', not an 'edict', wherein the religious aspirations often hidden by syncretism are taken seriously.[143] It is thus a process, a natural development that comes from below and is not imposed from the top. Syncretism could act as a bridge to cross from non-Christian to Christian belief. Authentic syncretism occurs when the culture is being Christianized rather than when the gospel is being culturalized. The focus should be on the message of Jesus

---

[141] Bautista, 'The Rebellion and the Icon', p. 296.
[142] Bautista, 'The Rebellion and the Icon', p. 297.
[143] Luzbetak, *The Church and Culture*, p. 370.

and the values of the gospel to be inculcated in our lives. The core values of the Christian faith are preserved and translated into cultural norms that are meaningful to people.

Leonardo Boff believes the future of Catholicism depends on its ability to syncretize: Since catholicity implies universality, the ability to integrate diverse cultural elements is needed to remain relevant and meaningful.[144] While Boff emphasizes the challenges and shortcomings of Roman Catholicism, the same thing can be said about Christianity in general. If we understand Catholicism, or Christianity for that matter, as a perfect religion, then syncretism is a threat to be avoided. For those who desire to live out their faith together with other religious expressions, syncretism is a natural process. However, our knowledge of syncretism usually comes from defenders of ecclesiastical teachings who are critical of syncretism. Even *Ad Gentes*, the Vatican II document that promotes accommodation to other cultures, teaches that 'every appearance of syncretism and of false particularism will be excluded'.[145]

If syncretism involves simply mixing foreign elements in a superficial and disparate manner, resulting in dilution and confusion, then it is to be avoided at all costs. Syncretism is to be welcomed if one religion uses the categories and cultural expressions of another religion to translate or convey its core message. For Christianity, a religion that needs to incarnate itself in different cultures, syncretism is a valid process, despite the fact that, at times, it might threaten the integrity of the faith. The religious diversity and pluralism in the world require that Christianity open itself to the richness of religious expressions to create a new image relevant today.[146]

There is no such thing as pure Christianity. Religions are syncretic by nature because the divine, mediated by human agency, is always dialectical. Thus, there will always be tensions between the prophetic and priestly movements. Concretely present, the Church is the 'historical-cultural expression and religious objectification of Christianity'.[147] The Church as a human institution is as syncretic as other religious

---

[144] Leonardo Boff, *Church: Charism and Power – Liberation Theology and the Institutional Church* (London: SCM Press, 1984), p. 89.

[145] *Ad Gentes*, On the Mission Activity of the Church, http://www.vatican.va/archive/hist_councils/ii_vatican_council/documents/vat-ii_decree_19651207_ad-gentes_en.html, no. 22.

[146] Boff, *Church: Charism and Power*, p. 92.

[147] Boff, *Church: Charism and Power*, p. 92.

Idiosyncrasies of Syncretism

institutions. In fact, Catholicism is 'a grandiose and infinitely complex syncretism'.[148] It affirms its own Christian identity while accepting and incorporating older religious values in a new syncretism. Not issuing directly from the hands of God, religion is a cultural expression of human relations with the divine. A gift from God, religion is a human construct whose origin is supernatural. Dialectical in nature, syncretism is not necessarily a threat to religion. It is a normal process of how human beings express their spiritual longings.

True syncretism comes about when the core Christian message is embodied in another cultural framework, when there is a conversion of the culture to gospel values. Otherwise, the Christian identity is totally absorbed by another culture. The process of syncretism takes place once there is conversion to the Christian faith.[149] The Christian identity is developed in another culture through borrowing 'from the customs and traditions of their people, from their wisdom and their learning, from their arts and disciplines, all those things which can contribute to the glory of their Creator, or enhance the grace of their Saviour, or dispose Christian life the way it should be'.[150]

It could also happen that another religion enters into Christianity, syncretizing its elements and thus absorbing the Christian identity. This does not mean that the new religion is useless or false. It simply means that it falls outside the theological boundaries established by the Church authorities. Like popular piety, non-Christian religion is also God's gift of salvation. It may have absorbed some Christian values or elements into its system, but it is not Christianity per se. Examples of such religious beliefs are found in Latin America, like the *yoruba* religion in Brazil.[151] The role of the Church should be to transform this native religion by proclaiming the Christian faith and syncretizing those local elements that are compatible with Christian belief. Scripture and the tradition of the universal Church are the criteria used for true Christian syncretism.[152]

---

[148] Boff, *Church: Charism and Power*, p. 92.

[149] Boff, *Church: Charism and Power*, p. 101.

[150] *Ad Gentes*, On the Mission Activity of the Church, http://www.vatican.va/archive/hist_councils/ii_vatican_council/documents/vat-ii_decree_19651207_ad-gentes_en.html, no. 22.

[151] Boff, *Church: Charism and Power*, p. 102.

[152] Boff, *Church: Charism and Power*, p. 104.

The Christian identity is not synonymous with the Greco-Roman structure of Western Christianity. It is not a historical replica, but an experience and a way of life related to that of Jesus of Nazareth, his life, death, and resurrection as recounted in the New Testament. To participate in the salvation offered by Jesus is not about joining a Christian community; it is to live the same experience of Christ, to obey his command to love one another.

True Christian syncretism will lead to greater participation in the building of God's kingdom, where justice, fraternity, and love between persons flourish. The future of Christianity lies in its ability to devise new syncretism. This means the Church must have the courage to abandon its old syncretism and formulate a new one, accepting and purifying the values of other cultures. In other words, the Church must go through the paschal experience, for it is only through dying to ourselves that we can rise again to new life. The deeper our faith in the incarnation of Jesus Christ, the more willing we are to accept the challenges of a new syncretism.

Topics for discussion and reflection

- Looking at the evolution of syncretism, were there more positives or negatives for the development of Christianity?
- Numerous studies indicate that the numbers of religious believers have been on the rise. Assuming this trend continues, how might syncretism act as a positive lever to bridge the gap between Christians and believers of other faiths?
- Taking a macroscopic view and following the posits from Lord Herbert of Cherbury or Raimon Panikkar, or the Asian readiness to integrate multiple religious practices, what could Christian leaders do to optimize the positives of syncretism while truthfully maintaining Christian faith?

Chapter 4

Sociological Perspective

Fools say in their hearts, 'There is no God' (Psalm 14:1).

Belief in the supernatural is a universal phenomenon. Some form of religion is found in every known culture and is usually accepted by the community. The practice of religion includes celebrations of festivals, rituals and ceremonies, prayers and meditations, marriages and funerals, offering sacrifice to the divinities or service to the poor. As such, religion is a social institution with established rules regarding the beliefs and behaviour of its believers centred on social needs and norms.

As social scientists explore religious experiences, beliefs and rituals, they often apply three paradigms in sociology to understand the relationship between religion and society: i. functionalism, ii. symbolic interactionism, and iii. conflict theory. With functionalism, religion provides the answer to spiritual mysteries or comfort to those suffering. Another important function of religion is providing space for social interaction and community building. Symbolic interactionism examines, for example, how the cross, as a sacred symbol, communicates to believers about Jesus Christ's suffering, death and resurrection. With conflict theory, researchers analyse the power dynamics in religion, and how it can be used to enslave or liberate people. Very often, religion is a mere reflection of social and economic forces, but at times, it can also generate a liberating power to reform society. Marx asserts that nineteenth-century capitalism colluded with religion, exploiting and enslaving the population. However, if religion can be self-critical, it can be a source of power to expose exploitation and halt alienation.

This chapter examines the relationship between religion and society in the writings of Karl Marx (1818–83, Friedrich Engels (1820–95), Émile Durkheim (1858–1917), and Max Weber (1864–1920). These thinkers generally agreed that religion is a projection of human longing and aspirations, but they were all conditioned by their respective historical circumstances: Marx's perception of religion was essentially negative, whereas Durkheim and Weber acknowledged the positive role faith could play in promoting human solidarity and economic prosperity. This chapter also attempts to show that, like most social phenomena, the development of religion is not linear but dialectic. Many early social theorists predicted that secularization would signal the end of religion. Yet, recent history has revealed that religion is here to stay, albeit sometimes in different forms.

Marxist Criticism

Influenced by Ludwig Feuerbach's *The Essence of Christianity* (1841), Marx believes that religion and divinities are projections of people. Theology begins with the study of God as pre-existing and as the creator of humankind; Marx, however, argues that it was human beings who created God. In his criticism of religion, Marx exposes how human beings have misled themselves when they attempted to cope with the difficulties of life. People have an innate desire to search for a superhero, but have found nothing but reflections of themselves. Marx is convinced that religion is manufactured by humans: 'religion is the self-consciousness and self-feeling of man who has either not yet found himself or has already lost himself again.'[153] Put simply, human beings created God, not God human beings. It is society that produces religion to serve as its moral guide, as the ground for consolation, and as justification for its existence.

To obtain true happiness, Marx believes that it is necessary to abolish religion, or more accurately, the condition that allows the flourishing of such belief, which can only offer 'illusory happiness'. Hence, his famous

---

[153] Karl Marx and Friedrich Engels, *On Religion* (New York, NY: Schocken Books, 1964), 41. See also Frederick E. Sontag and John K Roth, 'Is the Criticism of Religion the Premise of All Criticism?' *Philosophy of Religion and Theology: 1976 Proceedings*, edited by Peter Slater (Missoula, MT: Scholars Press of for the American Academy of Religion, 1976), p. 104.

saying: 'Religion is the sigh of the oppressed creature, the heart of a heartless world, just as it is the spirit of a spiritless situation. It is the opium of the people.'[154] Opium gives temporary relief to the sufferings of the oppressed, who are often exploited by the wealthy. Marx maintains that we must get rid of such a condition that allows injustice to exist. It is the responsibility of human beings 'to unmask self-alienation in its holy forms'.[155] It is high time, he felt, that people understand the danger of adverse effects of this 'drug' that they have been taking. In other words, we must destroy the illusion and the self-deception caused by religion.

Be that as it may, rich people also need religion. In fact, the history of Christianity has shown that many Christians came from the privileged classes. Revising Marx's phrase, sociologist Rodney Stark says, 'Religion often is the opium of the dissatisfied upper classes, the sigh of wealthy creatures depressed by empty materialism.'[156] Perhaps prejudice against the wealthy class prevented Marx from perceiving such a possibility.

Marx's understanding of religion is dialectic. The sufferings of the people are real and religious belief is a great source of consolation. Opium is both a medicine and a destructive narcotic, depending on how we use it. It is cheap and beneficial; it is used as a painkiller in surgeries. Many farmers make a living cultivating opium poppy. Famous artists, poets and writers such as Thomas De Quincey, Samuel Taylor Coleridge, and Marx himself used opium. Opium is equally relevant for both oppressor and oppressed. Thus, for Marx, opium is a multivalent metaphor for religion.[157]

Christianity teaches that human beings, born in original sin, are equal and in need of salvation. Engels believes this teaching supports the idea that Christianity is the religion of the slaves and oppressed. Such an emphasis on equality promotes common ownership and solidarity among the followers. However, this sense of equality among Christians comes to an end when there is a distinction between priests and laity.[158]

---

[154] Marx and Engels, *On Religion*, p. 42.
[155] Marx and Engels, *On Religion*, p. 42.
[156] Rodney Stark, 'SSSR Presidential Address, 2004: Putting an End to Ancestor Worship', *Journal for the Scientific Study of Religion* 43, no. 4 (2004), p. 473.
[157] Roland Boer, 'Opium, Idols and Revolution: Marx and Engels on Religion', *Religion Compass* 5, no. 11 (2011), p. 703.
[158] Marx and Engels, *On Religion*, p. 145

Equality as an expression of justice is a recent historical development, Engels asserts, as such an idea did not exist in ancient societies where slavery was prevalent. To speak of equality among Greeks, Romans, barbarians, and freemen, etc., would be an offence or an insult among the ancients. Catholicism, however, teaches that all human beings before God are sinners. We are equal as children of God redeemed by the blood of Jesus Christ. Thus, in the beginning, Christianity attracted slaves, the banished, the dispossessed, the persecuted and the oppressed.

The ambitious Constantine saw the adoption of Christianity as the best means to exalt himself as emperor. Christians became the privileged group and pagans, heretics, and unorthodox were relegated to the bottom of the heap. Here again, we witness the dialectic tension when Christianity 'entered into a resolute antithesis to all previous religions'.[159] In its initial stage, Christianity was the faith of slaves who had to console themselves that a better life was possible. Engels writes: 'for such consolation of their consciousness, for this flight from the external world into the internal, were necessarily among slaves'.[160] Christianity could only flourish in such an unjust situation, where social divisions, slavery, and poverty existed.

Competing with many beliefs in the Middle East, Christianity won, according to Engels, in the 'Darwinistic struggle for ideological existence', becoming a universal religion.[161] The reasons for its success in this natural selection among the competing sects are as follows: Christianity accepted all peoples, with no cultural or national barriers to membership. Most countries have their own national gods, but Christianity has a universal God that embraces all humankind. Christianity's teaching on sin, the culpability of humankind for their wickedness, struck a chord of empathy with many who lamented the moral decadence of this world. The idea of atonement to avert the wrath of a deity and the self-sacrifice of its founder for the sins of the world expressed the universal guilt and gratitude of people conscious of their own wickedness.[162] In other words, Christianity makes sense to many who believe the world is corrupt and in need of salvation; it is a religion based on faith and reason.

---

[159] Marx and Engels, *On Religion*, p. 202.
[160] Marx and Engels, *On Religion*, p. 202.
[161] Marx and Engels, *On Religion*, p. 204.
[162] Marx and Engels, *On Religion*, pp. 203–4.

Engels points out that the history of early Christianity resembles that of the modern working-class movement. Christianity was originally a movement for people who were deprived of their rights and controlled by Rome. Both Christianity and workers' socialism emphasize liberation from slavery and suffering. For Christianity, such salvation would come in the next world, in the afterlife, in heaven; for socialism, it would happen when society is transformed. Members of these two movements are persecuted and despised, looked upon as enemies of the human race and of the state, respectively. In spite of persecutions and sufferings, both Christianity and socialism persevered and flourished.

Indeed, within three hundred years of its foundation, Christianity became the state religion in the Roman Empire. Likewise, socialism eventually was recognized as a workable political system, one which would conquer the world. In medieval times, persecuted peasants and urban plebeians took part in mass uprisings, which appeared to be motivated by religious fervor. Engels asserts that behind every religious upheaval, there are always material or economic motives.[163]

In sum, Marx and Engels suggested that religion is essentially man-made, a reflection of society. There is nothing supernatural about religion as they saw it. Influenced by Darwin's evolutionism and Hegel's dialecticism, Marx and Engels believed religion, like every social phenomenon, evolved, transformed and would eventually disappear. Since they believed that religion, like 'opium', does more harm than good, it was important to them to expose its side effects and deceptions; in other words, to promote atheism.

Can Christians Be Marxists?

Marx held that religion was a kind of false consciousness, which eventually will pass away as society progresses. Critics consider Marx's understanding of society – defined as merely the material system of economic production and distribution – as too narrow. The notion of a religious ideology serving as a tool for the material interests of the rich against the poor is not necessarily false, but it must always be verified.[164] Religion is not just a form of alienation, but can also advance aspirations

---

[163] Marx and Engels, *On Religion*, pp. 317–18.

[164] Patrick Collinson, 'Religion, Society, and the Historian', *Journal of Religious History* 23, no. 2 (1999), 158. For a detailed refutation of the theses of

and strengthen the identities of social classes and nations. To the extent that it practices self-criticism, religion can be a source of power for the downtrodden.

Marx considered atheism to be one condition to establish a socialist society, but Jesuit Arthur McGovern holds that it is not inseparable from Marx's method of analysis. In other words, a Christian can adopt Marxist ideas or Marxist analysis, and his or her religious conviction can be separated from atheism. Marxism is not a set of dogmas that cannot be changed; it is a social theory open to revision because this movement is a product of changing historical circumstances.[165] Influenced by their own historical conditions, Marx and Engels advocated atheism as a condition for socialism because they viewed religion as an alienating force in human existence. Marx was a humanist who viewed religious belief as a kind of slavery that must be abolished for human beings to be free again.

In the spirit of the Enlightenment and supporting Marx's atheism, Engels argued that, eventually, science and materialism would replace religion. Marx and Engels believed that the inability of human beings to control nature led to the creation of religious beliefs. Anthropologists and naturalists, however, have not found any evidence that primitive people were afraid of nature or could not control it.[166] For them, religion is about rites of passage such as birth, marriage, death and the celebration of life. Religion not only functions as an escape from misery or as justification of the status quo, but can also function as a liberating force.

There is also a difference between 'religious feelings' which motivate people to work for social change and 'religious institutions' that serve the social order.[167] Marxism is also protected by its own ideology once it is established as a regime since it is the nature of institutions to protect and maintain their status quo. Institutionalized Marxism serves as the ideological foundation and justification of one-party rule in Communist nations, with dissent rarely tolerated.

Marx, Durkheim and Weber, see Stark, 'SSSR Presidential Address, 2004', pp. 465–75.

[165] Arthur F. McGovern, 'Atheism: Is It Essential to Marxism?' *Journal of Ecumenical Studies* 22, no. 3 (1985), p. 488.

[166] McGovern, 'Atheism: Is It Essential to Marxism?' p. 494.

[167] McGovern, 'Atheism: Is It Essential to Marxism?' p. 494.

Marx diagnosed religion as a social illness that was alienating, and prescribed atheism as the remedy. History has shown that his view of religion was limited, but such prejudice against religion did not contradict his commitment to humanity. Furthermore, Marxism is not a religion: it is a social theory that can be revised, updated, and changed. If Marx could see the positive side of religion as a formidable force for social transformation, we can safely conclude that atheism might not be essential or intrinsic to Marxism.[168] As a humanist, Marx's fundamental aim was human emancipation, and the abolition of religion was just a condition which could be changed.

The Marxist critique of religion exerted great influence, especially on the Frankfurt School of critical theory. Critics may agree or disagree with a Marxist reading of religion, but the shadow of Marx and Engels is always present when they discuss the social dimension of faith.

Critical Theory

The Frankfurt School theorists view religion, such as Christianity, as 'a heterogeneous phenomenon that intersects at many levels with social existence'.[169] Religion, as a part of society, mediates and constitutes it. As an institution, religion merges communities, and churches provide societies with a common language to express joy and sorrow. Although it plays an integral role in social evolution, religion has never been exhausted by this process of change. In fact, according to the Frankfurt School, religion inspires the development of critical thinking and the formation of new cultures, and is itself 'indoctrinated into the service of new and more acute forms of domestication and pacification'.[170] From the lens of critical theory, it has also been used as a socio-political tool.

The Frankfurt School's critical theory attempts 'to think religion *with* religion and *against* religion' and 'to rescue theology for the sake of reason'.[171] Simply put, it tried to expose the falsity of superstition so that people can be free from the bondage of irrational fear through the

---

[168.] McGovern, 'Atheism: Is It Essential to Marxism?' p. 497.

[169.] Eduardo Mendieta, 'Introduction: Religion as Critique', in *The Frankfurt School on Religion: Key Writings by the Major Thinkers*, edited by Eduardo Mendieta (New York, NY: Routledge, 2005), p. 8.

[170.] Mendieta, 'Introduction: Religion as Critique', p. 9.

[171.] Mendieta, 'Introduction: Religion as Critique', p. 9.

'demystification of social reality'.[172] Formulating a 'negative theology', critical theorists emphasize the absence of God or the exile of God from creation as resulting in the sufferings of humanity.[173] Rejecting Christianity's salvation history, critical theory attempts to prove that progress is an illusion as revealed by the destruction of our environment. It simply cannot accept a God that is reconciled with the miseries of this world. Theology cannot be an excuse for the sufferings that are so much part of our social reality, suffering that has increased up to modern times.

The negative or atheistic theology promoted by the Frankfurt School rejects God for the sake of God. As Adorno asserted, 'God, the Absolute, eludes finite beings. Where they desire to name him, because they must, they betray him. However, if they keep silent about him, they acquiesce in their own impotence and sin against the other, no less binding, commandment to name him.'[174] Thus we must refute and reject religion when it is used as a tool for totalitarianism. In the opinion of critical theorists, when religion is useless, it is true, and if it is useful, it is not true. The Frankfurt School theorist Ernst Bloch said, 'Only an atheist can be a good Christian; only a Christian can be a good atheist.'[175] In other words, scepticism and doubt help us be better Christians, in that we do not take our faith and its teaching for granted but rather expose them to reason and criticism. Frankfurt School theorists call this negative theology.

This negative theology is reason in search of hope and truth, as Horkheimer asserts. 'Faced with the sciences and the entire present situation, my idea of expressing the concept of an omnipotent and benevolent Being no longer as a dogma, but as longing that unites all men so that the horrible events, the injustice of history so far would not be permitted to be the final, ultimate fate of the victims, seems close to the solution of the problem.'[176] This yearning for a benevolent being is Horkheimer's desire for a just society. Here, theology is drawn into the service of social justice and peace. The Frankfurt School theorists attempt to find out what makes religion a source of conflict and alienation as well as a source of hope and redemption. They also

---

[172.] Mendieta, 'Introduction: Religion as Critique', p. 10.
[173.] Mendieta, 'Introduction: Religion as Critique', p. 10.
[174.] Quoted in Mendieta, 'Introduction: Religion as Critique', p. 10.
[175.] Quoted in Mendieta, 'Introduction: Religion as Critique', p. 11.
[176.] Quoted in Mendieta, 'Introduction: Religion as Critique', p. 11.

encourage interreligious dialogue in which the nature of faith can be analysed as opium or as genuine hope. In spite of its chequered history, a religion like Christianity can aid in human flourishing. In fact, Edmund Arens argues that religion can help cement members in a community through its cultic worship and rituals.

Arens asserts that religion is essentially a 'way of life' or 'a praxis of life'; it copes with contingency and the faith is to be practiced in 'communicative praxis'.[177] Communication is fundamental to human life: no society can exist if there is no communicative exchange. Religion is profoundly linked to communication through speech and action, revealing reality and its nuances. Communication comes in the form of texts, traditions, rituals, prayers, worship, prophesy and more. One of its functions as praxis is coping, overcoming, and accepting contingency. In fact, the problem of contingency lies at the heart of all philosophical and religious inquiries. Thus, the function of religion is to deal with eventuality. Rituals cannot change anything, but they serve to confirm what exists, like the consecration of a new church, the blessing of a new home and the inauguration of a new president. The question of truth is also irrelevant in the study of religion, because what really matters, according to Hermann Lübbe, is whether the religion can cope with contingency through accepting it.[178] Further, religion is not affirmed for its own sake, but functions as a tool to promote stability and harmony in society. Lübbe appears to treat religion like a placebo, a fake drug. Oblivious of the harsh realities of life, this is an empty 'alienated bourgeois religion' that merely supports the socio-political status quo.[179]

In theistic religion, worship is a 'central ritual praxis'.[180] The act of ritual worship or celebration is viewed as a cult, essentially 'an event of communication',[181] whereby a community performs actions that come into contact with the supernatural power and with one another. In these ritualized actions, the authority and roles of the participants are carefully distributed. It takes place at a particular time and location. 'The cult gives divine reality space and time; gives it presence in the

---

[177] Edmund Arens, 'Religion as Ritual, Communicative, and Critical Praxis', in *The Frankfurt School on Religion: Key Writings by the Major Thinkers*, edited by Eduardo Mendieta (New York, NY: Routledge, 2005), pp. 373–4.
[178] Arens, 'Religion as Ritual, Communicative, and Critical Praxis', p. 376.
[179] Arens, 'Religion as Ritual, Communicative, and Critical Praxis', p. 377.
[180] Arens, 'Religion as Ritual, Communicative, and Critical Praxis', p. 381.
[181] Arens, 'Religion as Ritual, Communicative, and Critical Praxis', p. 381.

celebrating community; and thereby reveals, opens, and qualifies reality itself. Cultic action is at the same time communicative. It creates, strengthens and transforms community.'[182] In cultic worship, language, music and gestures are integrated into highly elaborated rituals and dramas. The cult is indispensable for the practice of religion because it expresses the human encounter with divinity and also its members' experience of the community. To Arens, religion only takes place in a cultic realm and through ritual action or liturgical ceremony.

The cult, a ritual action, can also degenerate into magic and destroy communities. This happens when the cult is threatened by power and corruption. Ritual action is deeply shaped by power, and from time to time, cultic actions have been criticized and their legitimacy questioned. For example, Old Testament prophets denounced the false worship of the Israelites when cultic practices had been corrupted by power and money, thus destroying the community.[183] The antithesis is the prophetic critique which serves the purpose of integrating society in a more holistic community living where there is sharing of spiritual and material resources.

Believing and Belonging

Émile Durkheim's pioneering study, *The Elementary Forms of Religious Life* (1912), provides us with valuable insights regarding the early stages of religious development. In fact, Durkheim's text remains a classic, a standard to which all other works are compared. His research throws light on the historical development of human response to absolute mystery. Durkheim envisioned the possibility of religious revival, the birth of new gods, and occasions for the flourishing of human lives. He believed that religious life would survive despite the growing secularism we witness in the West. His study of religion from a sociological perspective has advanced our understanding of human existence.

Durkheim researched totemism, the aboriginal religion in Australia, as a paradigm to understand a permanent feature in human existence – spiritual aspiration. He concluded that 'if religion generated everything that is essential in society, this is because the idea of society is the soul

---

[182] Arens, 'Religion as Ritual, Communicative, and Critical Praxis', p. 381.

[183] Arens, 'Religion as Ritual, Communicative, and Critical Praxis', p. 382.

of religion'.[184] For Durkheim, religion is comprised of beliefs, ideas and practices that shape our moral outlook in society. In his study of totemism, Durkheim argues that society and the symbol of religion are two sides of the same coin, as it were. The god of the clan must be the clan itself, 'but transfigured and imagined in the physical form of the plant or animal species that serve as totems'.[185] Religion is a force that binds individuals to society. It follows that the ideas and practices of society invariably acquire a religious dimension that influences all aspects of the community.

Durkheim also maintains that '[a] religion is a unified system of beliefs and practices relative to sacred things ... things set apart and surrounded by prohibitions – beliefs and practices that unite its adherents in a single moral community called a church'.[186] This means that believing and belonging must go hand in hand. As a member of a religion, you need to belong to a community or a church. Hence, religion is a set of beliefs and practices by which a community represents itself to itself. The spiritual and social aspects of life are inextricably linked. Thus, if we feel dependent on God, we are dependent on society in a symbolic way. If we are afraid of God's justice and punishment, it is because we are afraid of breaking the laws of society. We revere God because we want to protect our society. Our belief in the immortality of the soul reflects our desire for the continuity of our community life. The basis of society lies in its religious belief: the secular and sacred are two sides of the same coin.

Society, a moral community which Durkheim calls the church, is comprised of collective forces, which anoint many objects. Thus the Church is sacred; so too are the clergy, the laity and even the objects used in rituals and ceremonies. There is no religion without this moral community in which members think and act in the interest of the community, which is sacred. Religion is a binding force that cements the members in a common cultic practice. Durkheim identifies sacred practices with the activities of the moral community and profane practices with the activities of individuals pursuing self-interested goals. The profane is not inherently

---

[184] Émile Durkheim, *The Elementary Forms of Religious Life*, translated by Carol Cosman and edited by Mark Sydney Cladis (Oxford: Oxford University Press, 2008), p. 314.
[185] Durkheim, *The Elementary Forms of Religious Life*, p. 154.
[186] Durkheim, *The Elementary Forms of Religious Life*, p. 46.

evil, but it is in direct opposition to the sacred. The division between the sacred and the profane parallels the social division between common life and private lives of individuals.[187]

Like in Judeo-Christian tradition, institutional specialization of religion involves the establishment of a church, the formation of priesthood, and the separation between sacred and secular spaces. The formulation of doctrines, development of ecclesiastical organizations, and differentiation of religious community from society all contributed to the specialization of religion in institutional form. The segregation between the sacred cosmos and the secular world is often matched by specialization of religious roles and the establishment of groups claiming to be religious.[188] Religion helps to cement individuals in the social order and to preserve the status quo. Ironically, 'institutionally specialized religion' may eventually come into conflict with the society that supports it. This specialized religion becomes a dynamic social force that begins to develop its own 'logic', and tension emerges between special religious experience and ordinary secular life.[189] As witnessed in history, Christianity, Islam and Buddhism develop conflicts with non-believers or adherents of other faiths. The dialectic tension, thesis and antithesis, between religion and society are present within the structures of these beliefs.

Sacred and Profane

Durkheim further asserts that categories of human thought emerged from the distinction between the sacred and profane. For example, the category of time arose from the need to set apart religious festivals as distinct from secular work. 'Space' is created due to the need to divide the sacred from the profane. Science and logic also developed from this sacred and profane distinction when they began to move away from a religious worldview. Thus religion encompasses everything: 'the concepts of totality, society, and deity are really just different aspects

---

[187] Durkheim, *The Elementary Forms of Religious Life*, p. xxii.
[188] Thomas Luckmann, *The Invisible Religion; the Problem of Religion in Modern Society* (New York, NY: Macmillan, 1967), p. 68.
[189] Luckmann, *The Invisible Religion*, p. 67.

of one and the same notion'.[190] These aspects, including moral and scientific activities, constitute the legal and socio-linguistic frameworks in which people live out their lives.

An important thesis of Durkheim is the division of human life into two aspects: mundane and moral. The mundane refers to our daily private routine existence, and the moral refers to our collective and elevated life. This dichotomy is symbolised by body and soul, profane and sacred. If members exclusively pursue their private mundane life, the community would eventually disintegrate. Religious life links individuals together through the sharing of goods and values. Through sacred symbols, religion helps to revive the collective existence of the people, that is often threatened by self-centred and utilitarian pursuits. In other words, religion promotes a shared life against individualism and selfishness.

Durkheim also highlights a distinction between religion and magic. Magic is strictly a utilitarian activity pursued by the individual, associated with the profane in opposition to the sacred. Circulated among individuals in groups, it is used for private purposes. One hires a magician for his services, like paying a consultation fee to a medical doctor. Durkheim asserts, 'A church of magic does not exist ... the magician has a clientele, not a church.'[191] Their relationship is accidental, transitory, and purely for individual needs. The practice of magic seems to have been popular and in vogue during Durkheim's times. He emphasises a religious spirit that promotes justice and human dignity. Magic, in his opinion, is an individualistic and selfish pursuit that does not contribute to the common good.

Durkheim's contrast between religion and magic stresses the importance of the sacred in human flourishing. Today's enchanted 'magic' could be the technological advancement and economic prosperity that we enjoy in this digital age. However, this new miracle cannot solve all aspects of our spiritual and moral malaise. The remedies must come from 'religion': we need to develop new sacred symbols, rites and practices so that love, justice and equality can flourish in society. Durkheim was interested to establish a secular morality as a substitute for Church teachings.

[190.] Durkheim, *The Elementary Forms of Religious Life*, 337, no. 2.
[191.] Durkheim, *The Elementary Forms of Religious Life*, p. 43.

As a trusted civil servant of the French republican government who supported the Third Republic, Durkheim promoted the idea of secular (*laïque*) morality in his effort to wrestle control of education from the influence of the Catholic Church. Secular morality would replace religion in moral education in public schools. He advocated 'an education that is not derived from revealed religion, but that rests exclusively on ideas, sentiments, and practices accountable to reason only – in short, a purely rationalistic education'.[192] Here, secular morality is associated with reason and rationality. Durkheim acknowledged that, historically, religion and morality had been inextricably bound together: 'we must discover the rational substitutes for those religious notions that for a long time have served as the vehicle for the most essential moral ideas.'[193] In other words, we must continue to engage with religion in order to construct a secular morality.

As mentioned, Durkheim's pioneering work has inspired other thinkers to pursue a critical study of religion, highlighting people's sufferings and earthly hopes rather than their eschatological expectations. Nonetheless, Durkheim's research and writings raise a few serious problems. Critics find Durkheim's study of Australian aboriginal totemic beliefs too simplistic and narrow to support a universal theory of religion. Some claim that the distinction between sacred and profane does not exist in many religious traditions. It seems that Durkheim interpreted Australian aborigines' belief through the lens of his Judaic-Christian tradition. Some critics even question the existence of the totem as a distinct religious structure. Religions in modern society hardly exhibit the simplistic patterns perceived by Durkheim.

Durkheim's study of religion, present in Australia among the aboriginals, did not take into account the other features found in other faiths. There have been great religious reformers, like Buddha and Jesus, who actually preached and acted against societal norms and expectations, which Durkheim totally ignored. In the Old Testament, prophets such as Amos spoke out against the Jewish society of his time. Durkheim also has nothing to say about the phenomenon of mysticism,

---

[192.] Quoted in Horii Mitsutoshi, 'Historicizing the Category of "Religion" in Sociological Theories: Max Weber and Émile Durkheim', *Critical Research on Religion* 7, no. 1 (2019), p. 32.

[193.] Quoted in Horii, 'Historicizing the Category of "Religion" in Sociological Theories', p. 32.

which occurs in individuals. For example, Buddhism and Hinduism teach about the importance of detachment, the life of the individual ascetic or monk who challenges and changes the values of society.

The British historian Patrick Collinson argues that Durkheim's assertion about religion as a function seems too narrow: 'Was society worshiping itself?'[194] Assuming a perfect fit, Durkheim practically made society identical with religion, which is too simplistic; both terms, 'society' and 'religion', have their own shared history. The Japanese sociologist Mitsutoshi Horii believes that Durkheim was unwittingly promoting French imperialism. Horii remarks that Durkheim's investigation into the elementary forms of religious life poses a challenge to 'many of its intellectual premises, which were themselves grounded in Europe's self-understanding as a civilizational zenith (and the consequent inferiority of "primitive" societies) as well as the normalized ethnocentrism of the Euro-American human sciences'.[195] Durkheim's work is seen as providing moral sanction for French colonial policy.

The writings of Durkheim and Weber need to be read within the context of European expansionism in the late nineteenth and early twentieth centuries, namely the French Third Republic and the German Empire, respectively. Weber was interested in world religions, such as Hinduism, Buddhism, Confucianism, Taoism, and of course, Protestant Christianity. Despite his use of the term 'in a completely value-neutral sense', Weber's writings clearly imply the superiority of Protestant Christianity and Western civilization.[196] We shall now look in more detail into the writings of Weber.

Weberian Perspective

In every religious phenomenon, Max Weber observes, there is an evolutionary process from rationalism to irrationalism. Once a religion has moved beyond fulfilling material needs, people begin to reflect on their relationship with the divine. At the same time, practical considerations or needs begin to recede. People no longer look for the worldly success that

---

[194.] Collinson, 'Religion, Society, and the Historian', p. 161.

[195.] Quoted in Horii, 'Historicizing the Category of "Religion" in Sociological Theories', p. 31.

[196.] Horii, 'Historicizing the Category of "Religion" in Sociological Theories', p. 30.

their religious beliefs can offer, and their religious behaviour becomes more irrational. Eventually, this irrational trait or non-economic goal becomes the distinguishing feature in their religious disposition.[197] According to Durkheim, Weber's focus is on religion as a force of social change, not as a force for stability in society.

Weber first developed a conception of primitive religion in *The Sociology of Religion*, in which he asserted that every society possesses some ideas of the supernatural order in the form of spirits or extraordinary forces different from the ordinary and natural word. People in ancient times took these supernatural forces or events seriously and attempted to control them. Anthropological studies have confirmed that, like language, the supernatural is universal, prevalent in all cultures and civilisations. Weber's emphasis is not on the transcendent aspect of primitive religion, but on its practical usefulness, such as curing diseases, defeating enemies, maintaining harmony in society, etc. In other words, religious behaviour is pragmatic, worldly-oriented, and rational.

Priest and Magician

Human beings relate to supernatural forces in two ways: through cultic worship in religion and through magical coercion, also known as sorcery. In religion, we worship divinities or 'gods' in contrast to 'demons', which the magician attempts to control.[198] It can happen that priestly power can suppress an old cult in favour of a new religion, thus forcing the old gods to survive as demons. Weber also makes a distinction between the priest and the magician. Put simply, the priest influences gods by means of worship while the magician coerces demons by means of magic. Further, a magician deals with spiritual issues in an ad hoc manner, while the priest functions as part of an organized cult. The office of priesthood may be hereditary or associated with an organisation, in contrast to magicians who are often self-employed. All these distinctions are by no means clear-cut. There are always exceptions to the norm. According to Weber, for example, not all priests have an official post and magicians may belong to an organised guild or occasionally as members of a caste that perform magic for the community.

---

[197] Max Weber, *The Sociology of Religion*, Beacon Series in the Sociology of Politics and Religion (Boston, MA: Beacon Press, 1964), p. 28.

[198] Weber, *The Sociology of Religion*, p. 28.

Generally, religion is related to the worship of divinity in an organised setting for the purpose of guiding human destiny. Magic or sorcery, on the other hand, can be manipulated or harnessed to serve the needs of the individual with correct formulae or incantations. As in all sociological phenomena, the distinction between religion and magic is fluid, with no absolute differences. For example, forms of divine worship including prayer and sacrifices have their origin in magic: 'even the Catholic priest continues to practise something of this magical power in executing the miracles of the mass and in exercising power of the keys'.[199] Sacrifice performed by priests can persuade or coerce the gods or form a pact between believers and the deities. Sacrifice is also used as a means of deflecting the anger of a god onto a scapegoat. The sacrificial offering of animals conducted in the ceremony of a meal eaten together produces 'a fraternal community between the sacrificers and the god'.[200] The first fruits may also be offered as a sacrifice so that the gods will not deprive the people of their remaining produce.

Weber also critiques totemism as a social institution that displays a natural object, such as an animal, and its relationship to a particular social group. This totemic animal becomes 'a symbol of kinship': 'the animal symbolized the common possession by the group of the spirit of the animal, after it has been consumed by the entire group'.[201] With the promotion of kinship, laws are established to govern the particular community, such as regulation of sexual behaviour or the prohibition to kill and consume the animal except during worship. Some primitive groups believe they have descended from the totem animal. Weber also holds that totemism serves the division of labour between males and females as well as regulation of trade beyond the group.

Prophet and Peasant

Besides priest and magician, Weber also writes about the office of the prophet, an individual who, by virtue of his personal charisma, proclaims a message or divine commandment. What distinguishes a prophet from a priest is his personal calling: a priest has a claim to authority by virtue of his sacred office, whereas a prophet's claim is based on his personal

---

[199.] Weber, *The Sociology of Religion*, p. 25.
[200.] Weber, *The Sociology of Religion*, p. 26.
[201.] Weber, *The Sociology of Religion*, p. 39.

appeal and revelation. As such, no prophet has ever emerged from the priestly class, except in Zoroastrianism, according to Weber. The priest preaches salvation by virtue of his office even though he may have specific charisma. It is the religious authority that confers on the priest the power to dispense salvation. The prophet, on the other hand, exercises power like the magician because he possesses certain gifts, such as personal revelation. However, it is important to discern that the core mission of the prophet is his message, doctrine or command, not magic.[202]

The idea that the peasant is pious is a modern invention, according to Weber. With a few exceptions, such as in Zoroastrianism, the peasant has not been highly regarded in East Asian religions. During the period of the Pharisees, the Jewish rural peasantry was regarded as godless and second class. Unable to fulfil ritual laws, it was not easy for a peasant to live a pious life according to Judaism, Hinduism and Buddhism. In Christianity, the peasant was simply a pagan. Thomas Aquinas, the medieval theologian, considered the peasant a Christian of lower rank.[203] The piety of the peasant is a modern development found in Lutheranism which came into conflict with rationalism and political liberalism. However, this was not the position of Martin Luther.[204] Weber maintains that the glorification of the peasant's piety has nothing to do with the holiness of the rustic folk, but, rather, is largely due to reaction against the modern rationalism found in urban areas.

In fact, the city is regarded as the site of piety. Christianity, after all, was an urban religion. Churches and sectarian movements develop in urban surroundings and Christian communities flourished in the cities. It is in the cities that we discover the 'transcendence of taboo barriers between clans, the concept of office, and the concept of the community as an institution (*Anstalt*), an organized corporate identity serving specific realistic functions'.[205] At the same time, strengthened by Christianity, these concepts and ideas facilitated the growth of the medieval cities in Europe. As an ethical religion of salvation, Weber writes, Christianity took roots and flourished in urban environments.

Finally, Weber remarks that 'capitalism' existed in all religions in ancient and medieval times but not quite to the extent of the modern capitalism that we know. Weber associates Protestantism with the

---

[202] Weber, *The Sociology of Religion*, pp. 46–7.
[203] Weber, *The Sociology of Religion*, p. 83.
[204] Weber, *The Sociology of Religion*, p. 84.
[205] Weber, *The Sociology of Religion*, pp. 84–5.

Sociological Perspective 93

spirit of modern capitalism. In *The Protestant Ethic and the Spirit of Capitalism* (1905), Weber examines the relationship between ascetic Protestantism and the development of modern capitalism. Calvinism, with its teaching on predestination, provides the impetus for the growth of modern capitalism. In Protestantism, the pursuit of profit received a new sanction. Thus, prosperity is a sign of God's blessing. When pushed to the extreme, capitalism becomes a religion. In fact, Christianity today is big business, especially in the United States, Singapore and in many major cities in the world.

Christianity and Capitalism

Critical theorist Walter Benjamin held that capitalism performs the same function as religion when it helps us to deal with worries, anguish and anxiety. For him, capitalism is 'a pure religious cult' in the sense that it has no special dogma, no theology, no ordinary days and feast days but is an 'extreme exertion of worship'.[206] Without dream or mercy, capitalism is not a repenting cult but a blaming one. Developed on the back of Christianity, the history of capitalism is essentially the history of parasites: 'the spirit that speaks from the ornamentation of banknotes'.[207] Capitalism promotes inequality, widens the gap between rich and poor, and destroys the environment through excessive and mindless consumerism and wastage of resources. Benjamin blames the Reformation for evolving Christianity into capitalism.

In fact, there is an inner relationship between the traditional Protestant spirit and our modern capitalist culture, as asserted by Weber. First, Weber traces the idea of 'calling' to Luther's *sola fide* (by faith alone). Critical of the monastic life, which withdraws from temporal responsibilities, Luther looked upon secular life as a 'calling', 'an expression of brotherly love'.[208] He believed that performance of worldly

---

[206.] Walter Benjamin, 'Capitalism as Religion', in *The Frankfurt School on Religion: Key Writings by the Major Thinkers*, edited by Eduardo Mendieta (New York, NY: Routledge, 2005), p. 259.
[207.] Benjamin, 'Capitalism as Religion', p. 260.
[208.] Max Weber, *Protestantische Ethik und der Geist des Kapitalismus* (Florence: Taylor & Francis Group, 2001), p. 41. This work, *The Protestant Ethic and the Spirit of Capitalism*, was originally published in 1905.

duties is to do the will of God, and therefore any legitimate calling is acceptable to him. The effects of this moral and religious justification of secular work as a 'calling' led to an increase in organised labour.

Weber also highlights Calvin's doctrine of predestination: 'This doctrine must above all have had one consequence for the life of a generation which surrendered to its magnificent consistency ... A feeling of unprecedented inner loneliness.'[209] Weber believes the capitalist spirit emerged from this anguish. If we believe we are saved, we will work hard and succeed in this life, and our success is a testimony of our having been chosen by God. Success in secular calling becomes a sign of salvation, evidence that we are one of the elect. Hence, in the Protestant ethic, accumulation of wealth combined with sober living received moral and religious sanction. Weber underscores that Calvinism, with its strict discipline, work ethic and ascetic lifestyle, provided the dynamism for the flourishing of modern capitalism.

It would be a mistake to assume that Weber is proposing Protestantism or Calvinist ethics to be the cause of capitalism. Weber is not interested in the origins of capitalism per se, only in the *spirit* of capitalism. He explores the relationship between economics and faith and its possible consequences. His research has been focused on 'certain correlations between forms of religious belief and practical ethics'.[210] Thus it is essential that we pay attention to the many nuances and reservations Weber made in his argument.

The publication of *The Protestant Ethic and the Spirit of Capitalism* in 1905 sparked debate, controversy and misunderstanding. Like Marx's, Weber's influence is phenomenal. Christians in the United States are often afraid to criticize capitalism, which has become fundamental to their way of life. In fact, some believe that 'a good Christian can be, indeed should be, a good capitalist'.[211] Capitalism has taken on such a sacred image that to question its social ramifications is like committing heresy. Christians have generally failed to confront the greed that is destroying the fabric of society and widening the gap between the rich and the poor. Evangelical Christians are generally supporters of modern capitalism, though they struggle to find biblical justification

---

[209] Weber, *Protestantische Ethik und der Geist des Kapitalismus*, p. 60.
[210] Collinson, 'Religion, Society, and the Historian', p. 166.
[211] Quoted in Ryan C. McIlhenny, 'Introduction', in *Render Unto God: Christianity and Capitalism in Crisis*, edited by Ryan C. McIlhenny (Newcastle-upon-Tyne: Cambridge Scholars Publisher, 2015), p. xi.

for it because nowhere in scripture can we find a 'defense of the legal personification of the corporation, that exorbitant debt (with outrageous interest) augments consumer power'.[212] Nonetheless, modern capitalist policies in the 1970s and 1980s are taken for granted as if it were part of Providence.

In defending capitalism, Christian apologetics asserts that it is a sin to steal, and thus, private property needs to be protected. Unfortunately, the modern situation is more complicated than this simplistic reasoning. Capital 'is not a thing but a process in which money is perpetually sent in search of more money'.[213] Capitalism in fact promotes greed, the desire for more possessions. Marx and Engels wrote: 'The need of a constantly expanding market for its products chases the bourgeoisie over the entire surface of the globe.'[214] There is no evidence that Scripture supports modern corporate capitalism and one could also argue that globalisation does more harm than good to developing nations.[215]

In spite of criticism, capitalism has a way of transforming itself, appearing as beneficial and concealing its negative impact. It continues to absorb and interiorize everything that comes its way. In other words, it consumes the environment and human beings. Capitalism leads to encompassing consumption, feeding on itself, devastating and depleting natural and human resources. Capitalists use the 'surplus value' they gain from exploiting workers to sustain institutions such as churches, schools, commercial enterprises, etc., and to convince people that the system is working well and thus cannot and need not be changed.[216]

Liberation theologians attempt to dissociate Christianity from capitalism, to expose its devastating effects, or as they call it, 'structural sin'.[217] The duty of Christians should primarily be to render absolute allegiance to God and not the mammon created by capitalism. After the fall of communism, many are convinced that capitalism per se cannot

---

[212] McIlhenny, 'Introduction;, pp. xii–xiii.
[213] Quoted in McIlhenny, 'Introduction', p. xiii.
[214] Quoted in McIlhenny, 'Introduction', pp. xiii–xiv.
[215] See Chamsy El-Ojeili and Patrick Hayden, eds., *Critical Theories of Globalization* (Basingstoke: Palgrave Macmillan, 2009), p. 51.
[216] McIlhenny, 'Introduction', p. xv.
[217] See Conor M. Kelly, 'The Nature and Operation of Structural Sin: Additional Insights from Theology and Moral Psychology', *Theological Studies* 80, no. 2 (June 2019), pp. 293–327.

be eliminated, that it is the only system that works. Churches, however, need to arouse the conscience of their flock to the potential harm that capitalism can cause to humans and the environment.

Throughout the Scriptures, God chastises the rich, especially those who accumulate wealth at the expense of the poor. For the poor, the lack of material goods has been added to a lack of knowledge and training, which prevents them from escaping their state of humiliating subjection.[218] While critical of communism, the late Pope John Paul II was also aware of the danger of 'unbridled capitalism': 'In spite of the great changes which have taken place in the more advanced societies, the human inadequacies of capitalism and the resulting domination of things over people are far from disappearing'.[219] John Paul II, however, accepted a capitalist system that recognizes the positive role of the market, private property and free human creativity in the economic sphere.

The Future of Religion

In his study of the social order of his time, Durkheim concluded that religion, including Christianity, is on the decline. Looking at the organic nature of belief and taking an evolutionary approach, he assumed that a religion, like any social phenomenon, is established, develops and eventually will die or transform. He also held that the more primitive a society is, the more influence religion will have on the people. Similarly, the more modern a society is, the less influence religion will have. As time goes by, institutions like politics, economy and science would free themselves from the clutches of the Church; individual freedom is celebrated.[220] Durkheim believed religion would be transformed and retreat into the private domain. Convinced that religion would change as society changes, he also argued that as long as people live in communities, they will have religion.

---

[218] John Paul II, *Centesimus Annus*, http://www.vatican.va/content/john-paul-ii/en/encyclicals/documents/hf_jp-ii_enc_01051991_centesimus-annus.pdf, no.33.

[219] John Paul II, *Centesimus Annus*, http://www.vatican.va/content/john-paul-ii/en/encyclicals/documents/hf_jp-ii_enc_01051991_centesimus-annus.pdf, no.33.

[220] J. Beyers, 'Obituaries and Predictions: A Sociological Perspective on the Future of Religion', *Acta Theologica* 33, no. 1 (2013), p. 15.

Peter Berger reckons that religion would not only survive against the onslaught of secularization, but would even flourish. In the European context, secularization refers to the 'widespread alienation from organized Church' or 'a shift in the institutional location of religion'.[221] Berger has identified a religious revival in our modern society, offering three reasons supporting this religious upsurge: i. in times of uncertainty, religion can provide some kind of certainty; ii. religion can be used to resist a secular elite that threatens society's core beliefs and values; iii. it is part of human nature to search for meaning that transcends earthly existence.[222]

Thomas Luckmann also believes that religion is still an important aspect of society but 'is empty of specific empirical content'.[223] Unlike institutionalized faith, religion will become 'a private affair'.[224] The emergence of modernity and rationalisation in society results in people becoming more individualistic. In the past, religious identity was associated with collective identity, but now Berger defines 'personal identity as a universal form of individual religiosity'.[225] This means that religion has been transformed to suit the individual rather than the community.

Further, the pluralistic nature of modern society allows the flowering of different religious traditions. Durkheim and Weber researched religion within a relatively homogeneous European context. However, in our modern pluralistic society, the individual has the option to choose from an array of faiths, all competing for members. As such, religious pluralism may help to advance greater religious participation.[226]

Weber believes religion would not last forever due to rationalism and economic progress. When people are rational, they stop believing in magic and become disenchanted with the world. The process of rationalisation leads to demystification, which means the world is devoid of magic and mysteries: 'As intellectualism suppresses belief in magic, the world's processes become disenchanted, lose their magical significance, and henceforth simply "are" and "happen" but no longer signify anything. As a consequence, there is a growing demand that the

---

[221] Quoted in Beyers, 'Obituaries and Predictions', p. 17.
[222] Quoted in Beyers, 'Obituaries and Predictions', p. 17.
[223] Luckmann, *The Invisible Religion*, p. 78.
[224] Luckmann, *The Invisible Religion*, p. 86.
[225] Luckmann, *The Invisible Religion*, p. 70.
[226] Beyers, 'Obituaries and Predictions', p. 19.

world and the total pattern of life be subject to an order that is significant and meaningful'.[227] Weber calls this a 'world-feeling intellectualist religion', which, arguably, is one of the roots of secularism. Rationalism leaves no room for the transcendental as every empirical phenomenon can be explained and, thus, religion becomes obsolete.

Following Weber, theories of secularization trace their origins to Protestantism. Secularization implies that religion, Christianity in particular, no longer plays an important role in Western society. According to Berger, secularisation is 'the process by which sectors of society and culture are removed from the domination of religious institutions and symbols'.[228] Following Durkheim's distinction, this means the strict division between the sacred and the secular is disappearing, followed by the diminishing of organized religion's influence on society, especially in areas such as marriage and education.

In the process of secularization, Berger discerns 'privatised religion' as a matter of choice and preference.[229] No longer is religion a public matter; now it is a personal choice. While the move towards secularization does not mean the complete disappearance of religion, nonetheless it is a significant shift towards new expressions of the transcendental or the sacred. The growth of the modern economy is also a contributor to the demise of religion. Berger assumes that any society that engages in modern economic policies and technological innovations (first industrialisation and now digitalization) will eventually be secularised.[230] Berger emphasises the role of economics and politics in shaping religion and contributing to the secularizing trend in modern society.

Weber and Durkheim also acknowledge that the process of secularization is occurring, though they also anticipate a religious revival: the old gods may be growing old and dying, but others could be born. Their understanding of the secularizing trend is also dialectical because secularization need not lead to the disenchantment of the world but rather to a transformation of religion itself.

---

[227] Weber, *The Sociology of Religion*, p. 125.

[228] Peter L. Berger, *The Sacred Canopy: Elements of a Sociological Theory of Religion* (New York, NY: Anchor Books, 1990), p. 107.

[229] Berger, *The Sacred Canopy*, p. 133.

[230] Peter L. Berger, *A Rumor of Angels: Modern Society and the Rediscovery of the Supernatural* (Garden City, NY: Doubleday, 1969), p. 20.

Topics for discussion and reflection

- Several dichotomies mentioned in this chapter inform the development of religion: for example, Christianity and Marxism, Christianity and capitalism. Are these relevant to your community, and if so, how?
- Religiousization or secularization? Institutionalized faith or a private affair? Choose one position to argue on the trend of religion in the next five years.
- Which theory or proposition discussed in this chapter do you disagree with? What is your argument?

Chapter 5

Challenge of Secularism

In the conclusion of the previous chapter, we discussed the future of religion, including the process of secularization, which challenges Christianity's influence on Western society. Secularism relegates religion to the private domain, insists that the state remains neutral in religious affairs, and hence promotes religious pluralism.

Secularization and secularism look somewhat similar in spelling, leading none-too-careful writers to use the two terms interchangeably. It is pivotal, though, to note that they carry very different meanings and connotations. Secularization refers to a historical process tracing the advancement of scientific truths and principles from the mid-seventeenth century. The modernization of society that gradually pushed religion out of public life was dominated by these scientific discoveries and the principle of evidence-based truths.

Secularism, on the other hand, is a worldview where gods, divine revelation, religious dogmas and supernatural practices have no role in civil society. Each individual is free to follow his or her natural inclination in matters of worship and prayer, but that individual cannot impose his/her set of beliefs on others. Religion is thus a private matter which must not impose itself on the government of the day. The outcome is the strict separation between the state and religious institutions, and people of different religious beliefs and those without any religion are equal before the law.[231]

[231.] See José Casanova, 'The Secular and Secularisms', *Social Research* 76, no. 4 (Winter 2009), pp. 1049–66. The material in this chapter is taken from

This chapter attempts to trace the relationship between secularism and Christianity, focusing on the dialogues between Jürgen Habermas and Joseph Ratzinger in *The Dialectics of Secularization*. In view of the growing religious pluralism in the West, the conflict between secularism and Christianity has somewhat abated. Meanwhile, some people have discovered that Eastern philosophies such as Confucianism, Taoism, and Buddhism may also contribute to our post-secular society. This chapter concludes with Joseph Ratzinger's call for a 'healthy secularism' which can help to build a society where different traditions, cultures, and religions can flourish.

Threat to the Church

It is well known that Joseph Ratzinger (Pope Emeritus Benedict XVI) has always been concerned with the threat of aggressive secularism and relativism, as revealed in many of his writings and discourses. His preoccupation with this profound problem is not a reactionary stance. It is more the position of a priest who is deeply concerned about secularization, not only of Western society but also of the Church itself, in that many Catholic schools and institutions have lost a sense of being Catholic. In his address to the plenary members of the Council for Culture entitled, 'The Church and the Challenge of Secularization', Ratzinger says:

> This secularization is not only an external threat to believers, but has been manifest for some time in the heart of the Church herself. It profoundly distorts the Christian faith from within, and consequently, the lifestyle and daily behaviour of believers ... They live in the world and are often marked, if not conditioned, by the cultural imagery that impresses contradictory and impelling models regarding the practical denial of God: there is no longer any need for God, to think of him or to return to him.[232]

Ambrose Mong, *Are Non-Christian Saved? Joseph Ratzinger's Thoughts on Religious Pluralism* (London: Oneworld Publications, 2015), 92–101, 104–15 and *Dialogue Derailed: Joseph Ratzinger's War Against Pluralist Theology* (James Clarke & Co., 2015), pp. 118–27, 130–40, 142–5.

[232] Benedict XVI, 'The Church and the Challenge of Secularization', *Christ to the World 53*, no. 5 (September 2008), p. 390.

In addition to this denial of transcendence inherent in secularization, Ratzinger also laments the 'death of God' taught by intellectuals and resulting in selfish individualism. We are thus in danger of 'drifting into spiritual atrophy and emptiness of heart'. To counteract this disposition, he encourages us to appeal to the lofty values of existence that give meaning to life: the dignity of the human person, the equality of men and women, and the meaning of life and the afterlife.[233]

Besides this address in 2008, in the first speech of his historic state visit to the United Kingdom in September 2010, Joseph Ratzinger, as Pope Benedict XVI, urged Britain to maintain its respect for religious traditions and warned against 'aggressive forms of secularism'. He said, 'Today, the United Kingdom strives to be a modern and multicultural society … in this challenging enterprise, may it always maintain its respect for those traditional values and cultural expressions that more aggressive forms of secularism no longer value or even tolerate'.[234]

In November 2010, the Pope surprised Spain with strong words against what he described as 'aggressive secularism' on the part of the government. Since 2004, the Spanish government had legalized gay marriage, relaxed abortion legislation, and eliminated compulsory religious education in schools. He said, 'The renaissance of modern Catholicism comes mostly thanks to Spain. Nevertheless, it is also true that laicism, a strong and aggressive secularism, was born in Spain, as we saw in the 1930s … This dispute is happening again in Spain today. The future of faith and the relations between faith and secularism have Spanish culture as its epicenter.'[235]

As we shall see, Ratzinger is not against secularity per se, but rather secularism as an ideology that marginalizes God and does not allow breathing space for Christianity. In fact, Ratzinger has argued that the secular tradition is necessary to correct the extremes and temptations of religion. Since Vatican II, the Church has come to recognize the secular,

---

[233] Benedict XVI, 'The Church and the Challenge of Secularization', p. 390.
[234] 'Pope Benedict XVI Warns against "Aggressive Secularism" in Britain', *The Daily Telegraph*, http://www.telegraph.co.uk/news/newstopics/religion/the-pope/8006272/Pope-Benedict-XVI-warns-against-aggressive-secularism-in-Britain.html.
[235] 'In Spain, Pope Benedict XVI Lambasts "Aggressive Secularism"', *The Christian Science Monitor*, 7 November 2010, http://www.csmonitor.com/World/Europe/2010/1107/In-Spain-Pope-Benedict-XVI-lambasts-aggressive-secularism.

neutral state as a positive value and cultural achievement. Martin Rhonheimer says it is significant that in Benedict XVI's Christmas address to the Roman Curia on 22 December 2005, he referred positively to the 'model of a modern state' which originated in the American Revolution. He also distinguished this American model from the Jacobin model of the French Revolution, which no longer allows the Church any freedom.[236]

One thing is clear: much like John Henry Newman, Joseph Ratzinger is unquestionably opposed to the liberal spirit of secularism and relativism that has adverse effects on the Church and its faithful. In the next section, we will explore the relationship between secularism and Christianity.

Christian Origin of Secularism

In many ways, secularization is more a threat to the Church than to the Christian faith.[237] Paradoxically, secularism has its roots in Christianity. Owen Chadwick claims that the Reformation 'baptized' the secular world by levelling the differences between the clergy and the laity.[238] This implies that all secular callings are also a vocation from God. Furthermore, it was Christian conscience that made Europe secular by teaching people to be tolerant and inclusive. Gradually, the West allowed religious pluralism to flourish and abolished state religion.

According to Peter Berger, the Reformation in the sixteenth century started the process of secularization when the reformers placed sole emphasis on scripture and private interpretation of the Bible. Research and advanced studies in scripture by Protestant scholars in the eighteenth and nineteenth centuries led to the 'disenchantment of the world'. The Protestant Reformation ignited a resurgence of secularizing forces previously kept in check by Catholicism. Chadwick writes, 'If the drama of the modern era is the decline of religion, then Protestantism

---

[236] See Martin Rhonheimer, 'Christian Secularity, Political Ethics and the Culture of Human Rights', *Josephinum Journal of Theology* 16, no. 2 (Summer-Fall 2009), p. 321.

[237] Nancy A. Dallavalle, 'Cosmos and Ecclesia: A Response to Richard Lennan', *Philosophy & Theology* 17, no. 1-2 (1 January 2005), p. 285.

[238] Owen Chadwick, *The Secularization of the European Mind in the Nineteenth Century* (Cambridge: Cambridge University Press, 1975), p. 8.

can aptly be described as its dress rehearsal.'[239] Many intellectuals, including theologians, think that modern society has no place for religious beliefs, which are perceived as superstitious and primitive. It seems that a truly modern person must be 'godless' and the unfolding of history is a secularizing process in which human beings try to get rid of the gods.[240]

In the context of mission, Vinoth Ramachandra asserts that Christianity had a 'powerful secularizing thrust' in its attitude towards local language and culture because it stood in stark contrast to Muslim and Hindu 'notions of eternal, divine tongues', referring to Arabic and Sanskrit respectively. The Christian mission destroyed the powerful myth of Christendom and led to the successful separation of Church and state, and of religion and territory. Eventually, the modern secular culture resulted in the 'rejection of Christianity on the basis of Christian social and cultural achievements'. Hence Henrikus Berkhof writes, 'Secularization is a child of the gospel, but a child who sooner or later rises against his mother.'[241] Thus, the notion of 'secular' clearly has a Christian origin.

If secularization has a Christian origin, we can say that the Church has unwittingly given birth to secularism, and is now trying to control this rebellious child with little success. This 'child', in turn, has been adopted by modern societies who have forgotten its Christian origin. It was Jesus himself who said, 'Render to Caesar the things that are Caesar's, and to God the things that are God's' (Mark 12:17). This could arguably be quoted as the original source of secularism. Therefore, it is not surprising that secularism is flourishing in Europe, the heart of Christendom.

One of the main features of secularization is the distinction between the public and private sectors in society; it applies to all aspects of life, both tangible and intangible. It follows that religion belongs exclusively

---

[239] Chadwick, *The Secularization of the European Mind in the Nineteenth Century*, p. 138.

[240] Hastings writes that it is hard to prove that in the past, society was ever very religious. Furthermore, society evolves and religious beliefs find ways and means to express and adapt themselves to different times and places. Adrian Hastings, *A History of English Christianity, 1920–1990* (London: SCM Press, 1991), p. 669.

[241] Vinoth Ramachandra, 'Learning from Modern European Secularism: A View from the Third World Church', *European Journal of Theology* 12, no. 1 (1 January 2003), p. 37.

to the private domain and has no place in the public life of the nation so as to safeguard the people against state intolerance and assure that the state remains neutral in religious matters. At the same time, religion or the Church cannot intervene or interfere in public affairs. In this way, secularization liberates science and learning from religious influence. This process of secularization already existed even before we coined the word for it.[242] This banishment of God from the public arena, in secularism, is also a legacy of the Enlightenment.

The Enlightenment

In his introduction to Joseph Ratzinger's *Christianity and the Crisis of Cultures*, Marcello Pera recognizes that the rationality of the Enlightenment bore marvelous fruit, for, without it, there would not have been many of the great scientific, technological, economic and political advances that changed the lives of many in Europe.[243] However, in Ratzinger's opinion, these advances were also accompanied by scourges such as 'marginalization, the triumph of subjectivity, and the imprisonment of the divine, of the sacred, of God in a ghetto' and in Europe, the banishment of God from the public square.[244] Ratzinger writes:

> This same rationality [of the Enlightenment] leaves its imprint on all the world today in a much deeper way, thanks to the technological culture that science has made possible. Indeed, in a certain sense, scientific rationality is imposing uniformity on the world. In the wake of this form of rationality, Europe has developed a culture that, in a manner hitherto unknown to mankind, excludes God from public awareness. His existence may be denied altogether or considered unprovable and

---

[242.] Chadwick, *The Secularization of the European Mind in the Nineteenth Century*, 2. See also Charles Taylor, *A Secular Age* (Cambridge, MA: The Belknap Press of Harvard University Press, 2007), pp. 1–22.

[243.] Joseph Ratzinger, *Christianity and the Crisis of Cultures* (San Francisco, CA: Ignatius Press, 2005), p. 13.

[244.] Ratzinger, *Christianity and the Crisis of Cultures*, p. 14.

uncertain and, hence, as something belonging to the sphere of subjective choices. In either case, God is irrelevant to public life.[245]

Ratzinger admits that the Enlightenment has a Christian origin and has drawn attention to its Christian values. Since Vatican II, the Church has also tried to establish harmony between Christianity and the Enlightenment by reconciling itself with modernity. Martin Rhonheimer says Western Enlightenment is a prodigal son of Christianity in whom the father recognizes himself. After due correction and reconciliation, perhaps incomplete, this son acquires the right to live in the father's house. Rhonheimer also thinks that it was Christian culture that gave rise to the modern secular state. Christianity may be necessary to prevent the secular political culture from turning into 'an all-absorbing monism' that is hostile to religion.[246]

Influenced by the Enlightenment, contemporary philosophies are characterized by an anti-metaphysical element that denies the existence of God. Thus Ratzinger writes, 'They are based on a self-limitation of the positive reason that is adequate in the technological sphere but entails a mutilation of man if it is generalized. The result is that man no longer accepts any moral authority apart from his own calculations.'[247]

The philosophy of the Enlightenment is incomplete because it deprives itself of its original sources. This radical detachment from its roots will eventually lead to treating human beings as no different from other living things.[248] As a result, secularization, influenced by this philosophy, originally a positive development, turns against itself, resulting in people losing their identity and experiencing alienation. Ratzinger highlights this theme when he speaks of the crisis of catechesis in *Handing on the Faith in an Age of Disbelief*:

> In the technological world, which is a self-made world of man, one does not immediately encounter the Creator; rather, initially, it is only himself that man always encounters.

---

[245] Ratzinger, *Christianity and the Crisis of Cultures*, p. 30.
[246] Rhonheimer, 'Christian Secularity, Political Ethics and the Culture of Human Rights', p. 329.
[247] Ratzinger, *Christianity and the Crisis of Cultures*, p. 40.
[248] Ratzinger, *Christianity and the Crisis of Cultures*, p. 42.

The fundamental structure of this world is feasibility, and the manner of its certainty is the certainty of what can be calculated. Therefore, even the question of salvation is not geared to God, who appears nowhere; rather, once again, it is geared to the ability of man, who wants to become the engineer of himself and of history ... For him, creation is silent with regard to morality; it speaks only the language of mathematics, of technological utility.[249]

Man Is the Measure of All Things

Ratzinger vehemently rejects the Enlightenment's motto – 'Man is the measure of all things' – a theory which has convinced the West of our human ability to build a world of justice and reason. According to this motto, everything is possible for human beings; we do not need God. Discoveries and scientific and technological advancements have followed, but unexpectedly, disillusionment, alienation, and scepticism have also arrived. Commenting on technology and scientific advancement, Ratzinger says it is not the method but the power of its success that threatens to destroy the earth. This has resulted in the unification of 'technical' civilization, which in turn has caused 'the fragmentation of the philosophical consciousness and the dissolution of its specific content, namely, the question of truth'.[250]

One way out of this situation, Ratzinger asserts, is to make philosophy 'wholly "positive"', which means that only what is empirical and scientifically proven is acceptable. Thus, the question of the truth of God and of spiritual things is abandoned. However, 'pure positivism' is unbearable in the long run, and so truth becomes the product of human beings and is replaced by practical results. Truth, too, is produced 'scientifically'.[251] This implies that human beings can create an ideal future solely with their practical skills and expertise, and with no need for any divine assistance. As mentioned earlier, Ratzinger believes that this Enlightenment thinking with its anti-metaphysical trait is incomplete

---

[249.] Joseph Ratzinger, *Handing on the Faith in an Age of Disbelief* (San Francisco, CA: Ignatius Press, 2006), pp. 13–14.

[250.] Joseph Ratzinger, *The Nature and Mission of Theology* (San Francisco, CA: Ignatius Press, 1993), p. 77.

[251.] Ratzinger, *The Nature and Mission of Theology*, p. 77.

because it is divorced from its original source, neglecting its ontology. The stress on the Being as foundation is one of the great philosophical concerns of Ratzinger, given the threat of aggressive secularism as well as theological and religious pluralism.

On Metaphysics

Ratzinger raises this issue in *The Nature and Mission of Theology*, where he claims that philosophy and theology cannot do without ontology. However, it seems that contemporary philosophers and theologians are both hostile to ontology. This is why they are 'indissolubly dissociated' because the ontology they deny could give them a solid foundation and a common ground on which to base their dialogues.[252] Philosophy and theology need this dimension of thought if they are to work together, just as faith and philosophy confront the basic question of human death. Such a question implies the need to live meaningfully, while at the same time it lets people find their origin and destination. Ratzinger writes, 'Death, the one question which it is impossible to ignore forever, is thus a metaphysical thorn lodged in man's being … Faith hears the answer because it keeps the question alive.' When Christian faith speaks about the resurrection, it is not talking about an unknown future, but 'the comprehension of man's being within the whole of reality'.[253]

In view of the above, Ratzinger argues that the fundamental problem concerning justice and hope and the relationship between history and ethos has remained essentially the same throughout history, though these are formulated differently from time to time. The relationship, however, can progress in the exchange of question and answer in philosophical and theological reflections. From the perspective of faith, the dialogue of human thought gives us one aspect, and from the perspective of philosophy, another aspect.[254] Consequently, both must remain in a mutual relationship to provide a complete picture of reality.

Ratzinger argues that faith furthers an ontological claim when it asserts that there is a God who has power over us all, implying that he is the creator and saviour of the whole universe, and reaches beyond the specific religious community that proclaims him. The prophets of

---

[252.] Ratzinger, *The Nature and Mission of Theology*, p. 22.
[253.] Ratzinger, *The Nature and Mission of Theology*, p. 23.
[254.] Ratzinger, *The Nature and Mission of Theology*, p. 23.

Israel see in God 'the primordial creative ground of all reality'.[255] God is the creator and saviour, not only of one specific community but of the whole world. Ratzinger believes this is a breakthrough in thinking about God because it perceives him beyond a symbolic representation in a particular religion. It is also an appeal to our reason, as is evident in the writings of the prophets and Wisdom Literature in the Old Testament, proclaiming the true God in contrast to man-made idols. Hence, the faith of Israel goes beyond a particular people's way of worship, but rather is put forth as a universal claim. Ratzinger asserts that it is universal, because it is rational.[256]

Christianity is a universal religion on the basis of the above claim. It is this critique of religion, found in the very heart of Israel, resulted in the successful synthesis of secular Greek thought and the Bible, which the early Church Fathers sought to achieve.[257] Thus, the universality of faith makes missionary endeavour 'meaningful and morally defensible', and only this kind of faith directs itself beyond the symbolism of a specific religion towards an answer that appeals to people's common sense. The question of God thus requires that theology takes a philosophical position in the debate while, at the same time, philosophy 'must open itself to faith's claim on reason'.[258]

Ratzinger believes this debate to be an anthropological problem. If a human being's spiritual life is to remain intact and his spiritual life not to be allowed to disintegrate into a 'flat rationalism' dominated by technology or 'dark irrationalism', then faith and reason must be brought into a proper relationship.[259] The 'wave of esotericism' we now witness is caused by human beings' inability to integrate into 'positivistic rationalism', resulting in the resurgence and even the flourishing of superstitions. Positivism doubts a person's capacity to know the truth and confines knowledge to what can be produced and verified. Meanwhile, irrational forces dominate outside this scientific domain, and human beings become servants of 'inscrutable powers'.[260]

[255.] Ratzinger, *The Nature and Mission of Theology*, p. 24.
[256.] Ratzinger, *The Nature and Mission of Theology*, p. 24.
[257.] Ratzinger, *The Nature and Mission of Theology*, p. 24.
[258.] Ratzinger, *The Nature and Mission of Theology*, p. 25.
[259.] Ratzinger, *The Nature and Mission of Theology*, p. 102.
[260.] Ratzinger, *The Nature and Mission of Theology*, p. 102–3.

The Christian faith, on the other hand, responds to the primordial questions of man with respect to his origins and goals: 'What can I know? What may I hope for? What is man?' Concomitantly, these primordial questions also constitute the essential core of philosophy. Thus, faith is related to truth. Only if a human being is capable of truth can he find freedom.[261] According to Gianni Vattimo, who presents us with a different perspective, this understanding of Being as the foundation in metaphysics is essentially a medieval, European way of thinking that is untenable in our pluralistic world.

Postmodern Pluralism

Unlike Ratzinger, Gianni Vattimo believes that, in twentieth-century philosophical thinking, it is no longer possible to think of Being (ontology) as the foundation because Europeans have come to recognize that other cultures cannot be considered 'primitive' just because they fall behind the West in terms of 'progress'.[262] He asserts that our pluralistic world cannot be based on an ideology that seeks to unify 'at all costs in the name of a sole truth'. This would also go against the ideals of democracy.[263] Vattimo also claims that 'since God can no longer be upheld as an ultimate foundation, as the absolute metaphysical structure of the real, it is possible, once again, to believe in God ... not the God of metaphysics or of medieval scholasticism,' but the 'God of the Bible'. Once we discover that the idea of Being as the eternal structure of metaphysics is untenable, 'we are left with the biblical notion of creation, namely with the contingency and historicity of our existing'. Translating this into secular and philosophical terms, Vattimo argues that in our experience of postmodern pluralism, 'we can think of Being only as event, and of truth ... as a historical message that must be heard and to which we are called to respond'.[264]

The Church must accept the influence of modernity, Vattimo insists, which means recognizing 'the profoundly Christian meaning of secularization'. The Christian's vocation consists of 'deepening its own

---

[261] Ratzinger, *The Nature and Mission of Theology*, p. 102–3.
[262] Gianni Vattimo, *After Christianity* (New York, NY: Columbia, 2002), p. 4.
[263] Vattimo, *After Christianity*, p. 5.
[264] Vattimo, *After Christianity*, p. 6.

physiognomy as source and condition for the possibility of secularity'.[265] Secularization is seen as a 'purification of the Christian faith' – a return to the 'faith's authentic essence'.[266] Vattimo makes this startling assertion that 'secularization is the way in which kenosis, having begun with the incarnation of Christ ... continues to realize itself more and more clearly by furthering the education of mankind concerning the overcoming of originary violence essential to the sacred and to social life itself'.[267]

One of the features of Christianity is a universalism, 'the awareness of a plurality of cultures and of a lay space where these can confront one another'. To become a true partner in cultural dialogue, Vattimo says, 'Christianity cannot put aside this essential feature of its heritage and identity; it must present itself as a bearer of the idea of secularity for the sake of its own specific authenticity'.[268] He thus calls for the development of Christian lay vocations. This implies acknowledging the secularized character of Christianity and also recognizing this essential feature of the Christian faith as being unique, compared to other religious traditions. Christianity can take part in interreligious dialogue by referring to its 'specific lay orientation' which is not emphasized as much in other cultures and religions.[269]

In view of our pluralistic and multi-cultural societies, Gianni Vattimo argues that Christianity can recover its universalizing function only by stressing its missionary inclination as 'hospitality' and establishing its laity.[270] This means that in interreligious dialogue, Christians should be ready to acknowledge that others might be right. It is the 'principle of charity' realized in the form of 'hospitality in the dialogue between religions and cultures'. It includes listening and giving voice to others.[271] In other words, the new mission of Christianity should be moving from an emphasis on universality to understanding the particularities of other faiths in order to establish a dialogue.

---

[265] Vattimo, *After Christianity*, p. 98.
[266] Gianni Vattimo, *Belief* (Stanford, CA: Stanford University Press, 1999), p. 47.
[267] Vattimo, *Belief*, p. 48.
[268] Vattimo, *After Christianity*, p. 99.
[269] Vattimo, *After Christianity*, p. 100.
[270] Vattimo, *After Christianity*, p. 100.
[271] Vattimo, *After Christianity*, p. 101.

Dialectics of Secularization

The Dialectics of Secularization by Habermas and Ratzinger is a good place to examine, in depth, Ratzinger's thoughts on secularism. This book is a transcript of their dialogue on an agreed subject: 'The pre-political Moral Foundations of a Free State'. Ratzinger posed this provocative question to his audience at the Catholic Academy of Bavaria: Is religion 'an archaic and dangerous force that builds up false universalisms, thereby leading to intolerance and acts of terrorism?'[272] The context for the question was a debate between himself, then Prefect of the Congregation for the Doctrine of the Faith, and Habermas, a liberal, secular philosopher who proclaimed himself to be 'tone-deaf in the religious sphere'.[273] Ratzinger did not deny the fact that religion could be an archaic and dangerous force, and Habermas did not defend his commitment to a neutral, universally accessible reason as defence against the claims of any revealed religion.

Foundations of the Secular State

Habermas admits that free, secular states have arisen, as in the case of his native Germany, from a 'common religious background and a common language'.[274] However, he is more concerned with whether such states, as they exist today, can justify their commitment to neutral, non-religious principles of reason. He thinks that regardless of whether citizens are themselves motivated by a particular ethic or perceived revelation, the liberal state can 'satisfy its own need for legitimacy in a self-sufficient manner'.[275] Its uniting bond is the 'democratic process itself – a communicative praxis ... exercised only in common and that has as its ultimate theme the correct understanding of the constitution'.[276] Habermas says democracies can maintain legitimacy without having to ground themselves in any singular worldview or metaphysical understanding. He admits, however, that democracies do demand the solidarity and the commitment of their citizens to the process itself.[277]

[272.] Habermas and Ratzinger, *The Dialectics of Secularization*, p. 64.
[273.] Habermas and Ratzinger, *The Dialectics of Secularization*, p. 11.
[274.] Habermas and Ratzinger, *The Dialectics of Secularization*, p. 32.
[275.] Habermas and Ratzinger, *The Dialectics of Secularization*, p. 29.
[276.] Habermas and Ratzinger, *The Dialectics of Secularization*, p. 32.
[277.] Habermas and Ratzinger, *The Dialectics of Secularization*, p. 29.

As the trend for globalization moves society beyond the confines of a particular political system, it frees the global economy from many political constraints. However, there is no law to guarantee human rights in the globalized world, and the secular state faces destabilization as people increasingly feel compelled to act in their self-interest. Therefore, many people are losing hope in this process of globalization. Habermas does not say the secular forces of communicative reason do not work in a global and pluralistic society. He is simply saying that these forces should be treated 'undramatically, as an open, empirical question'.[278] He admits that reason has its limits, and we must become aware of them. Consequently, reason cannot claim to know what 'may be true or false in the contents of religious traditions'.[279]

In view of the above, Habermas acknowledges the feasibility of alternative claims and admits that there is something to learn from religious traditions, something which reason does not provide. Religions, he says, have kept alive and continue to reformulate contextual interpretations of redemption, of 'salvific exodus from a life that is experienced as empty of salvation'.[280] This task cannot be performed by secular philosophers alone. Regarding 'the substance of biblical concepts accessible to a general public that also includes those who have other faiths and those who have none', secular societies must learn to transpose these concepts into a context that is relevant for everyone. For example, the biblical idea of 'man in the image of God' can be translated as referring to the dignity of all human beings.[281] In other words, secular philosophers must learn to appreciate that religious traditions have a contribution to make. The bonding of a secular democratic process with a society depends on the faith and commitment of the people whose religions play an important part in their lives.

---

[278] Habermas and Ratzinger, *The Dialectics of Secularization*, p. 38.
[279] Habermas and Ratzinger, *The Dialectics of Secularization*, p. 42. In *The Dialectic of Enlightenment*, Horkheimer and Adorno claim that reason has gone astray, 'giving rise to a totally administered world' and 'to the manipulation of consciousness'. Gianni Vattimo, *The Transparent Society* (Cambridge: Polity Press, 1992), p. 82.
[280] Habermas and Ratzinger, *The Dialectics of Secularization*, p. 43.
[281] Habermas and Ratzinger, *The Dialectics of Secularization*, p. 45.

Habermas, a 'methodical atheist', agrees that the heart of European culture is Christian in origin. It also depends on Christianity for its nourishment.[282] In *Times of Transitions*, he writes:

> Christianity has functioned for the normative self-understanding of modernity as more than a mere precursor or a catalyst. Egalitarian universalism, from which sprang the ideas of freedom and social solidarity, of an autonomous conduct of life and emancipation, of the individual morality of conscience, human rights, and democracy, is the direct heir to the Judaic ethic of justice and the Christian ethic of love ... To this day, there is no alternative to it. And in light of the current challenges of a postnational constellation, we continue to draw on the substance of this heritage. Everything else is just idle postmodern talk.[283]

Like Ratzinger, Habermas also regards political philosophy, which has given birth to secularism in Europe, as influenced by the covenantal theology of the Old Testament and Hellenistic philosophy. The liberal secularism of modern Europe thinks it has freed itself from religious faith, but in fact, it has merely suppressed or forgotten its religious roots. Ideas such as liberty, conscience, and human rights, which are fundamental for liberal secularism, are continually nourished by these roots.[284] Likewise, Gianni Vattimo would even say the secularizing trend in modern Europe consists not only in exposing the errors of religion, but also in the survival of these 'errors' in some degraded forms. It follows that 'a secularized culture is not one that has simply left the religious elements of its tradition behind, but one that continues to live them as traces, as hidden and distorted models that are nonetheless profoundly present.'[285]

---

[282] Gary D. Glenn, 'Is Secularism the End of Liberalism? Reflections on Europe's Demographic Decline Drawing on Pope Benedict, Habermas, Nietzsche and Strauss', *Catholic Social Science Review* 13 (2008), p. 93.

[283] Quoted in Glenn, 'Is Secularism the End of Liberalism?' p. 94.

[284] Glenn, 'Is Secularism the End of Liberalism?' p. 94.

[285] Vattimo, *The Transparent Society*, p. 40.

Friedrich Nietzsche and Leo Strauss

According to Gary Glenn, Habermas' acknowledgement of the Christian roots of European secularism reflects not only Ratzinger's conviction, but also that of Friedrich Nietzsche, who opposed Christianity.[286] In *Twilight of Idols*, Nietzsche writes:

> If you give up Christian faith, you pull the *right* to Christian morality out from under your feet. This morality is simply *not* self-evident ... Christianity is a system, a view of things that is conceived as a connected *whole*. If you break off a major concept from it, faith in God, you break up the whole as well; there are no necessities left to hold onto any more. Christianity presupposes that human beings do not know, *cannot* know, what is good and evil for them: they believe in God, who is the only one who knows it. Christian morality is a commandment; its origin is transcendent; it is beyond all criticism, all right to criticism; it is true only if God is truth – it stands and falls with faith in God.[287]

Therefore, according to Nietzsche, if the New Testament God is rejected, secular morality would be groundless, inconsistent, and incoherent. Western society's continued preference for some of the political and moral fruits of Christianity, like tolerance and humaneness, are now without any foundation and lack the energizing spirit to sustain the personal and political sacrifices needed for stability. Nietzsche teaches that the only consistent inferences from the rejection of the Christian God are that the strong would do what they like to the weak and that without that 'God', there would be no rational basis for sacrificial love.[288]

Agreeing with Nietzsche, Leo Strauss claims European relativism (rather than secularism) tends to be liberal rather than ruthless because it is inconsistent. At times it prefers Judeo-Christian values instead of the strict dictates of secularism. It follows, therefore, that 'the inconsistent reliance on Christian morality, while jettisoning the Christian God, shows that its secularism is liberal or "post Christian"'.[289] It would be

---

[286.] Glenn, 'Is Secularism the End of Liberalism?' p. 94.
[287.] Quoted in Glenn, 'Is Secularism the End of Liberalism?' pp. 94–5.
[288.] Glenn, 'Is Secularism the End of Liberalism?' p. 95.
[289.] Quoted in Glenn, 'Is Secularism the End of Liberalism?' p. 96.

rational to condemn or suppress evil, but relativism teaches that such knowledge of good and evil is not available, and hence, we must tolerate it. However, Strauss observes, 'Absolute tolerance is altogether impossible; the allegedly absolute tolerance turns into ferocious hatred of those who have stated most clearly and most forcefully that there are unchangeable standards founded in the nature of man and the nature of things.'[290] Strauss claims that 'liberal relativism has its roots in the natural right tradition of tolerance or in the notion that everyone has a natural right to the pursuit of happiness as he understands happiness; but in itself it is a seminary of intolerance'.[291] Such an assertion agrees with Ratzinger's analysis that the more relativism becomes the accepted norm of thinking, the more it becomes intolerant.[292]

That Which Holds the World Together

It is interesting to note that Ratzinger did not put forward his religion or any metaphysical basis as the legitimizing force behind Western democracies. He agrees with Habermas that the adherents of secular reasoning and those with religious convictions should learn from each other. He also demands something more active, something as revolutionary to secular democracies as secular democracies are to the European churches. He provides a brief analysis of the dynamics of power and law. He says that the law cannot be the arm of the strong because law is the only thing built strongly enough to oppose those with power. It offers strength to those who are weak. Law is the 'antithesis of violence' because the true function of the law is equality for all.[293]

Ratzinger argues that 'revolt against the law, will always arise when law itself appears to be no longer the expression of a justice that is at the service of all, but ... the product of arbitrariness and legislative arrogance'.[294] He asserts that democracy is the most appropriate form of political order only when the law is 'the expression of the common

---

[290] Quoted in Glenn, 'Is Secularism the End of Liberalism?' p. 96.
[291] Leo Strauss, *Natural Right and History* (Chicago, MI: The University of Chicago, 1953), p. 6.
[292] Joseph Ratzinger and Marcello Pera, *Without Roots* (New York, NY: Basic Books, 2007), p. 128.
[293] Habermas and Ratzinger, *The Dialectics of Secularization*, p. 58.
[294] Habermas and Ratzinger, *The Dialectics of Secularization*, p. 58.

interest of all'.[295] However, total consensus is hard to achieve among human beings, and the vagaries of the majority can be blind and unjust.[296] While Habermas has great faith in democratic systems of law, Ratzinger thinks they are hard to sustain because of pluralism and globalization. Doubting the reliability of reason, Ratzinger is afraid that religious believers will come to no longer trust in the protection of secular systems.

As to whether religion is to be blamed for the acts of terrorism and intolerance that occur when conflicting worldviews collide, Ratzinger admits that it is often true. As to whether religion should be placed under the guidance of reason, Ratzinger asserts that reason has taken humanity not only as far as the atomic bomb, but even further, to the point where 'man is now capable of making human beings, of producing them in test tubes … man [has become] a product … he is no longer a gift of nature or of the Creator God.'[297] One could debate the advantages and disadvantages of genetic engineering, but it is hard to argue with Ratzinger's point that the pace of the effort is out of control and that the sense of life being a gift is disappearing. Thus, he rightly asks, 'Does this then mean that it is reason that ought to be placed under guardianship? But by what or by whom?'[298] Ratzinger's position is a balanced one: that reason and religion should restrict each other by setting boundaries for each other.

Ratzinger does not say that religious belief can be the saviour of a world gone astray; nor does he believe that the answers are to be found in a debate between secular reason and religion. He goes further than Habermas and suggests that the classic debate between a 'neutral' secular reason and a Christian-dominated worldview in the West is not even a universal debate. Both are global in their reach but are 'de facto not universal'.[299] Ratzinger admits that there are 'pathologies' in religion, but he believes 'pathologies' are also found in secular reason.[300] He agrees with Habermas that secular reason and the Christian religion need to learn from each other because of the necessary relationship between faith and reason.

---

[295] Habermas and Ratzinger, *The Dialectics of Secularization*, p. 59.
[296] Habermas and Ratzinger, *The Dialectics of Secularization*, pp. 59–60.
[297] Habermas and Ratzinger, *The Dialectics of Secularization*, p. 65.
[298] Habermas and Ratzinger, *The Dialectics of Secularization*, p. 66.
[299] Habermas and Ratzinger, *The Dialectics of Secularization*, p. 75.
[300] Habermas and Ratzinger, *The Dialectics of Secularization*, p. 77.

Divergence and Convergence of Views

Ratzinger and Habermas have radically different worldviews, but what is interesting is that they have expressed a willingness to learn from each other and hope for something that neither of them has yet experienced. Inherent in their respective positions is the commitment to pursue something new as well as the commitment to redeem what is old. Both men explore how a liberal state can transcend its majoritarian relativistic foundations. Habermas thinks that a state with a neutral worldview can generate its view and give legitimacy to the people so that they can begin to vote, relate sincerely to one another and share a will that can be democratically realized.

Contrary to Ratzinger, Habermas thinks that no religion or exterior source is required to establish these values in the community. The state is legitimate because the citizens assist in formulating the laws and shaping the political culture. The process of democracy yields 'the fruit of a socialization in which one becomes accustomed to the practices and modes of thought of a free political culture'.[301] Habermas claims that political liberalism can establish the values a state needs, from within the community, except when it faces 'external threats' such as capitalism. According to him, capitalism may lead to the isolation of people from each other within society, people acting on the basis of their self-interest, and so on, and the state would lack the values to counteract the situation.[302] Habermas admits that religion can provide the resources needed to fight such external threats and suggests that philosophy could secularize some useful religious concepts, like the dignity of the person, in order to provide a common ground.[303]

It is intriguing to find in this dialogue that it was Habermas who suggested that religion ought to play a greater role in public life and even more surprising to hear Ratzinger proclaiming that religion, unchecked by rational critique, can become an ideology with terrible consequences. Both men are sceptical of the absolute claims of science. They agree that, even in our pluralistic world, 'philosophy must continue to seek to salvage truth or succumb to a postmodern collapse into relativism, and the shared pragmatic recognition of the vital epistemic and discursive contributions that spiritual worldviews can positively contribute to the

---

[301] Habermas and Ratzinger, *The Dialectics of Secularization*, p. 30.
[302] Habermas and Ratzinger, *The Dialectics of Secularization*, p. 35.
[303] Habermas and Ratzinger, *The Dialectics of Secularization*, p. 45.

organization of civil society in light of a deflated and overly rationalistic conception of human nature'.[304] They are aware of the threat to human solidarity of a globalized world with a relentless capitalism, and they also agree that the state, with the help of religion, can revive some forms of solidarity.

Polyphonic Relatedness: East and West

Since secularism is most developed in Europe, Habermas and Ratzinger offer little reflection on how non-Western cultures could contribute to a better understanding of our post-secular age. This absence is all the more striking when Ratzinger himself has said:

> It is important that both great components of the Western culture learn to *listen* and to accept a genuine relatedness to these other cultures, too. It is important to include the other cultures in the attempt at a polyphonic relatedness, in which they themselves are receptive to the essential complementarity of reason and faith, so that a universal process of purifications (in the plural!) can proceed.[305]

In view of Ratzinger's call for a 'polyphonic relatedness', Jonathan Bowman suggests that non-Western modes of thought must be regarded as equal partners in this dialectic (between secularism and Christianity) and viewed as 'authoritative sources of potential redaction of Enlightenment and Christian ideologies'.[306] Bowman calls for an ambitious, 'multi-faceted purification' of secular ideology, using Eastern

---

[304] Jonathan Bowman, 'Extending Habermas and Ratzinger's *Dialectics of Secularization*: Eastern Discursive Influences on Faith and Reason in a Postsecular Age', *Forum Philosophicum* 14 (2009), p. 40. Charles Taylor refers to this as a 'post-secular' Europe where we see not the reversal of the decline of religion of the last century, but rather that 'the hegemony of the mainstream master narrative of secularization will be more and more challenged'. Taylor, *A Secular Age*, p. 534.

[305] Habermas and Ratzinger, *The Dialectics of Secularization*, p. 79.

[306] Bowman, 'Extending Habermas and Ratzinger's *Dialectics of Secularization*', p. 41.

religious teachings: the Confucian 'notion of the rectification of names', the Taoist 'idea of truth disclosure' and the Buddhist 'practice of right speech'.[307] However, in spite of the call for a 'polyphonic relatedness', the dialogue focuses only on the European scene. Habermas, the champion of the Frankfurt School of critical theory, naturally speaks of human rights, and Ratzinger, schooled in the patristic tradition, speaks of natural law.

Human Rights and Natural Law

Habermas argues that there is a need to translate spiritual values into secular language given the fact that the world has been badly battered by market forces and growing government interference in the public sphere. Market forces seek to increase their capital while an expanding governmental bureaucracy seeks to increase its power. As mentioned earlier, one example of the possible translation of the spiritual into the secular is the reference to the Judeo-Christian notion of the human being created in the image of God, which in turn is translated into the notion of the dignity of the human person. This forms the basis of human rights.

On the other hand, Ratzinger points to natural law as the moral basis of the modern state. Although he does not grant equal weight to claims about truth in all religions, he believes the situation created by globalization and the mass media can provide a means of utilizing other traditions as a check on the claims to universality made by Enlightenment proponents and, in my opinion, also found in some aspects of Church dogma. Such an attempt might lead to a new version of universally held values. Ratzinger writes, 'Ultimately, the essential values and norms that are in some way known or sensed by all men will take on a new brightness in such a process, so that that which holds the world together can once again become an effective force in mankind.'[308] In spite of their differences, both Habermas and Ratzinger share the same insight that spiritual influence in the public sphere can help people discover the truths about human nature.

[307.] Bowman, 'Extending Habermas and Ratzinger's *Dialectics of Secularization*', p. 42.
[308.] Habermas and Ratzinger, *The Dialectics of Secularization*, pp. 79–80.

The Role of Religion in Society

Habermas' view in this dialogue demonstrates that he recognizes the importance of the religious dimension, including tolerance between the Church and state, in his political-ethical project.[309] He rejects the transformation of science as an alternative religion.[310] Habermas admits that the modernization project started by the Enlightenment has become the victim of a society that can lose its ability to control things. What he means is that when the dynamics of a globalized economy and markets in general are 'clearly outside the control of consensual rational judgments ... [the] citizens become "depoliticized", but they seem to show indifference to the glaring inequalities' between people in different parts of the world.[311] He also admits that we are entering into a post-secular phase where societies are becoming more open to the questions of the spirit because they have developed the habit of critical enquiry. Hence, 'there is a ready audience for the theory that the remorseful modern age can find its way out of the blind alley only by means of the religious orientation to a transcendent point of reference'.[312]

The interesting point to note here is that Habermas is willing not only to acknowledge the continued existence of religion in our secular societies, but also to take up the 'cognitive challenge' of this phenomenon.[313] Perhaps the most surprising thing that Habermas articulates is the concession he gives to religion when he says:

> We find in sacred scriptures and religious traditions intuitions about error and redemption, about the salvific exodus from a life that is experienced as empty of salvation ... This is why something can remain intact in the communal life of the religious fellowship – provided of course they avoid

---

[309] Virgil Nemoianu, 'The Church and the Secular Establishment: A Philosophical Dialog between Joseph Ratzinger and Jürgen Habermas', *Logos* 9, no. 2 (Spring 2006), p. 22.

[310] Nemoianu, 'The Church and the Secular Establishment', p. 23.

[311] Nemoianu, 'The Church and the Secular Establishment', pp. 25–6.

[312] Habermas and Ratzinger, *The Dialectics of Secularization*, p. 37.

[313] Habermas and Ratzinger, *The Dialectics of Secularization*, p. 38.

dogmatism and the coercion of people's consciences – something that has been lost elsewhere and that cannot be restored by the professional knowledge of experts alone.[314]

In this, Habermas implies that there are 'societal pathologies' and people whose lives have gone astray. He speaks of 'the failure of individuals' plans for their lives' and 'the deformation and disfigurement of the lives that people share with one another'.[315] It is clear that Habermas disapproves of those who wish to keep religion out of the public sphere, for he believes 'it is in the interest of the constitutional state to deal carefully with all the cultural sources that nourish its citizens' consciousness of norms and their solidarity'.[316] He advocates mutual understanding and tolerance in a society that allows space for religious discourse. In spite of growing secularism, Habermas understands that religious fellowship is here to stay.

The Purification of Reason and Religion

The position of Ratzinger regarding secularism is made even more interesting by the fact that he did not begin his response with a comment on religion. Instead, he gave an analysis of the state of the world today: globalization, the increased human potential for construction and destruction, and a relativism which weakens the possibility for common ethical ground. Few would disagree with him that power should be subordinate to the law. However, this is not so easy in practice because injustice can be committed by majority vote and diverse cultures may not agree on the norms for civil rights.[317]

Regarding the abuse of both reason and religion, Ratzinger proposes that reason should accept that it has limits and be willing to listen to the great religious traditions of humanity. At the same time, Christianity, which currently is not yet capable of establishing a set of universally acceptable principles, must go through a critical and cleansing process of rational inquiry.[318] Ratzinger writes, 'Religion must continually allow

---

[314.] Habermas and Ratzinger, *The Dialectics of Secularization*, p. 43.
[315.] Habermas and Ratzinger, *The Dialectics of Secularization*, p. 44.
[316.] Habermas and Ratzinger, *The Dialectics of Secularization*, p. 46.
[317.] Nemoianu, 'The Church and the Secular Establishment', pp. 27–8.
[318.] Nemoianu, 'The Church and the Secular Establishment', p. 29.

itself to be purified and structured by reason; and this was the view of the Church Fathers, too.'[319] This implies that religion and reason are correlated: both are called to engage in mutual purification and healing.

Ratzinger has clearly stated that the two branches of Western civilisation – Christianity and scientific rationalism – can gain acceptance only by acknowledging the multicultural nature of our pluralistic world. A renewed spiritual culture can be established through a two-pronged dialogue that takes into account the 'apprehensions of these alternative cultures towards both Christianity ... and ... scientific rationalism'. However, the fact remains that these two branches are only intelligible to and accepted by a small section of humankind. They are far from universal. Non-Western cultures, spiritual in their nature, are very suspicious of 'domineering rationalism' and 'crass materialism'.[320]

According to Virgil Nemoianu, Ratzinger is not a political conservative, but more like a kind of 'moderate social democrat'.[321] Nemoianu believes that there are few places left in the world where reason can find a home other than inside the Catholic Church. Thus, it is understandable that faith and reason become the basis for building bridges to thinkers like Habermas who, although 'tone deaf in the religious sphere', still seeks connection with the world's religious traditions.[322]

Ratzinger, for his part, believes that reason and religion must purify one another. In fact, they need each other. He admits that Christianity and scientific rationalism are only accepted by a small percentage of people globally – it is not as universal as we think. This means that we must interact with non-Western cultures. Ratzinger acknowledges that the secular is a legitimate sphere with its own autonomy, privileges and limits. He is not against secularism as such, but only as an aggressive ideology that systematically seeks to discredit religion.

Healthy Secularism

From *The Dialectics of Secularization*, we can see that Ratzinger's understanding of secularism is nuanced and balanced. He does not say Christianity could be the saviour of our broken world and that it would

---

[319] Habermas and Ratzinger, *The Dialectics of Secularization*, p. 77.
[320] Nemoianu, 'The Church and the Secular Establishment', p. 30.
[321] Nemoianu, 'The Church and the Secular Establishment', p. 31.
[322] Nemoianu, 'The Church and the Secular Establishment', p. 32.

eliminate the malaise of humankind. However, he is fighting against an aggressive ideology that threatens our freedom and pushes God out of human existence. The secularism experienced in Western society is no longer a neutral influence that opens up space for religious freedom; it is being transformed into an ideology that penetrates politics and does not allow a Christian vision to exist. Thus, the Christian faith runs the risk of being something purely private and disfigured.

In an interview in *La Repubblica*, the Italian daily, on 19 November 2004, Ratzinger said, 'We must defend religious freedom against the imposition of an ideology which is presented as if it were the only voice of rationality when it is only the expression of a "certain" rationalism.' In this interview, Ratzinger recognized that a just secularism allows freedom of worship and that the state should not impose religion but rather, allow space for religious belief. It allows various religions to be co-builders of society. Whereas, when secularism is transformed into an ideology, to speak of God is seen as an attack on the freedom of unbelievers: God has been marginalized in the world of politics.[323]

Christianity cannot regard itself as being in conflict with secular reality because 'God so loved the world that he gave his only Son, that whoever believes in him should ... have eternal life' (John 3:16). Secular reality is not unknown to the Christian faith. Pope Paul VI said the Church 'has an authentic secular dimension, inherent to her inner nature and mission, which is deeply rooted in the mystery of the Word Incarnate, and which is realized in different forms through her members'.[324] Perhaps the tension in Western society is not a conflict between religion and the secular, but between those who search for deeper meaning in life and those who believe that human life has no meaning beyond this earthly existence. Perhaps the conflict is actually between faith and an ideology of secularism which believes that there is no answer to the fundamental questions concerning life and death.[325]

In his address to the new Ambassador to the Holy See of the Republic of San Marino, Ratzinger asserted that a condition of 'healthy' secularism is needed 'for building a society where different traditions, cultures, and religions may peacefully co-exist'. He says we will go into a blind alley if we entirely separate public life from traditions. Therefore, 'it is essential

---

[323] 'Church in the World', *The Tablet*, https://thetablet.co.uk/article/1866.
[324] Quoted in Donal Murray, 'The Secular Versus Religion?' *Origins* 37, no. 26 (6 December 2007), p. 412.
[325] Murray, 'The Secular Versus Religion?' p. 413.

to redefine the sense of a secularism that emphasizes the true difference and autonomy between the different components of society' and also to preserve the specific competences of each component in working towards the common good. This 'healthy' secularism suggests that it may be possible for each sector of society to be governed according to its own rules, but secular society must not neglect the fundamental ethical base in human beings.[326]

In sum, the healthy secularism that Ratzinger supports should include a separation of Church and state, as well as a neutral stance towards religion, which is required in a pluralistic society. This means that no religion is given privileged status, there is equality between people of different religious beliefs, and people have the freedom to believe or not to believe. Healthy secularism should also maintain a harmonious relationship between the adherents of different faiths, hence the importance of engaging in interreligious dialogue at all levels.[327] Secularism is not just an end in itself but can be a means towards democracy and religious pluralism. If such is the case, the secularist principle of separation of Church and state should include equal participation of all citizens in the democratic process as well as a free exercise of their religion.[328]

An Exceptional Phenomenon

José Casanova reminds us that the term 'secularization' has its roots in Western Christian discourse, that of *saeculum*, just as the term 'religious' is derived from Western secular modernity. These categories evolved within the European context as the result of the interaction between Christianity and Western culture. This recognition should allow a 'less Eurocentric comparative analysis of patterns of differentiation and

---

[326] 'Healthy Secularism for a Peaceful Coexistence', *L'Osservatore Romano*, 2070, Wednesday, 19 November 2008, p. 6.

[327] See the foreword by Charles Taylor, in Geoffrey Brahm Levey and Tariq Modood, *Secularism, Religion and Multicultural Citizenship* (Cambridge: Cambridge University Press, 2009), pp. xi–xii.

[328] José Casanova, 'The Secular, Secularizations, Secularisms', in *Rethinking Secularism*, edited by Craig Calhoun, Mark Juergensmeyer and Jonathan VanAntwerpen (Oxford: Oxford University Press, 2011), p. 72.

secularization in other civilizations and world religions'.[329] Casanova argues that the secularization of Western Europe is not a universal but an exceptional phenomenon, unlikely to be repeated in other parts of the world. It is particularly a European, 'Christian and post-Christian historical process'.[330]

Furthermore, through Western colonial expansion, the process of secularization became globalized and entered 'into dynamic tension with the many different ways in which other civilizations had drawn boundaries between "sacred" and "profane", "transcendent" and "immanent", "religious" and "secular"'.[331] Casanova argues that in other civilizations, the 'transcendent' is not necessarily 'religious' and the secular is not necessarily 'profane'. As such, we need to be more open to non-Western analysis of secular dynamics and be critical of Western secular categories to better understand this complex phenomenon.[332]

Casanova's theory of secularization confirms Ratzinger's observation that aggressive secularism is a European phenomenon that strikes at the heart of the Christian faith and poses a threat to the Western Church. Ratzinger also fears that this threat may spread to the rest of the Church. However, the spread of secularism has not led to a decline of religious belief and practice in Asia. In fact, various religious beliefs are flourishing in Asia, as can be seen by the many temples, mosques, and churches there. Even in communist China, where the government pursues an atheistic policy and persecutes underground churches, Christianity continues to spread. According to the 2007 Chinese Spiritual Life Survey conducted by Fenggang Yang and the Institute for Religion at Baylor University, only 15 per cent of the Chinese population can be regarded as 'pure atheists'.[333] This suggests that the Church must rethink and reformulate its doctrines and policies regarding pastoral care and mission in Asia.

In this chapter we have examined Ratzinger's concern for the rise of aggressive secularism in Europe and its negative effect on Christianity. Secularism is related to relativism because the confinement of religious

---

[329] Casanova, 'The Secular, Secularizations, Secularisms', p. 61.
[330] Casanova, 'The Secular, Secularizations, Secularisms', p. 64.
[331] Casanova, 'The Secular, Secularizations, Secularisms', p. 72.
[332] Casanova, 'The Secular, Secularizations, Secularisms', p. 73.
[333] Richard Madsen, 'Secularism, Religious Change, and Social Conflict in Asia', in *Rethinking Secularism*, edited by Craig Calhoun, Mark Juergensmeyer and Jonathan VanAntwerpen (Oxford: Oxford University Press, 2011), p. 268, note 6.

beliefs to the private sphere implies that all religions are equally valid as paths to salvation. Besides the widespread rise of secularism, the rise of religious pluralism has led to an interest in Eastern religions and philosophies such as Confucianism, Taoism, and Buddhism in the West.

Topics for discussion and reflection

- This chapter separates the definitions and, more importantly, the implications of secularisation and secularism in our society. Do you agree? Please expand.
- In your world, do you see the changes in and challenges of secularism, as described in this chapter, threatening the Christian faith? If so, how do you maintain your faith?
- Several lenses have been introduced to explore what reinforces and challenges the future of Christianity. For example, ontology and pedigree (original source), cultures of the East and the West, individualism vs. worldviews, laws of humans or nature, etc. Choose one lens to discuss the pros and cons.

Chapter 6

The Challenge of Religious Pluralism

The phrases 'religious plurality' and 'religious pluralism' have at times been used interchangeably, though they have different meanings. 'Religious plurality' describes the state of the world: there exist many different religious beliefs and traditions. 'Religious pluralism', in distinction, indicates a stance or a belief that no single religion is the exclusive source of truth. It rejects the premise that God reveals himself solely through Jesus Christ and suggests that all genuine religions are valid paths to the divine. In discussing the challenges of religious pluralism that the Church faces, this chapter examines the three paradigms in the Christian theology of religion, exclusivism, inclusivism and pluralism. Highlighting the teaching of Vatican II on non-Christian religions, this chapter also discusses the approaches of the late Pope John Paul II and Pope Emeritus Benedict XVI (Joseph Ratzinger) to dialogue with other religions.

Christianity and Religious Pluralism

Christianity was born within the milieu of Judaism and mystery religions. As Christianity separated itself from Judaism, it encountered Greek philosophy, which led it to attempt the interpretation of the gospel in Hellenistic philosophical terms. Regarding Christianity's encounter with Greek philosophy, Ratzinger writes:

> The Christian faith opted ... against the gods of the various religions and in favor of the God of the philosophers, that is, against the myth of custom and in favor of the truth of Being

itself and nothing else ... the early Church did indeed reject the whole world of the ancient religion, declaring none of it to be acceptable and sweeping the whole system aside as empty custom that was contrary to the truth.[334]

Later the threat of Gnosticism led to the formation of the biblical canon and the composition of the creeds. It was the challenge of the Gnostic heresy that also instigated the process of understanding Christianity in terms of exclusivity. The Christological doctrine taught by the Church upheld Christianity's claim to uniqueness and normativeness.[335]

This understanding of Christianity as a unique and true religion continued with the writings of Church Fathers like Justin, Irenaeus, Tertullian, Clement, and Origen, who were much influenced by the Greek notion of *Logos*. The theological dispute in the early Church culminated in the long and crucial dispute between Arius and Athanasius over the nature of the relationship between God the Father and God the Son. Harold Coward claims that the significance of this dispute is that Arius' position of subordinating Jesus to God would have made Christianity more open to other religions.[336] However, Athanasius' view dominated the period, became orthodox teaching, and resulted in a closed, exclusive Christianity that proclaimed Jesus as the 'only true incarnation' and the sole savior of humanity.[337]

By 500 AD this version of Christianity, which was based on exclusivity, had destroyed the previous Greek and Roman religions, and the Catholic Church began to identify itself with the Kingdom of God on earth. In the seventh century, Christianity had to compete with Islam as another missionary religion. In the sixteenth century, Western Christian missionaries encountered the ancient and venerable religions of Asia in

---

[334] Joseph Ratzinger, *Introduction to Christianity* (San Francisco, CA: Ignatius Press, 2004), p. 142. The material in this chapter is taken from Ambrose Mong, *Are Non-Christian Saved? Joseph Ratzinger's Thoughts on Religious Pluralism* (London: Oneworld Publications, 2015), pp. 24–9, 34–40, 42–3 and *Dialogue Derailed: Joseph Ratzinger's War Against Pluralist Theology* (Cambridge: James Clarke & Co., 2015), pp. 25–41, 46–52.

[335] Harold Coward, *Pluralism in the World Religions* (Oxford: Oneworld Publications, 2000), p. 58.

[336] Coward, *Pluralism in the World Religions*, p. 58.

[337] Coward, *Pluralism in the World Religions*, p. 59.

the forms of Hinduism, Buddhism, Taoism, and Confucianism. In spite of all these contacts, or perhaps because of them, Western Christianity maintained its claim to be the one, true religion.[338]

Thus, it was not surprising that in 1442, the Council of Florence-Ferrara declared that the Holy Church of Rome firmly believed that no one – not just heathens, but also Jews, heretics and schismatics – outside the Catholic Church could be saved unless they were received into the Church before they died. Edward Schillebeeckx says such thinking was acceptable at that time. For centuries, Catholics ardently proclaimed exclusivism and put their beliefs into action, even resorting to physical force.[339] However, at Vatican II, we heard a different message: those who did not know the gospel through no fault of their own, but nevertheless sought God with a sincere heart could also be saved.[340] As we can see, these two official church teachings appear to be diametrically opposed. However, Vatican II does not make clear what 'seeking God' really means, so it could be interpreted as explicitly searching for God or as doing charitable work.[341]

According to Schillebeeckx, the council fathers at Florence-Ferrara were right in proclaiming Jesus as the only way to God, because they could not imagine any other means in which people could be saved. However, they were mistaken to think that God could not work outside Christianity for the salvation of humankind. At a deeper level, the mistake lies in confusing a personal conviction with a truth that can be known objectively. Schillebeeckx argues that although dogmas have become irrelevant with the passing of time, they remain important for our understanding of faith. As Christians, we have to confess that Jesus Christ 'is the only way of life *for us*', though God leads others in different ways. We can remain sincere Christians without condemning others as heretics or infidels.[342] The multiplicity of religions is not just a historical fact but a matter of principle and there are genuine religious experiences in other faiths which are never realized in Christianity.[343]

[338.] Coward, *Pluralism in the World Religions*, p. 59.

[339.] Edward Schillebeeckx, *Church: The Human Story of God* (New York, NY: Crossroad Publishing Company, 1990), p. xvii.

[340.] *Lumen Gentium*, Dogmatic Constitution on the Church, http://www.vatican.va/archive/hist_councils/ii_vatican_council/documents/vat-ii_const_19641121_lumen-gentium_en.html, no. 16.

[341.] Schillebeeckx, *Church: The Human Story of God*, p. xvii.

[342.] Schillebeeckx, *Church: The Human Story of God*, p. 43.

[343.] See Jacques Dupuis, *Toward a Christian Theology of Religious Pluralism* (Maryknoll, NY: Orbis Books, 1997), pp. 386–7.

It is against this historical background that the Church now seeks to formulate an appropriate theological response to the reality of religious pluralism as the new context within which to witness the gospel. Christians now have to deal with this reality as a fact of contemporary life. In spite of Christian missionary efforts, religious diversity is here to stay. The Christian theology of religions seeks to account for the diversity of world religious traditions and to discover appropriate responses to this phenomenon. This particular theology attempts to understand other religions' doctrines and evaluate the relationship between the Christian faith and the beliefs of other religious traditions. In his contact with the history of religions, Paul Tillich realized that 'every individual doctrinal statement or ritual expression of Christianity receives a new intensity of meaning'.[344] This realization means that the future of Christian theological endeavor lies in the attitude Christianity adopts to religious pluralism. This linking of systematic theology with the history of religions, in positive engagement, is crucial for revitalizing the self-understanding of Christianity. Tillich draws our attention to the fact that religious pluralism is the context for Christian faith and practice.

Three Dominant Paradigms

We will now briefly discuss the standard typology in the Christian theology of religions – exclusivism, inclusivism and pluralism.[345] There have been various criticisms of this categorization. However, I agree with Paul Hedges that this typology is useful as a 'descriptive and heuristic' guide, and it is not meant to be 'prescriptive'.[346] Ratzinger

---

[344] Paul Tillich, *The Future of Religions*, edited by Jerald C. Brauer (New York, NY: Harper & Row, Publishers, 1966), p. 91. See also Alan Race, *Christians and Religious Pluralism* (Maryknoll, NY: Orbis Books, 1982), p. 4.

[345] The three-fold typology of exclusivism-inclusivism-pluralism was introduced in the late 1970s and early 1980s by Alan Race and John Hick. Paul Knitter has expanded it and classified the typology options into four models, namely 'The Replacement Model', 'The Fulfilment Model', 'The Mutuality Model', and 'The Acceptance Model'. See Paul F. Knitter, *Introducing Theologies of Religions* (Maryknoll, NY: Orbis Books, 2002) and Robert McKim, *On Religious Diversity* (Oxford: Oxford University Press, 2012).

[346] Paul Hedges, 'A Reflection on Typologies: Negotiating a Fast-Moving Discussion', in *Christian Approaches to Other Faiths*, edited by Alan Race and Paul M. Hedges (London: SCM Press, 2008), p. 22.

The Challenge of Religious Pluralism

rightly thinks that many advocates of the various positions are too quick to equate the issues of religion with the question of salvation. They cannot discriminate between the various types of religion because not all religious faiths consider salvation to be their primary concern. The various positions stated above – exclusivism, inclusivism and pluralism – offer too simplistic a view of religions which 'by no means all lead men in the same direction but which above all do not, each in themselves, exist in one single form'.[347]

S. Mark Heim also argues that the typology of exclusivism, inclusivism and pluralism in the theology of religions is fully coherent only if it is assumed that salvation is the same for one and all. This assumption is dubious and limited. If we take religion seriously in its historical and empirical contexts, the inevitable approach is the exclusivist one. Thus, for Buddhists, *dharma* is the only way; for Christians, it is Christ.[348] The fact that some people follow both Buddhist and Confucian paths reinforces the point that each tradition constitutes a unique way of obtaining 'distinct fulfilments', although they are 'compatible and complementary'. If they are not exclusive religions, then there is no need to follow two different ways because they both reach the same goal.[349] Another person who disagrees with this typology is Joseph S. O'Leary, who laments that 'the pontifications of theologians about inclusivism, exclusivism, pluralism, and relativism are part of that in-house ecclesiastical wrangling that is the mark of a theology disengaged from a living context'.[350]

In spite of its limitations, this standard typology is useful for examining Ratzinger's position regarding Christianity in relation to other religions. In *Truth and Tolerance*, Ratzinger has offered a critique of these three paradigms, and thus, it is fitting that we use it to ascertain his position. This typology also deals with two underlying theological principles in each category – the universal salvific will of God and the claim that only in Jesus Christ (or his Church) can human beings be saved. Each paradigmatic position places different emphases on one or both of these

---

[347] Joseph Ratzinger, *Truth and Tolerance* (San Francisco, CA: Ignatius Press, 2004), p. 53.

[348] S. Mark Heim, *Salvations* (Maryknoll, NY: Orbis Books, 1995), p. 4.

[349] Heim, *Salvations*, p. 5.

[350] Joseph S. O'Leary, 'Toward a Buddhist Interpretation of Christian Truth', in *Many Mansions? Multiple Religious Belonging and Christian Identity*, edited by Catherine Cornille (Maryknoll, NY: Orbis Books, 2002), p. 42.

axioms.[351] This issue is an important one when we explore Christianity as a particular religion, an historical event in time and place, with a universal role, and also, when we examine its relationship with other religions.

Exclusivism

The New Testament presents Christian faith as absolute and final: 'And there is salvation in no one else, for there is no other name under heaven given among men by which we must be saved' (Acts 4:12). Jesus, in the fourth gospel also says, 'I am the way, and the truth, and the life; no one comes to the Father, but by me' (John 14:6). Thus, throughout its history, the Church's predominant attitude has been to regard other religious beliefs as false. In the Catholic Church we have the axiom, *Extra Ecclesiam nulla salus* (outside the Church there is no salvation). Initially, the people referred to were heretics and schismatics, but later, it also came to include non-Christians.[352] In recent times, exclusivism in the theology of religions is more a product of Protestant than of Catholic theology due to its strong reliance on the New Testament as the starting point for faith.

Alan Race thinks that the current emphasis on dialogue has led to the adoption of exclusivism as a defence mechanism. Dialogue can pose a serious threat to the traditional belief in the uniqueness of Christ and Christianity. Proponents of exclusivism in the Christian theology of religions want to expose this potential threat. Exclusivists stress that the revelation in Jesus Christ is the 'sole criterion' to judge all religions, including Christianity.[353]

In his *Church Dogmatics* (Vol 1/2), Karl Barth presents a theory that represents the most extreme form of exclusivism: 'The Revelation of God as the Abolition of Religion'. Barth believes that only the Christian faith can save people. Other religions do not lead to salvation, and nor does Christianity as a religion. He distinguishes religion and revelation.

---

[351] Gavin D'Costa, *Theology and Religious Pluralism* (Oxford: Basil Blackwell, 1986), p. 18.

[352] See Francis Sullivan, *Salvation outside the Church? Tracing the History of the Catholic Response* (New York, NY: Paulist Press, 1992), pp. 22–3 and Dupuis, *Toward a Christian Theology of Religious Pluralism*, pp. 84–109. See also Ambrose Ih-Ren Mong, 'Crossing the Ethical-Practical Bridge: Paul's Knitter's Regnocentrism in Asian Perspective', *The Ecumenical Review* 63, no. 2 (July 2011), pp. 187–8.

[353] Race, *Christians and Religious Pluralism*, p. 11.

Barth believes that religion is contrary to faith; religion consists of human attitudes constructed to reach God. His guiding principle is the revelation of God in Jesus Christ as given in the scripture. Thus, he considers religion as a kind of unbelief, and it is false and blind. As an attempt by human beings to redeem themselves, religion is a futile endeavor and 'an activity of unbelief', if practised without the benefit of revelation.[354] Barth is determined to defend the absolute freedom of God to act in his exclusive divine initiative. Any attempt by a human being to 'supply criteria out of his own reason by which the gospel may be interpreted, is a direct contradiction of the meaning and act of revelation'.[355] According to Barth, 'Revelation is God's sovereign action upon man or it is not revelation'.[356]

This radical separation between revelation and religion becomes the criterion by which Barth judges other religious traditions. Genuine faith, however, is a gift from God, who reaches out to save us personally. Barth believes that it is the 'presence and reality of the grace of God' that differentiates Christianity from others as the true religion. The gospel is linked to revelation, but 'other faiths are the product of "religion"' – this is Barth's understanding of the Christian revelation. He condemns Christianity and other religions when they are not centred upon the revelation of Jesus Christ. Thus, other faiths cannot be judged in comparison with Christianity as a historical religion, but only with the gospel of Jesus Christ. Therefore, Christians are more likely to be condemned if they fail to live up to the gospel.[357]

Paul J. Griffiths holds that the theory of exclusivism, which teaches that one's religion is uniquely privileged with regard to the possession of truth, is not widely accepted. This theory commits anyone who holds this position to the claim that none of the teachings in other religions is identical with his or her own. If, for example, one's religion teaches that there is only one God who alone is worthy of being worshipped, then an exclusivist who adheres to such a belief must say that no other religions teach this doctrine. If there is such an 'instance of identity', it follows that if the relevant teaching of one's own religion is true, then it applies to other religions as well.[358]

---

[354] Race, *Christians and Religious Pluralism*, p. 12.

[355] Race, *Christians and Religious Pluralism*, p. 13.

[356] Quoted in Race, *Christians and Religious Pluralism*, p. 13.

[357] Quoted in Race, *Christians and Religious Pluralism*, p. 13.

[358] Paul J. Griffiths, *Problems of Religious Diversity* (Oxford: Blackwell Publishers, 2001), p. 54.

Regarding exclusivism, Ratzinger claims that giving an absolute value to a religion is not unique to monotheism; it also applies to mysticism and enlightenment. He asserts that everyone sets up an 'absolute value' to what they believe to be true, not just Christians. Some follow Radhakrishnan who teaches the relativity of all religions and at the same time gives the experience of mysticism an absolute value.[359] Ratzinger says this is no less arrogant than 'offering the absolute value of Christ to the non-Christian'.[360] He also remarks that no one takes the position of exclusivism in the sense of denying salvation to all non-Christians, not even Karl Barth. However, he thinks Barth's radical view of exclusivism is 'contradictory and illusory'. According to Ratzinger, faith must express itself in religion and through religion, but it cannot be reduced to religion alone.[361]

Lai Pan-chiu challenges the traditional reading of Barth as an exclusivist. Lai does concede that, for Barth, the true nature of religion refers only to the revelation of God in Christ Jesus, meaning that religion without the revelation of God is a futile human undertaking. Nevertheless, Lai alerts us to the fact that Barth does not say *all* religions are false except Christianity. In fact, unbelief can also be found in Christianity itself. Only God can judge whether a religion is true or false, but this should not prevent us from appreciating the grace and goodness of other religions. Barth affirms that besides Christ being the true light, there might be other lights such as those of Confucius, Buddha and Mohammed. This suggests that Christianity must not attempt to push other religious traditions out of its ken because, in so doing, it will only manifest an attitude of arrogance and self-righteousness. Lai argues that a close reading of the latter part of *Church Dogmatics* reveals the inclusivist nature of Barth's theology of religions, namely that salvation wrought by Christ is not exclusive and the revelation of God cannot be confined to Christianity alone. Hence, Christianity should not 'absolutize' itself because grace is not its exclusive possession.[362]

---

[359] Ratzinger, *Truth and Tolerance*, p. 30.

[360] Ratzinger, *Truth and Tolerance*, p. 31.

[361] Ratzinger, *Truth and Tolerance*, p. 50.

[362] See Lai Pan-chiu, 'Barth's Theology of Religion and the Asian Context of Religious Pluralism', *Asia Journal of Theology* 15, no. 2 (1 October 2001), pp. 250–3.

Inclusivism

Inclusivism implies 'an acceptance and a rejection' of other religions. On the one hand, it accepts other religions as possessing some truths. On the other hand, it rejects them as valid paths for salvation as they do not recognize Christ who alone can save. Inclusivists believe that non-Christian religious truths belong, ultimately, to Christ alone, and thus, they need to delineate the 'lines between the Christian faith and the inner religious dynamism of other faiths'. Inclusivism attempts to integrate non-Christian religions into Christian reflection. It aims to hold together two fundamental principles: God's grace operates in all the great religious traditions of the world and the uniqueness of the manifestation of this grace in Christ.[363]

Since Vatican II, the Roman Catholic Church has adopted the inclusivist position in the theology of religions. The most important representative of this inclusivist position is Karl Rahner, who is always associated with the theory of 'Anonymous Christianity'. Rahner believes there is such a thing as an 'anonymous Christian' in the sense that someone who has no concrete, historical contact with the explicit Christian message can nevertheless be justified and live in the grace of Christ. This person possesses God's gift of supernatural self-communication in grace, accepts it and, in reality, really accepts the essentials of Christianity. Rahner adds that the incarnation appears as the necessary beginning of the 'divinization' of the entire world.[364]

For non-Christian religions, Rahner stresses that 'many have already encountered Christ who did not know that they had grasped the very one into whose life and death they entered as into their blessed and redeemed destiny, that they had encountered the very one whom Christians correctly name Jesus of Nazareth'.[365] Consequently, anyone who accepts his existence in faith, hope and charity, in patient silence, is already acknowledging Christ even if he does not know it. Anyone who accepts his and others' humanity fully has already 'accepted the Son of Man because in him God has accepted man'. Scriptures say, 'whoever loves his neighbor has fulfilled the law' and the ultimate

---

[363.] Race, *Christians and Religious Pluralism*, p. 38.
[364.] Karl Rahner, *Foundations of Christian Faith* (New York, NY: The Crossroad Publishing Company, 2010), p. 181.
[365.] Rahner, *Foundations of Christian Faith*, pp. 227–8.

truth is that 'God himself has become his neighbor': 'He who is at once nearest to us and farthest from us is always accepted and loved in every neighbor.'[366]

Karl Rahner teaches that Jesus Christ is also present in non-Christian religions. Christians cannot deny such 'presence' of Jesus Christ throughout the history of salvation if they believe in Jesus as the savior of all humanity. This understanding refers especially to non-Christians of goodwill who have nothing to do with Christ. Thus, there is no reason to deny a priori a partial, positive function to non-Christian religions for people who have no chance to hear the gospel.[367] According to David Cheetham, Rahner's understanding is based on his reflection on what it is to be a human being rather than his desire to understand other religions in relation to Christianity.[368] This idea of the 'anonymous Christian' is connected to 'Rahner's ideas about our basic humanity as supernatural'. Therefore, it is crucial to recognize that he is not making a theological judgment or observation on other religions as such.[369]

This inclusivist approach, apparently found in the New Testament, is based on the doctrine of Christ's pre-existence as the *Logos*. The idea that Jesus has been actively present throughout creation implies the universality of Christianity. Thus, the inclusivists would see Christ's presence in all authentic religions. Nonetheless, this has not been the basic understanding of Christology in the Latin Church. Even when taken seriously, this approach tends to reduce other religions to vassals of Christianity, 'something less than they themselves claim to be'. This universal claim of Christianity runs the risk of promoting religious imperialism.[370] Furthermore, according to Cheetham,

> inclusivism ... supplies an unwarranted hermeneutical layer that precludes ... the other religion's self-interpretation ... it is a patronizing approach that assumes at the outset what is really going on in another religion. Worst still, it may even

---

[366] Rahner, *Foundations of Christian Faith*, p. 228.
[367] Rahner, *Foundations of Christian Faith*, pp. 312–13.
[368] David Cheetham, 'Inclusivisms: Honouring Faithfulness and Openness', in *Christian Approaches to Other Faiths*, edited by Alan Race and Paul M. Hedges (London: SCM Press, 2008), p. 71.
[369] Cheetham, 'Inclusivisms', p. 72.
[370] Coward, *Pluralism in the World Religions*, pp. 21–2.

be deficient when it comes to engendering a proper attitude towards the other. Thus, the inclusivistic 'owning' of the other's discourse is essentially a refusal to learn about other religions on their own terms.[371]

In other words, our interpretation of other people's religions must be at least recognizable and acceptable to them. Otherwise, we will be 'playing god', forming an idea of others' faiths according to our own image.

Pluralism

Pluralist theories in the Christian theology of religion begin with the notion of 'tolerance', which is the hallmark of liberal Christianity.[372] Tolerant pluralism is an essential feature of this theology: knowledge of God is partial in all religions, including Christianity. Religions must acknowledge their need for one another if the full truth of the divine is to be known to humanity.[373] The pluralists hold that religious truth cannot escape its cultural conditioning. This means that the diverse forms of religious experience represent different cultural responses to the divine initiative. Therefore, no religion can claim a monopoly on truth.[374] Religious pluralism holds all legitimate religions to be the same – they can help us reach God or find salvation.

John Hick is the most prominent theologian to promote the pluralist paradigm in the Christian theology of religions. According to Hick, pluralism 'is the view that the transformation of human existence from self-centredness to Reality-centredness occurs in different ways within the contexts of all great religious traditions'.[375] Thus, there is a plurality of divine revelation, making possible diverse forms of human response to salvation. Hick asserts philosophically that religious pluralism views the great world religious traditions as embodying different perceptions and responses to the Real, or 'the Ultimate from within the major variant

---

[371] Cheetham, 'Inclusivisms', p. 77.
[372] Race, *Christians and Religious Pluralism*, p. 71.
[373] Race, *Christians and Religious Pluralism*, p. 72.
[374] Race, *Christians and Religious Pluralism*, p. 76.
[375] John Hick, *Problems of Religious Pluralism* (London: The Macmillan Press Ltd, 1985), p. 34.

cultural ways of being human'.[376] Thus the great religious traditions are regarded as different ways in which human beings can find salvation, liberation, enlightenment, or fulfilment.

John Hick uses an astronomical analogy in which he presents a Copernican revolution in the Christian theology of religions in the sense that Christians should see that God, not Christ, is the centre and that all religions revolve around God. First, he shifted from an obsolete *ecclesiocentrism* and *Christocentrism* (Ptolemaic paradigm) to a more adequate *theocentrism* (Copernican paradigm).[377] Later, Hick makes another radical change by shifting *theocentrism* to *reality-centredness*, since the concept of God is also culturally biased and limited. This paradigmatic shift, Hick believes, will end all sense of exclusivism and will facilitate interreligious ecumenism. Another important point that Hick makes is to see the incarnation of Christ as 'mythological'.[378] This means that Jesus as Word made flesh is not a unique saving event but a myth attached to salvation history.

Hick also makes the Kantian distinction between what exists independently, outside of human perception, and the phenomenal world that we perceive with our senses. The various religious responses are authentic but different in so far as there are different responses to the *noumenal* Real. It follows from this distinction between the Real as it is in itself and as it is experienced through our religion that we cannot apply to the Real *an sich* the characteristics by which we identify the Real in the physical world. None of the concrete descriptions that apply within our human experience can be transferred to the divine realm. This means that the phenomenal world is structured by our mind, but its noumenal ground is not.[379] Thus, according to Hick, we cannot say that the Real *an sich* is shown by its manifestations such as love of the Father.[380]

This relationship between the ultimate noumenon and its various phenomenal experiences 'makes possible mythological speech about the Real'. Hick defines a myth as a story that is not true but which evokes an appropriate disposition. The truth of a myth is a 'practical truthfulness' and a true myth is one that rightly allows us to understand,

---

[376] Hick, *Problems of Religious Pluralism*, p. 36.

[377] Gavin D'Costa, *The Meeting of Religions and the Trinity* (New York, NY: Orbis Books, Maryknoll, 2000), p. 24.

[378] D'Costa, *The Meeting of Religions and the Trinity*, p. 25.

[379] John Hick, *An Interpretation of Religion: Human Responses to the Transcendent*, 2nd edn. (Basingstoke: Palgrave Macmillan, 2004), p. 246.

[380] Hick, *An Interpretation of Religion*, p. 247.

The Challenge of Religious Pluralism

in the correct way, the reality that we cannot describe in non-mythical terms. Hick argues that 'we exist inescapably in relation to the Real'. Our attitudes and actions must be appropriate, not only for our physical environment but also for our ultimate environment. A true myth helps us to cultivate the right attitude and disposition towards the Real.[381] Hick insists that this divine noumenon is a 'necessary postulate' of our pluralistic society. The followers of every tradition regard the object of their worship as real; hence it is also important to regard the object of worship in other religious traditions as real.[382]

The implication of Hick's theory is that missionary endeavors should not be directed to people of other religions but the 'post-Christian majority of the nominally Christian countries'. Furthermore, instead of being concerned with explaining traditional doctrines, theologians should develop different approaches, in secular societies, to believe in a 'transcendent divine Reality' which gives meaning to human existence. Hick believes that outside the churches there is a strong desire for spiritual fulfilment that can never be satisfied by traditional Christianity as a 'self-enclosed faith claiming exclusive truth'.[383] At the same time, it now seems that an expansive spirituality that includes Christianity and other religious beliefs appeals to many open and searching minds. In this context, Hick argues that while traditional Christian doctrines have ceased to be of importance to most people, there is a widespread concern with ecological issues, with the meaning of human life, with the nature of good and evil, and with the question of life, death and the afterlife.[384]

It is important to recognize that pluralism, in the theology of religions, does not mean that all religions are equally valid as paths to salvation, but it implies that at least some are.[385] Perry Schmidt-Leukel says it is an option to assess 'at least some other religions as equally genuine and salvific on the basis of norms and criteria that are understood to be universally valid'.[386] Thus, pluralism is not to be equated with relativism.

---

[381] Hick, *An Interpretation of Religion*, p. 248.

[382] Hick, *An Interpretation of Religion*, p. 249.

[383] John Hick, *The Rainbow of Faiths* (London: SCM, 1995), p. 138.

[384] Hick, *The Rainbow of Faiths* p. 139.

[385] Perry Schmidt-Leukel, 'Pluralism: How to Appreciate Religious Diversity Theologically', in *Christian Approaches to Other Faiths*, edited by Alan Race and Paul M. Hedges (London: SCM Press, 2008), p. 86.

[386] Schmidt-Leukel, 'Pluralism: How to Appreciate Religious Diversity Theologically', p. 87.

The Second Vatican Council on Other Religions

For the first time in the history of the Catholic Church, during Vatican II, her teaching on other religions took on a positive note. It has taken the Church many centuries to acknowledge the wisdom and goodness of other religions. Here I would like to discuss two documents that have greatly impacted the Catholic understanding of other religious traditions: *Lumen Gentium* and *Nostra Aetate*. *Lumen Gentium* first teaches that 'All men are called to be part of this catholic unity of the people of God which in promoting universal peace presages it. And there belong to or are related to it in various ways, the Catholic faithful, all who believe in Christ, and indeed the whole of mankind, for all men are called by the grace of God to salvation.'[387] It then offers explicit teaching on Muslims by highlighting common ground: 'In the first place amongst these there are the Muslims, who, professing to hold the faith of Abraham, along with us adore the one and merciful God, who on the last day will judge mankind'.[388] The document suggests that there is saving efficacy in Islam because Muslims have acknowledged the creator who will come in judgment one day.

After the Muslims, *Lumen Gentium* also teaches that the divine presence is found in all God-seekers, other believers in God, even if it is 'in shadows and images' that they seek the unknown God. Therefore, those who through no fault of their own, 'do not know the Gospel of Christ or His Church, yet sincerely seek God and moved by grace strive by their deeds to do His will as it is known to them through the dictates of conscience' will also be saved.[389] Here we see Paul's speech in Athens, as presented by Acts 17, having a great influence on Vatican II's approach to other religions. It suggests that all human beings are called by God's grace to salvation (cf. 1 Timothy 2:4).

Lumen Gentium also teaches that 'whatever good or truth is found amongst them is looked upon by the Church as a preparation for the Gospel'.[390] Here Gerald O'Collins cautions us against thinking that this 'preparation for the Gospel' means people will enjoy the gifts of grace and truth only if they accept the gospel and baptism.[391] Vatican II never

---

[387] *Lumen Gentium*, no. 13.
[388] *Lumen Gentium*, no. 16.
[389] *Lumen Gentium*, no. 16.
[390] *Lumen Gentium*, no. 16.
[391] Gerald O'Collins, S.J., *The Second Vatican Council on Other Religions* (Oxford: Oxford University Press, 2013), p. 78.

states this. In *Lumen Gentium*, we are told that non-Christians can move from an implicit to an explicit knowledge of God and that they can also move from shadow and images to light.

Further, *Lumen Gentium* also maintains that through the Church's effort, 'whatever good is in the minds and hearts of men, whatever good lies latent in the religious practices and cultures of diverse peoples, is not only saved from destruction but is also cleansed, raised up and perfected unto the glory of God, the confusion of the devil and the happiness of man'.[392] In other words, those who are converted to Christianity already possessed elements of revelation inherited from their former religion. Nothing is lost or wasted. In fact, there is some continuity between their old religion and their newfound Christian faith. God's self-communication always includes revelation regarding the truth of the gospel and salvation regarding the influence of grace. The two cannot be separated.[393]

Nostra Aetate first considers the 'riddles of the human condition' and how different religions strive to respond. Then it reflects on the merits of Hinduism and Buddhism in their response to the human condition.[394] More importantly, this document also maintains that the Catholic Church rejects nothing that is true and holy in these religions. The Church believes they reflect a ray of truth that enlightens all men and women and encourages its members to enter into dialogue with adherents of other faiths to learn from them. This means looking at their 'precepts for life' and 'sacred doctrines'. The Church thus acknowledges some aspects of Hinduism and Buddhism, two of the religions that existed before the coming of Christ.

Besides commenting favorably on these two Asian religions, *Nostra Aetate* devotes an entire article to the Muslims, showing the importance of understanding and conducting dialogue with them. The document acknowledges major features in their understanding of God: 'They [Muslims] adore the one God, living and subsisting in Himself; merciful and all-powerful, the Creator of heaven and earth, who has spoken to men; they take pains to submit wholeheartedly to even His inscrutable decrees, just as Abraham, with whom the faith of Islam takes pleasure in linking itself, submitted to God.'[395] The declaration reveals its respect

---

[392] *Lumen Gentium*, no. 17.

[393] O'Collins, S.J., *The Second Vatican Council on Other Religions*, p. 81.

[394] Paul VI, *Nostra Aetate*, no. 2.

[395] Paul VI, *Nostra Aetate*, no. 3.

and esteem for the religious and moral life of the Muslims, the way they worship God in prayer, fasting, and almsgiving. In his encyclical *The Joy of the Gospel*, Pope Francis states, 'Our relationship with the followers of Islam has taken on great importance, since they are now significantly present in many traditionally Christian countries, where they can freely worship and become fully a part of society.'[396] Francis respects the Muslim's commitment to righteous living and compassion towards those in need. At the same time, he expects Muslims to respect the rights of Christians to worship and practice their faith in Islamic countries.

Interreligious Dialogue

Related to religious pluralism is the issue of interreligious dialogue, which is an important feature in the Church's understanding of mission and proclamation. Ratzinger's attitude towards interreligious dialogue differs from that of John Paul II. In his encyclical *Redemptoris Missio*, John Paul affirms that the 'Spirit's presence and activity affect not only the individuals but also society and history, peoples, cultures and religions'.[397] This means that John Paul acknowledges the mysterious working of the Spirit in other religions. Ratzinger, however, is much less willing to recognize the working of the Spirit in other religious traditions. The declaration *Dominus Iesus*, issued by the CDF under his prefecture, states: 'If it is true that the followers of other religions can receive divine grace, it is also certain that *objectively speaking* they are in a gravely deficient situation in comparison with those who, in the Church, have the fullness of the means of salvation'.[398]

---

[396] Apostolic Exhortation, Evangelii Gaudium of The Holy Father Francis to the Bishops, Clergy, Consecrated Persons and the Lay Faithful on the Proclamation of the Gospel in Today's World, http://w2.vatican.va/content /francesco/en/apost_exhortations/documents/papa-francesco_esortazione -ap_20131124_evangelii-gaudium.html, no. 252.

[397] John Paul II, *Redemptoris missio*, http://www.vatican.va/holy_father/john _paul_ii/encyclicals/documents/hf_jp-ii_enc_07121990_redemptoris-missio _en.html, no. 28.

[398] Congregation for the Doctrine of the Faith, Declaration 'Dominus Iesus' on the Unicity and Salvific Universality of Jesus Christ and the Church, http://

Critics of *Dominus Iesus* find this point objectionable. Jacques Dupuis rightly argues that the 'gravely deficient situation' of the 'others', taught by *Dominus Iesus*, sounds offensive, especially when they also 'possess an authentic religious faith in the practice of which they find their way to God and discover the meaning of human life. Comparisons can be odious and Christians should not indulge in them readily.'[399] Dupuis also laments that Christians and even church authorities tend to compare what is best in one's tradition to what is worst in others. This double standard needs to be corrected to have a more positive evaluation of other religious traditions.[400] Ratzinger, given his conviction as to the truth of Catholic Christianity, does not view it this way.

Some Catholics were scandalized when world religious leaders, Buddhists, Muslims, Jews, and Hindus prayed together with John Paul II in Assisi in 1986 and again in 2002. Ratzinger appeared sympathetic to some of these critics. He believes that the seriousness of faith was being undermined on such occasions.[401] While making an effort to say something positive about other religions, in the spirit of Vatican II, Ratzinger's emphasis in *Dominus Iesus* on evangelization and the necessity of conversion to Jesus Christ is done at the expense of interreligious dialogue. Thomas P. Rausch says the declaration fails to communicate the sense that entering into dialogue with another religious tradition can itself be part of witnessing to Jesus Christ and a way of approaching the mystery of God's truth.[402]

Ratzinger is cautious about interreligious dialogue because he insists that it is about truth and not mere tolerance. He thinks that pluralists seek harmony in interreligious dialogue at the expense of doctrine, surrendering the truth and thus, 'baptizing' relativism.[403] Ratzinger

---

www.vatican.va/roman_curia/congregations/cfaith/documents/rc_con
_cfaith_doc_20000806_dominus-iesus_en.html, no. 22.

[399] Jacques Dupuis, 'The CDF Declaration *Dominus Iesus* and My Perspective on It', in *Jacques Dupuis Faces the Inquisition: Two Essays by Jacques Dupuis on Dominus Iesus and the Roman Investigation of His Work*, edited by William R. Burrows (Eugene, OR: Pickwick Publications, 2012), p. 67.

[400] Dupuis, 'The CDF Declaration *Dominus Iesus* and My Perspective on It', p. 65.

[401] See Ratzinger, *Truth and Tolerance*, pp. 106–9.

[402] Thomas P. Rausch, *Pope Benedict XVI: An Introduction to His Theological Vision* (New York, NY: Paulist Press, 2009), p. 62.

[403] John L. Allen, *Pope Benedict XVI* (New York, NY: Continuum, 2000), p. 236.

insists on having some criteria of truth in order to do the right thing. The search for truth does not mean that we have the truth and others are searching for it. The quest for truth means that everyone is involved. This has relevance even for those who are Christians. The fruit of dialogue is learning: we live by faith, but we still do not know the entire truth. Ratzinger urges us to search for truth, but not to ignore the '"indispensable elements" of Christian revelation'. He also calls us to 'dwell in Christ, but remain vulnerable to an unpredictable dialogue that may actually change us'.[404]

Many theologians stress tolerance, harmony, and equality. However, Ratzinger is worried that such a liberal view ignores the differences in belief. Truth becomes relative and changeable according to each situation, and 'religious practices detachable from broader worldviews'.[405] Francis Xavier Clooney remarks, 'Oddly, Benedict's analysis aligns him with subaltern and post-colonial critics who insist that the West keeps distorting the religions and cultures of the wider world to maintain its own hegemony.'[406]

What is Christianity's position in the dialogue of religions? According to Ratzinger, the Christian faith has a mystical and an apophatic aspect. Thus, he argues that encounters with the great religions of Asia will remind Christians of this dimension of their faith and make them more tolerant.[407] He reminds us that God reveals and conceals himself in Jesus Christ; the Incarnate Word and the Crucified One far surpass all human words. There is a connection between truth and defencelessness, between truth and poverty.[408]

Ratzinger warns us that we cannot expect unification in the dialogue of religions; this is not possible within our historical time nor is it even desirable. He gives us three criteria to follow in interreligious dialogue. Firstly, in our encounter with other religions, we must not renounce the truth: 'Scepticism does not unite people. Nor does mere pragmatism'. The renunciation of truth and conviction makes man into a mere tool and 'robs him of his greatness'.[409] Thus, Ratzinger insists that we must

---

[404] Francis Xavier Clooney, 'Dialogue Not Monologue: Benedict XVI & Religious Pluralism', *Commonweal* (October 21, 2005), p. 14.
[405] Clooney, 'Dialogue Not Monologue', p. 14.
[406] Clooney, 'Dialogue Not Monologue', p. 14.
[407] Joseph Ratzinger, *Many Religions – One Covenant* (San Francisco, CA: Ignatius Press, 1998), p. 107.
[408] Ratzinger, *Many Religions – One Covenant*, p. 108.
[409] Ratzinger, *Many Religions – One Covenant*, p. 109.

The Challenge of Religious Pluralism

respect the beliefs of others and be ready to look for the truth in them, however strange it may appear to us. Such truths can correct us and deepen our own faith. He says too that we must also allow our narrow understanding of truth to be broken and acknowledge that we never possess the whole truth about God.[410]

Secondly, Ratzinger says we must look for what is positive in other religious traditions and what contains the precious pearl of truth. However, religions can also be perverted and destructive.[411] We must be ready to accept criticism of ourselves and our religion. Ratzinger warns that Christians can succumb to sickness and become superstitious. Thus, our faith must always be purified and based on truth, 'that truth which shows itself, on the one hand, in faith and, on the other hand, reveals itself anew through dialogue, allowing us to acknowledge its mystery and infinity'.[412] This comes close to the view of O'Leary who writes:

> although truth is an obstacle to dialogue when each of the partners believe themselves to be its sole possessor, nonetheless religions which forfeit their truth-claims hardly deserve to survive. Interreligious theology thus requires a concept of truth which is both firm and flexible, compatible both with a historical relativisation of all religious discourse and an affirmation of the referential objectivity of dogmatic language.[413]

Third, Ratzinger teaches that mission and dialogue must go hand in hand. Dialogue is not a conversation without any direction; it must seek to find the truth. We will meet people who are religious and try to relate to them meaningfully. The proclamation of the gospel must be a 'dialogical process'.[414] This means opening up the hidden depths in the religion of others. A dialogue of religions is listening to the *Logos*, who points us to the unity we share.[415]

In Ratzinger's *Many Religions – One Covenant*, one can see him adopting a kind of open inclusivism, as advocated by Griffiths, regarding the question of truth in the face of religious pluralism.

[410.] Ratzinger, *Many Religions – One Covenant*, p. 110.

[411.] Ratzinger, *Many Religions – One Covenant*, p. 110.

[412.] Ratzinger, *Many Religions – One Covenant*, p. 111.

[413.] Joseph Stephen O'Leary, *Religious Pluralism and Christian Truth* (Edinburgh: Edinburgh University Press, 1996), p. 3.

[414.] Ratzinger, *Many Religions – One Covenant*, p. 112.

[415.] Ratzinger, *Many Religions – One Covenant*, p. 113.

Ratzinger recognizes and admits that other religious traditions can teach the Church truths of great significance which it has not yet realized fully. Griffiths says, 'It is part of Catholic orthodoxy to think that the deposit of faith contains implicitly everything of religious significance; but this is compatible with the claim that the Church may learn what some of these implications are from those outside its boundaries'.[416] Although Ratzinger insists on the uniqueness of Christ and the universality of the Christian religion, he is quite disposed to accept truths found in non-Christian religions that are not yet explicitly taught by the Church.

Following St Augustine's teaching, Ratzinger states that Christianity is related to that divine presence that can be perceived by reason. Christianity is *religio vera* (true religion) in the sense that it is not based on legends but on rational knowledge.[417] Thus, he thinks that Hick is wrong to reduce religion to myth only. According to Ratzinger, Christianity is the worship of the 'true God' and enlightenment is part of this religion; it embodies 'the victory of demythologization, the victory of knowledge ... and the victory of truth'. It appears to be intolerant because it refuses to accept relativism and the interchangeability of gods or to be used for political purposes. Christianity is not just one religion among others, but the victory of perception and truth.[418]

Ratzinger believes that the Christian faith is convincing, and its success in the early years after its foundation was due to its linking of faith to reason. It is the synthesis of reason, faith and life that makes Christianity a *religio vera*.[419] This idea of synthesis of reason and faith is clearly a Hellenistic concept. This brings us to Ratzinger's Eurocentric view of Christianity.

Christianity: A European Religion?

Regarding the question of whether Christianity is a European religion, Joseph Ratzinger has highlighted the fact that Christianity did not originate in Europe but rather in the Levant, a strategic crossroads where East meets West. He stresses that it was not just geographical

---

[416.] Griffiths, *Problems of Religious Diversity*, p. 63.
[417.] Ratzinger, *Truth and Tolerance*, p. 169.
[418.] Ratzinger, *Truth and Tolerance*, p. 170.
[419.] Ratzinger, *Truth and Tolerance*, p. 183.

The Challenge of Religious Pluralism

contact, but also a spiritual encounter between Asia, Africa and Europe. Hence, 'interculturality' shaped Christianity, while Christianity also appropriated many things from the Greeks in terms of their ways of thinking and speaking. In this sense, Ratzinger says, Christianity has become European.[420]

This emphasis on the European connection in Christianity is forcibly brought out in his lecture as Pope, in Regensburg, in 2006:

> The encounter between the Biblical message and Greek thought did not happen by chance. The vision of Saint Paul, who saw the roads to Asia barred and in a dream saw a Macedonian man plead with him: 'Come over to Macedonia and help us!' (cf. Acts 16:6–10) – this vision can be interpreted as a 'distillation' of the intrinsic necessity of a rapprochement between Biblical faith and Greek inquiry.
>
> This inner rapprochement between Biblical faith and Greek philosophical inquiry was an event of decisive importance not only from the standpoint of the history of religions, but also from that of world history – it is an event which concerns us even today. Given this convergence, it is not surprising that Christianity, despite its origins and some significant developments in the East, finally took on its historically decisive character in Europe. We can also express this the other way around: this convergence, with the subsequent addition of the Roman heritage, created Europe and remains the foundation of what can rightly be called Europe.[421]

According to Ratzinger, it was no accident that the early apostles went to Macedonia, to the Greeks who were the leading intellectuals of the day. The early Christians encountered the best minds in Europe – found among the Greeks – and began to absorb many of their ideas. He believes it was part of God's plan that Christianity was cast in Hellenistic thought patterns and expressions. The Regensburg address is also a brief history of modern European philosophy rooted in the Old and New

---

[420.] Ratzinger, *Truth and Tolerance*, pp. 85–6.
[421.] Benedict XVI, 'Meeting with the Representatives of Science (Regensburg Lecture)', http://www.vatican.va/holy_father/benedict_xvi/speeches/2006/september/documents/hf_ben-xvi_spe_20060912_university-regensburg_en.html.

Testaments, in Greek and Roman thought. For Ratzinger, Europe is not just another continent but a cultural destination where reason and revelation met, and a symbiosis worked out.[422]

Ratzinger also notes that the Greek version of the Old Testament produced at Alexandria (the Septuagint) is more than a simple (and in that sense really less than satisfactory) translation of the Hebrew text: it is 'an independent textual witness' as well as a distinct and important step in the history of revelation. Thus, for Ratzinger, the relation between faith and reason cast in the Hellenistic mould is part of biblical revelation; it is 'part of the faith itself'.[423] This again means that the confrontation between Christian revelation and Greek philosophy did not happen by chance; it was providential.

In this lecture, Ratzinger traces the process of the 'de-Hellenization of Christianity' that emerged during the Reformation. He speaks about the attempt to develop Western thought beyond the synthesis between Christian faith and Greek reason and rejects metaphysics favouring *sola scriptura*. This separation of faith and reason was also present in the Protestant liberal theology of the nineteenth and twentieth centuries. Now pluralist theologians argue that the early synthesis of faith and reason under Hellenistic influence is not binding on other cultures. Ratzinger writes:

> In the light of our experience with cultural pluralism, it is often said nowadays that the synthesis with Hellenism achieved in the early Church was an initial inculturation which ought not to be binding on other cultures. The latter are said to have the right to return to the simple message of the New Testament prior to that inculturation, in order to inculturate it anew in their own particular milieux. This thesis is not simply false, but it is coarse and lacking in precision. The New Testament was written in Greek and bears the imprint of the Greek spirit, which had already come to maturity as the Old Testament developed.[424]

---

[422] James V. Schall, 'The Regensburg Lecture: Thinking Rightly about God and Man', http://www.ignatiusinsight.com/features2006/schall_regensburg_sept06.asp.

[423] Benedict XVI, 'Meeting with the Representatives of Science (Regensburg Lecture)'.

[424] Benedict XVI, 'Meeting with the Representatives of Science (Regensburg Lecture)'.

What Ratzinger means is that the Church sought to 'inculturate' itself into other cultures based on reason, something that all cultures have in common. According to James Schall, 'this reason is what was learned from Greek philosophy', but not identified with Greece itself. This confrontation of Bible and Greek thought was 'the first multicultural effort, the hellenization of the Christian understanding of itself'.[425] In this Regensburg lecture, Ratzinger insists that we must not attempt to get rid of this initial dynamism of the faith because 'the fundamental decisions made about the relationship between faith and the use of human reason are part of the faith itself; they are developments consonant with the nature of faith itself'.[426] This means that there is no such thing as pure Christianity—it comes clothed in Greek reason, as taught by Catholic tradition.

Ratzinger insists that any attempt to accommodate the local culture within the Christian faith must be done with great caution. However, we must differentiate between the original local tradition and what is a false claim to universality, in that it is simply European. However, he also reminds us that what is European can also be universal.[427] Ratzinger thinks that it is impossible to conceive of Christianity independent of any culture because he fears that 'such a transcultural vision of Christianity' could result in a loss of authentic Christian identity.[428] This means that we must accept the Hellenistic-Roman cultural expression of Christianity that comes to us as God-given. Thus, Ratzinger seems to presume that Western culture is the normative standard for Christian theology.

Claude Geffré also says there is no such thing as pure and abstract Christianity. The Christian message has always been 'inculturated' from the beginning of the Church. It has adopted the dominant culture of its place and origin – Semitic thought and Greek culture. Geffré believes in a fruitful and creative encounter between Christianity and non-Western cultures that are inseparably linked to their religious traditions.[429] The

---

[425] Schall, *The Regensburg Lecture*, p. 110.

[426] Benedict XVI, 'Meeting with the Representatives of Science (Regensburg Lecture)'.

[427] Joseph Ratzinger, *The Ratzinger Report* (San Francisco, CA: Ignatius Press, 1985), p. 194.

[428] Rausch, *Pope Benedict XVI*, p. 59.

[429] Claude Geffré, 'Double Belonging and the Originality of Christianity as a Religion', in *Many Mansions? Multiple Religious Belonging and Christian*

question now is whether Christianity should adopt the dominant culture as well as the religious values of any new place where it is planted. I agree with Geffré that it is wrong to conceive of inculturation in terms of a Christianity that ceases to be Western in order to become African, Chinese or Indian. It is essential, I believe, to retain the best of Semitic spirituality and Hellenistic thought in the process of adapting the gospel to our own local cultures.

Topics for discussion and reflection

- How successful has the Church been in formulating an appropriate theological response with historical backgrounds to inform contemporary religious life?
- Do you see Christianity as essentially a European religion or already successfully inculturated in different cultures? Please share examples from at least two different cultures or countries.
- In our VUCA (volatile, uncertain, complex, ambiguous) world, what are the roles and opportunities for Christianity in interfaith dialogues to promote peace, mutual understanding, and harmony?
- Of the three paradigms in the theology of religion, which one appeals to you more? How?

Identity, edited by Catherine Cornille (Maryknoll, NY: Orbis Books, 2002), pp. 95–6.

Chapter 7

Global Ethic

No world peace without peace between the religions.
No peace between the religions without dialogue between the religions.[430]

Given the socio-political, economic, and environmental crises we are facing, Hans Küng calls for a renewed ethic to save our planet from destroying itself. Our earth is deteriorating rapidly not because we are inherently evil or self-destructive, but because as the population increases or people become more affluent, they consume more goods and services, and they occupy more of our limited land area. The drive towards material prosperity and success often leads to political rivalries, conflicts, and trade wars between nations. Further, mindless consumerism has exhausted our natural resources and produced more waste and pollution, badly affecting our planet's biosphere, lithosphere, hydrosphere, and atmosphere. Many of the problems we face are not due to ill will or bad intentions but to the unforeseen or intentionally ignored consequences of industrialization, urbanization, and secularization. The earth is the only home we have, and Küng rightly believes we share a global concern and obligation to protect it from further destruction by adopting an ethic of responsibility in place of the ethic of prosperity.

This global responsibility includes restraining ourselves for the sake of future generations when using our natural resources. Ethics can no longer be confined to the private sphere; it is now a public concern in

---

[430] Hans Küng, *Global Responsibility: In Search of a New World Ethic* (New York, NY: Continuum, 2001), p. xv.

our postmodern world. If we need to keep the world intact, Küng insists that we need common goals, values, and visions. As a theologian, Küng believes religious leaders can contribute towards a renewed ethic that can save our planet. In spite of their ambivalent and chequered history, Christianity, Judaism, Hinduism, Buddhism, Confucianism and Taoism have contributed to the spiritual and moral progress of their adherents. Besides believers, Küng also includes non-believers in his grand project.

However, some non-believers, such as Marxists and humanists, prefer to have morality without religion. These so-called atheists or agnostics have a basic orientation towards leading a life of integrity, filled with compassion for others, but without the perceived trappings of religion. If one looks back in history, non-believers have fought hard for the cause of freedom of conscience, that is, freedom for and from religion. In fact, both believers and non-believers have defended human rights and dignity and supported Article 1 of the United Nations declaration: 'All human beings are born free and equal in dignity and rights. They are endowed with reason and conscience and should act towards one another in a spirit of brotherhood.'[431]

Human beings are rational creatures with a sense of autonomy, a sense of responsibility, and a fundamental grasp of reality. Hence, Küng insists that there must be mutual respect between believers and non-believers to cooperate so as to create a better world. With a joint effort, they can restore the basic rights of all human beings, alleviate poverty, protect the environment, and raise the living standard of poor people.

This chapter focuses on Küng's dissertations on global responsibility and his call upon representatives of major world religions to contribute towards formulating a global ethic. His arguments are explicated in two of his books, *A Global Ethic for Global Politics and Economics* (1998) and *Global Responsibility: In Search of a New World Ethic* (2001). While the rights and dignity of the human person are not stated directly in the Scriptures, nonetheless, we may be surprised to learn that the Christian churches had initially condemned the concept of human rights for various reasons. In fact, the churches felt threatened by the existence of human rights because they perceived them as an expression of unbridled freedom. It is thus the genius of Küng to turn to other religious traditions for help in formulating a world ethic.

[431.] Universal Declaration of Human Rights, https://www.un.org/en/about-us/universal-declaration-of-human-rights.

A controversial and influential Swiss theologian and Catholic priest, Küng died on 6 April 2021, at his home in Tübingen, south-west Germany. He had served as a theological advisor at Vatican II. In the years that followed, he had clashed with the Vatican; this culminated in 1979 when the Congregation for the Doctrine of the Faith (CDF) declared that Küng had 'departed from the integral truth of Catholic faith, and therefore he can no longer be considered a Catholic theologian nor function as such in a teaching role'.[432] The CDF cited his 1971 book, *Infallible? An Inquiry*, as containing ideas that are contrary to Church teaching.

No longer permitted to teach Catholic theology, Küng switched to ecumenical theology. From the 1990s, he promoted the idea of a 'global ethic', emphasizing common ethical values found in major world religions. Acknowledging the conflicts, rivalries, and divisions that religions have created in history, Küng believes religions still have the spiritual and philosophical resources in their traditions to inspire and improve the lives of people.

Merits of Religion

Religion can be interpreted as a projection of human longing (Feuerbach), but such a projection is not a proof that God does not exist. Religion can indeed be a form of consolation (Marx) promoted by interest groups or a psychological need for a fatherly figure (Freud). Nonetheless, religion can strengthen our identity and help us mature and be more aware of ourselves and others. Religion can act as motivation for the social transformation of society. In fact, ethical and moral norms in the West originate from the Judeo-Christian heritage.

Focussing on Abrahamic religions – Judaism, Christianity, and Islam – Küng maintains that these faiths can provide a basis for a universal ethical norm: the belief in God as the 'primal ground' or 'primal goal'. This belief in one God does not mean that we have no freedom, but rather provides us with security and orientation to live fully as human beings. Belief in God helps us 'to frame rules for one self and to accept personal

---

[432.] Sacred Congregation for the Doctrine of the Faith, 'Declaration', https://www.vatican.va/roman_curia/congregations/cfaith/documents/rc_con_cfaith_doc_19791215_christi-ecclesia_en.html.

responsibility': it is 'theonomy and not heteronomy'.[433] In other words, we live according to divine law and reason and not just according to our desires. We are responsible to God and to others for the way we live.

Religion provides us with teachings, dogmas, symbols, prayers, rites and festivals to satisfy our intellectual and emotional needs for both the masses and the elites. Tested by history and adapted to various cultures, religion can communicate the meaning of life and death. It offers us the highest ideals and supreme values, and also affords us a feeling of home, a sense of faith, hope, and security. Religion can provide us with the ground for protest and resistance against injustice and oppression committed by the government or the military, as we have witnessed in 2021 in Myanmar. For Küng, authentic religion is related to belief in one God, which he differentiates from pseudo-religion that idolises reason, progress, technology and capital. More importantly, he believes the world's religious traditions can contribute towards establishing a global ethic that we urgently need to navigate through the crises of our time.

Küng insists that human ethics cannot replace religion, which alone can communicate the depth of our human longing, positive feelings such as success and happiness, as well as negative feelings, such as suffering and guilt. Only religion can convey the ultimate meaning of life and issues such as suffering, death, and the afterlife. Religion attempts to answer questions regarding where we come from and where we are going. Further, religion attempts to give an answer to what a human's ultimate responsibility is and where our ultimate home is. Faith can move people to fight for justice through protest against unjust conditions even in the face of insurmountable difficulties. Religion is an expression of our longing for the 'Wholly Other'.[434] In the following section, we will briefly examine the teachings of various religious traditions in relation to human rights and dignity.

Jewish Tradition

The modern concept of human rights and dignity does not exist in the Bible nor in Jewish rabbinic texts. This notion of human rights is associated with property rights, for example, land legally acquired which

---

[433.] Küng, *Global Responsibility*, p. 53.
[434.] Hans Küng, *A Global Ethic for Global Politics and Economics* (New York, NY: Oxford University Press, 1998), p. 143.

the government must safeguard. There is great respect for property rights in the Jewish tradition, but God is regarded as the sole creator of the world. Thus in English, we call him 'Lord'. The only rights we have are given by God as his 'covenant partners'.[435] Judaism maintains the inalienable dignity of every human person because he or she is created in the image of God.

The relationship between the creator and his creatures is symbolized by this Jewish legal term, 'covenant'. Thus, human beings enjoy the highest status given by God among all his creations – they attain an almost god-like status because of their intimate relationship with the Lord. However, being a covenanted people, they are responsible for turning back to God (*teshuvah*) should they fall or sin.[436] It is a tremendous responsibility because they are also given the freedom to disobey or defy God. Even when a person is punished, if he repents, he is instantly forgiven. In Judaism, no human being can be denied this fundamental right, which God has bestowed upon all people.

Another important aspect of Jewish doctrine is the emphasis on justice and mercy. All human beings are equal in the eyes of God. Fundamental to Judaism is that all men and women are given the opportunity to develop their potential to the fullest. This includes the right to gainful employment, compensation, the acquisition of private property, to marriage and family, and everything that leads to a full human existence. Unfortunately, there are always powerful and unscrupulous people who will exploit the weak and the poor, and deny others the privileges and rights they enjoy. The treatment of foreigners or aliens in Judaism is admirable: 'When an alien resides with you in your land, you shall not oppress the alien. The alien who resides with you shall be to you as the citizen among you; you shall love the alien as yourself, for you were aliens in the land of Egypt: I am the Lord your God' (Leviticus 19:33–4). Thus human rights and dignity are accorded to all human beings irrespective of where they come from; they are given to residents and foreigners alike. Therefore, it is vital that a higher power safeguards those basic human rights and that dignity.[437]

---

[435] Eugene B. Borowitz, 'The Torah, Written and Oral, and Human Rights: Foundations and Deficiencies', in *The Ethics of World Religions and Human Rights*, edited by Hans Küng and Jürgen Moltmann, *Concilium* (London; Philadelphia, PA: SCM Press; Trinity Press International, 1990), p. 26.
[436] Borowitz, 'The Torah, Written and Oral, and Human Rights', p. 26.
[437] Borowitz, 'The Torah, Written and Oral, and Human Rights', p. 28.

Christian Tradition

Human rights in the modern era have their origin in English law. Christian churches opposed the concept of human rights mainly because this notion is not mentioned directly or clearly in the Bible. However, the negative attitude towards the social position of women and the use of torture in legal proceedings point to the fact that the churches violated human rights. During the Reformation, the rights of the individual and individual responsibility were taken seriously by the Church as the person's justification before God. Catholic authorities condemned the idea of human rights because in the English Bill of Rights of 1689 it was an expression of anti-Catholic sentiments. Furthermore, the North American Bill of Rights of 1791, which was backed by strong Protestant biblical piety, increased Catholic suspicion.[438] Protestant theology also displayed a negative attitude towards human rights, associating them with the Enlightenment, which was anti-religion.

Proponents of the Enlightenment had an optimistic view of the human person, while Christianity teaches that due to original sin, humankind has fallen. Thus, we have two contrasting images of the human being. Church authorities could not endorse the declarations on human rights because they were proclaimed by the French Revolution, which was anti-Church. The Catholic Church opposed human rights, perceiving these ideas as a 'doctrine of unbridled freedom' while the Protestant churches associated them with an authoritarian state.[439] There was no theological basis in their opposition, just ideological differences. The churches felt threatened by human rights, believing that the ideas could be used to destroy them.

The popes of the nineteenth and twentieth centuries condemned human rights because they believed the concept was influenced by secularism and permissiveness. John XXIII in his encyclical *Pacem in Terris* (1963) was the first pontiff to write unequivocally in support of human rights. Thus if we look at the church teachings and laws to support human rights, we will be disappointed. However, if we look at the gospel, we can discover that its teachings on the dignity of the

---

[438.] Knut Walf, 'Gospel, Church, Law and Human Rights: Foundations and Deficiencies', in *The Ethics of World Religions and Human Rights*, edited by Hans Küng and Jürgen Moltmann, *Concilium* (London; Philadelphia, PA: SCM Press; Trinity Press International, 1990), p. 35.

[439.] Walf, 'Gospel, Church, Law and Human Rights', p. 36.

human person is actually expressed within the social context: 'For in the one Spirit we were all baptized into one body – Jews or Greeks, slaves or free – and we were all made to drink of one Spirit' (1 Corinthians 12:13) or 'There is no longer Jew or Greek, there is no longer slave or free, there is no longer male and female; for all of you are one in Christ Jesus' (Galatians 3:28). The dignity of the individual is fully expressed in Jesus: 'He is the image of the invisible God, the firstborn of all creation' (Colossians 1:15).

Islamic Tradition

Islam, which means obedience to Allah, traces its origins to God, who according to Muslims is the author of *Tawrah*, the revelation given to Moses.[440] Like all revealed religions, it stresses the transcendent dimension of the human person, where human rights have their foundation in the divine. In line with the other Abrahamic religions, Judaism and Christianity, the concept of human rights in Islam is understood in terms of a relationship with God. Human beings are also given the freedom and responsibility to accept or reject God's law. While the Prophets reminded the people of the importance of doing God's will, freedom of conscience is also respected. There should not be any coercion in religion. Unfortunately, the word *jihad*, which means *effort*, has been wrongly translated as *holy war*, thus leading to much abuse. While violence is not excluded, it is only used against those who oppose Islam, but not to spread the faith.[441]

The Islamic community, which was founded by the Prophet Mohammed, first emerged in Mecca, and then migrated to Medina because of persecution; it was solely based on faith, following the example of Abraham in answering the call of God. The Shari'a, which developed from the Qur'an, contains laws governing the lives of Muslims. It states that everything belongs to Allah alone, and representatives on earth are responsible for

---

[440.] Most Muslims think that the current Hebrew text of Genesis and other books in the Bible are not a reliable record of the revelation of *Tawrah*. I would like to thank Professor Leo Lefebure for pointing out this to me.

[441.] Roger Garaudy, 'Human Rights, Islam: Foundation, Tradition, Violation', in *The Ethics of World Religions and Human Rights*, edited by Hans Küng and Jürgen Moltmann, *Concilium* (London; Philadelphia, PA: SCM Press; Trinity Press International, 1990), pp. 46–7.

managing these resources according to his will. For Muslims, duties come before rights, and thus the caretakers of Allah's property must safeguard it. It is a serious sin to accumulate wealth. In the Qur'an, *zakat* means to donate for the needy, and *riba* means an accumulation of fortune without labour or exploitative gain, which is not allowed.[442] This teaching in the Qur'an assists in closing the income gap: care of the poor and charitable work is fundamental to the Islamic way of life.

For most Muslims, the Qur'an must be read literally because it is the final word of God.[443] This sacred text has provided a firm foundation for human rights to be developed by virtue of being human. It teaches that one must not discriminate between Muslims and non-Muslims. In fact, general principles such as justice, equality, and freedom of religion can be found in the Qur'an in the early stage of its revelation in Mecca. The Qur'an composed during the Mecca period emphasised freedom of belief and equality of all human beings, regardless of religion or gender. Unfortunately, during the subsequent stage in Medina (622–32), the Qur'an incorporated verses and rules that discriminate against women and non-believers.[444] Perhaps, when the community became more powerful and wealthy, it became less tolerant, more abusive and authoritarian. When power corrupts, there is always a temptation to sacralise power and use religion as a tool to advance rule by religious or political leaders. Hence when interpreting these laws and rules, it is important to take into consideration other sources such as oral traditions and the context in which the Qur'an is understood.

Hindu Tradition

In principle, India is a secular nation. However, Hindu lawgivers there have the responsibility of promoting justice, peace and equality, and at the same time, to assist in the people's quest for transcendence in their

---

[442] Garaudy, 'Human Rights, Islam', p. 48.
[443] There exists also in Islam, the tradition of Sufi mystical and symbolic interpretation of the Holy Qur'an.
[444] Abdullah Ahmed An-Na'im, 'Qur'an, Shari'a and Human Rights: Foundations, Deficiencies and Prospects', in *The Ethics of World Religions and Human Rights*, edited by Hans Küng and Jürgen Moltmann, *Concilium* (London; Philadelphia, PA: SCM Press; Trinity Press International, 1990), p. 62.

daily lives. The religious and spiritual aspect of life is deeply embedded in Indian culture, and thus, the Hindu tradition has these broad duties. Practices, ethics and religious duties are closely related because Hindus believe the ultimate purpose of life is to be united with the Ultimate Being or Brahman: 'Only the teaching of the One Reality (Brahman) alone can truly bring about goodness and justice and not any teaching which promotes differentiations.'[445] In general, this is the essence of the Hindu religious tradition: the teaching of the One Reality or Brahman.

This emphasis on Brahman means that our human nature is intrinsically linked to nature but possesses the potential to transcend this temporal order. The *Upanishads*, sacred texts of Hinduism, state that the *atman* or the universal self of each person is the 'footprint of all pervasive Brahman'.[446] In other words, the *atman* is the essence, the soul, or the spirit of the person. This *atman* is present in the human personality but must be guided to live a righteous life, enabling the person to attain spiritual enlightenment. This is achieved through prayers, recollection, meditation and teachings as prescribed in sacred literature known as the *Śāstra*.[447] The teaching in *Śāstra* helps to awaken a person's consciousness of his or her true identity and destination, which are forgotten when we are distracted by worldly cares and concerns.

The focus of the *Śāstra* is on *dharma* or righteousness. *Dharma* has a wide connotation, including duty, virtue, morality, or religion itself. Hinduism teaches that all human beings are born with their tendencies and predilections known as *samskaras*, which means mental impressions or recollections. The law of *Karma*, i.e. the spiritual principle of cause and effect, states that an individual's good or bad actions determine his or her future mode of existence. Birth is regarded as the 'result of past actions and a given platform for future ones'.[448] The inequalities in life could be altered through righteous living. The extent that a person is aware of their true status as a creature, referring to their ability to reach spiritual awakening, is the foundation of the caste system in Hinduism.

[445.] *Bhagavatapurana*, quoted in Bithika Mukerji, 'The Foundations of Unity and Equality: A Hindu Understanding of Human Rights', in *The Ethics of World Religions and Human Rights*, edited by Hans Küng and Jürgen Moltmann, *Concilium* (London; Philadelphia, PA: SCM Press; Trinity Press International, 1990), p. 73.

[446.] Mukerji, 'The Foundations of Unity and Equality', p. 74.

[447.] Mukerji, 'The Foundations of Unity and Equality', p. 74.

[448.] Mukerji, 'The Foundations of Unity and Equality', p. 75.

Contrary to popular belief, the divisions in the caste system are not rigid. Hinduism teaches that all human beings are born equal because everyone has mixed qualities in their character. It is the action in this life that will determine one's caste in the next life. The teaching of One Reality and the spiritual quest for realizing the *atman* or self means that one must not be attached to pleasure and material possessions. Everyone, irrespective of caste, has the equal opportunity to pursue self-enlightenment. The Hindu caste system taught by ancient Vedic texts is the ideal yet the reality is that such a system has been exploited and manipulated by the upper caste to perpetuate their position and power.[449] Be that as it may, the social order based on caste divisions has served Hindu society for more than two thousand years, and it is here to stay.

I am aware that the above description of Hinduism is a broad generalization and does not do justice to the complexities of the faith. In fact, a unified Hindu view of ultimate reality and caste system do not exist. 'Hinduism' refers to a family of religious traditions that do not have a core set of values and beliefs. Furthermore, not all Hindus accept the caste system. Many practising Hindus condemn it as evil.

Buddhist Tradition

Buddhism emphasises the interrelatedness of life, compassion for all creatures, non-violence, and care for the earth and all that dwell in it. The Vietnamese monk Venerable Thich Nhat Hanh teaches the importance of mindfulness: paying particular attention to our senses, feelings, and actions in every moment of our waking hours. In line with Asian philosophy, Nhat Hanh also stresses non-dualism and the importance of being at peace with one's own life and acting as a peacemaker in society. Calling the world an extension of oneself, Nhat Hanh wants us to take good care of our environment. He founded a religious community known as Tiep Hien, which means 'Order of Interbeing'. He puts it this way: 'I am, therefore you are. You are, therefore I am. That is the meaning of the word interbeing. We inter-are.'[450] This Order of

---

[449.] Mukerji, 'The Foundations of Unity and Equality', p. 76.
[450.] Quoted in Sulak Sivaraksa, 'Human Rights in the Context of Global Problem-Solving: A Buddhist Perspective', in *The Ethics of World Religions and Human Rights*, edited by Hans Küng and Jürgen Moltmann, *Concilium*

Global Ethic

Interbeing was founded to address issues of social justice and peace, first by helping the members to understand their own behaviours in relation to the needs of the community, and at the same time, freeing them from rigid patterns of thinking and acting.

Revising the Five Precepts of Buddhism to address the issues of mind, speech and body more effectively, Nhat Hanh writes:

> First, do not kill and do not let others kill. We must find means to protect life. Thus, we avoid having an occupation that harms others and nature. Second, do not steal. Do not possess things that belong to others, respect others' properties. We must also prevent people from enriching themselves at the expense of others and the expense of the environment. Third, a sexual relationship is a commitment of love. We must respect the commitments and rights of others in addition to protecting our happiness. Fourth, be truthful. Do not spread fake news or gossip. Refrain from criticising or condemning others. Do not say things that will create discord and ill-feelings in the family and in the community. We must make every effort to promote reconciliation and to resolve conflict. Fifth, do not drink alcohol or take any intoxicating stuff. We must protect our bodies and avoid drugs that destroy our physical well-being. Destroying our body is tantamount to betraying our forebears, parents, and future generations.[451]

Grounded in Buddhist teachings, these principles and the practice of mindfulness can be the basis for social justice and peace. These precepts also help to counteract the tendency of people to be individualistic, self-centred and selfish. Nhat Hanh reminds us that there is a continuity between the inner and outer world and that we are all living on one planet, interconnected, hence we must collaborate with others to promote justice and peace.

(London; Philadelphia. PA: SCM Press; Trinity Press International, 1990), p. 88.

[451.] Summarized from Sivaraksa, 'Human Rights in the Context of Global Problem-Solving', p. 89.

Confucian Tradition

The Confucian concept of human rights emerges from a naturalist perspective – the *dao* of *tian* (天道). What follows *dao* (way) is good because it is from nature. *Tian* refers to nature, the source of goodness. Thus the goodness of human beings comes from the goodness of *tiandao* (天道). This idea of goodness is not based on an assertion or a judgment. Neither is the goodness of a person based on the dichotomy between good and evil. The Confucian idea of human rights has a naturalist foundation that springs from the goodness of heaven and earth. This goodness is not to be understood in the Western dualistic sense, such as good versus evil; it is simply natural goodness, such as the natural growth of trees and flowers. This goodness can also be the sustained effort of humans following the examples of heaven and earth (天地), translated as the natural order of things. Further, natural goodness is equated with good deeds that are 'resonant with natural cosmological sensibility'.[452] Confucian ethics is fundamentally ontological.

Thus to claim that human nature is good in the Confucian sense is to make a judgment regarding the completeness of human nature. The goodness of human nature is not based on dogmas or a religious foundation, but on creation. In other words, moral obligation is not based on transcendent sources but arises from moral roles or life itself. The moral sources of human action include the conscience one develops early in life, sympathy founded upon that conscience, wisdom acquired through social customs, and the established teachings of sages passed from generation to generation. All the above forms part of the cultural values of the family and society.[453]

Ancient classics provide moral wisdom and guidance for living. Contemporary moral ideals, especially those associated with human rights, are drawn from ancient texts. An example is the virtue of *ren ai* (仁爱), 'benevolent love'.[454] The call to human rights should not be seen

---

[452] Haiming Wen and William Keli'i Akina, 'A Naturalist Version of Confucian Morality for Human Rights', *Asian Philosophy* 22, no. 1 (2012), p. 7.

[453] Wen and Akina, 'A Naturalist Version of Confucian Morality for Human Rights', p. 9.

[454] Wen and Akina, 'A Naturalist Version of Confucian Morality for Human Rights', p. 9.

as a Western imposition; it arises from classical Chinese heritage. In fact, China could be an authority on human rights and a major contributor to a global ethic.

Unfortunately, history has shown that authorities can use Confucianism as a form of social control. The subjugation of women, the practice of foot-binding, and polygamy have been attributed to Confucianism. These practices could be argued to be 'human rights abuses' using today's Western-informed lens, although in the past they may have been understood differently. Nonetheless, none of these practices represents the true spirit of Confucianism, that is, the spirit derived from the canonical texts rather than historical practice. Authentic Confucianism promotes intellectual advancement and freedom. The Confucian equation of 'natural goodness-human nature' has at times inspired people to fight for human rights.[455] In spite of these merits, religion remains a divisive issue in many parts of the world.

What Divides Us?

Jews and Christians have common roots, but anti-Semitism and the annihilation of six million Jews in the Holocaust is a grim reminder of human wickedness and sin. For centuries, Jews and Muslims lived together in peace in Egypt, Spain and Istanbul, as well as many other places. However, during the past two centuries, Jews and Muslims have come into constant conflict and dispute in the Holy Land. Jews, Christians, and Muslims share a common father in Abraham. As mentioned in Chapter 1, this belief in a common father seems more mythical than historical.

In reality, Küng reminds us, there were five serious battles between Christians and Muslims. They are as follows:

i. During the seventh century, Muslims conquered and occupied the ancestral land of Christians, that is today's Palestine, Syria and Egypt.
ii. By the eighth century, the Islamic conquest included all of North Africa and Spain.

[455.] Wen and Akina, 'A Naturalist Version of Confucian Morality for Human Rights', p. 11.

iii. During the twelfth and thirteenth centuries, the Crusades temporarily recaptured the Holy Land, including Jerusalem. In Spain, we witness the reconquest of the peninsula by Christians up to 1492.
iv. During the fifteenth and sixteenth centuries, the Muslim Turks captured Constantinople and the Balkans and converted many of the people there, especially the Bosnians, to Islam.
v. During the nineteenth and twentieth centuries, colonial powers from the Christian West occupied Muslim territories such as North and East Africa, and the Middle and Far East, as far as Iran, India, Indonesia and Malaysia.[456]

Küng also reminds us that Islam is by no means just a radical fundamentalist religion. There are moderate Muslims who do not totally reject modernization and secularization. Fundamentalism also exists in Judaism as well as in Christianity. According to Küng, fundamentalism is not just religious; it has roots in the economic, political, and social spheres.

Overcoming Fundamentalism

The advent of modernization, which led to Westernization and secularization in the Islamic world, has caused an identity crisis and insecurity among many people. They look for a sense of direction and orientation in their religion to cope with the onslaught of modernity. Some ended up adopting fundamentalism and fanaticism. In view of this, Küng maintains that religious fundamentalism cannot be overcome with violent confrontation but must be approached with an open, understanding, tolerant, and democratic disposition. For example, in Turkey, there is an effort towards 'institutional integration' in which Islamic leaders who won in elections were able to form a government. This is better than the 'political polarization' in Algeria, where Islamic leaders who won elections were suppressed.[457] In other words, we must try to empathize with religious fundamentalists, and act to remove conditions that encourage such extremism. Fundamentalists should also

---

[456.] Küng, *A Global Ethic for Global Politics and Economics*, p. 146.
[457.] Küng, *A Global Ethic for Global Politics and Economics*, p. 147.

be reminded that there are teachings regarding freedom, pluralism and openness to other religious traditions in their own scriptures, whether those be the Qu'ran or the Bible.

Above all, Küng advocates dialogue and collaboration among religions. In order to escape the turbulence and antagonisms which are escalating in our time, he encourages religious leaders to search for a middle way, between modernism and fundamentalism, liberalism and exclusiveness, and laxity and aggressiveness. In spite of repeated failures, Küng believes that religions can contribute to peace by utilizing their spiritual resources, such as teachings in sacred texts which promote inner peace, to overcome violence and aggression in society. Peace between religions and nations is possible if there a 'basis of trust'.[458] This does not come about naturally but must be worked out by overcoming prejudices, resistance, ignorance and intolerance.

Basic Trust in Life

Küng maintains that a basic trust in life is the foundation of a healthy personality. Such trust must be cultivated during childhood: 'a child learns to trust literally at its mother's breast'.[459] Born into a middle-class family in Switzerland, Küng developed healthy and sound relationships with his parents and siblings, enabling him to possess this fundamental trust in life. He acknowledges that if a child is already damaged by psychological traumas or lack of sufficient attention at the time of weaning, this fundamental trust cannot be recovered. Küng's hope in humanity stems from this fundamental principle: 'The idea of Basic Trust is, therefore, for me, the foundation of a Basic Ethos that can unite us all. Without this "acceptance" of reality, without this positive, trusting Yes to reality despite all temptations to reject it, no one can behave ethically. Basic morality presupposes a Basic Trust in reality.'[460]

One need not be a Christian or a believer in any faith to possess this Basic Trust. Unbelievers and agnostics can cultivate this trust through healthy human relationships, meaningful work, and fulfilling

---

[458] Küng, *A Global Ethic for Global Politics and Economics*, p. 148.
[459] Hans Küng, *What I Believe* (London; New York, NY: Continuum, 2010), p. 1.
[460] Quoted in Jonathan Keir, 'From Religion to Business', *The Journal of Corporate Citizenship*, no. 62 (2016), p. 134.

occupations. In spite of the many crises, conflicts and challenges Küng faced, this Basic Trust, grounded in his belief in God, became a permanent self-identity in his life. He also realized that trust is an indispensable condition for a healthy society, in international politics and the global economy. Küng thus describes trust as the foundation of social life. It is this trust that motivated him to reach out to other religious leaders for dialogue and cooperation. His ingenuity lies in his courage and determination to consult world religious traditions for his work on a world ethic, without excluding other religious or secular resources.

Building Bridges

Acknowledging that it is not easy to build trust and confidence, Küng suggests some concrete measures to be implemented by leaders and representatives of various religions. This includes emphasis on what they have in common, such as the Golden Rule, rather than exaggerating their differences. Religious leaders must help to prevent crimes against humanity and the environment in the name of religion. They must also attempt to be mediators in violent situations through establishing ceasefires, negotiations and reconciliation. The more they engage with each other, the more understanding can be forged. Religious pluralism or multiplicity is not a threat but an enrichment of faith. Küng gives the following recommendations:

- dissolving hostile stereotypes,
- clearing up misunderstandings,
- working through traumatic memories,
- working through guilt complexes, socially and individually,
- demolishing hatred and destructiveness,
- reflecting on things that are held in common,
- taking concrete initiatives for reconciliation.[461]

In a situation of conflict, both sides must be able to present their perspectives and offer resolutions to be taken.

[461.] Küng, *A Global Ethic for Global Politics and Economics*, p. 150.

Minimal Basic Consensus

In 1993, Küng drafted the declaration on a global ethic for the Council of the Parliament of the World's Religions, which met for the first time in Chicago in 1893. A global ethic is not a substitute for the sacred texts of world religions; it is concerned with 'a minimal basic consensus relating to binding values, irrevocable standards and moral attitudes which can be supported by non-believers'.[462] The consensus of non-believers, including specialists in various disciplines, is important for a global ethic to be successfully implemented.

First of all, a global ethic demands that 'every human being must be treated humanely'. This means that there should not be discrimination on the basis of age, race, skin colour, language, religion, political views, etc. No one is 'above good and evil': all human beings must be respected and treated with dignity. Second, we must always 'do good and avoid evil'. This means we must follow the Golden Rule: 'what you wish done to yourself, do to others'.[463] These two principles are the most basic and minimal norms needed for society everywhere to function harmoniously. Based on them are four directives agreed upon by all religions:

  i. commitment to a culture of non-violence and respect for all life.
  ii. commitment to a culture of solidarity and a just economic order.
  iii. commitment to a culture of tolerance and a life of truthfulness.
  iv. commitment to a culture of equal rights and partnership between men and women.[464]

Relating to politicians, truthfulness plays an important role. All great religious traditions have taught us to speak and act truthfully. Unfortunately, many leaders in the world lack in this virtue. Lies, deceit, corruption and hypocrisy seem prevalent in our world. Some businesspeople, the media, scientists, researchers and religious leaders have also been guilty of not telling the truth. Küng says, 'There is no

---

[462] Küng, *A Global Ethic for Global Politics and Economics*, p. 109.
[463] Quoted in Küng, *A Global Ethic for Global Politics and Economics*, p. 110.
[464] Küng, *A Global Ethic for Global Politics and Economics*, p. 111.

global justice without truthfulness and humaneness!'[465] Thus our young people must be taught to be truthful in their thoughts and actions. Without an ethical education, they will not be able to separate facts from opinions, knowledge from information.

Six Perspectives

Besides the minimal basic consensus, Küng puts forward six ethical perspectives that the major world religions can contribute to the formulation of a global ethic:

> a. *Human wellbeing*. This refers to the protection of human life, integrity, freedom, and promotion of solidarity. In the Old Testament, we have the commandment to love God and to love one another. In the New Testament, we have the Sermon on the Mount. The Qur'an emphasizes justice, truth, and good works. Hindu *dharma* is about the right way of living or the path of rightness, while Buddhist doctrine emphasizes overcoming human suffering. Confucian teaching stresses harmony in the cosmic order and *humanum*, which is related to human well-being and dignity.[466]
> b. *Maxims of basic humanity*. These include the five basic commands: i. Do not kill; ii. Do not lie; iii. Do not steal (which includes corruption); iv. Do not practise immorality; v. Respect your parents and love your children. As a protection against libertinism, where everything is relative, these norms are absolute. At the same time, such norms are not to be applied rigidly, but they must take each specific situation into account. Ethics are neither dogmas nor tactics: they are norms that are governed by conditions.[467]
> c. *A reasonable middle way*. Küng acknowledges that there is a tendency for religions to be extreme and rigorous in the application of their doctrines. However, to convert more people, they must find a reasonable middle way. Balancing

---

[465.] Küng, *A Global Ethic for Global Politics and Economics*, p. 112.
[466.] Küng, *Global Responsibility*, p. 56.
[467.] Küng, *Global Responsibility*, p. 57.

between 'libertinism and legalism' means taking into consideration the complexity of human existence. In practical terms, religious teachings must strike a balance between greed and detachment, pleasure-seeking and asceticism, worldly and world-denying. Buddha stresses composure, Confucius speaks of wisdom, the Torah teaches duty in the world before God, and the teaching of Jesus is neither legalistic nor ascetic. In fact, all religions stress having the right dispositions, attitudes, and the cultivation of virtues to guide human lives.[468]

d. *The Golden Rule.* All great religions teach their adherents this fundamental rule: 'What you yourself do not want, do not do to another person' (Confucius, 551–489 BC). This teaching is also found in Judaism: 'Do not do to others what you would not want them to do to you' (Rabbi Hillel, 60 BC-10 AD). The same teaching is found in Christianity, phrased positively: 'Whatever you want people to do to you, do also to them' (Matthew 7:12; Luke 6:31).

e. *Moral motivation.* In spite of a lack of interest in religion among young people, faith still has the authority to motivate people to adopt a new attitude and a new lifestyle. Jesus, Buddha, Confucius, Lao Tze, and Mohammed are role models whose teachings inspire people to find meaning in life. Their ancient wisdom and teachings can be translated into a contemporary setting relevant to peoples' lives today.[469]

f. *A horizon of meaning and identification of a goal.* In the face of emptiness and meaninglessness in many peoples' existence, religions have the unique authority to offer answers to the questions of life, suffering, death and the afterlife. Judaism and Christianity preach about resurrection and eternal life. In Islam, this is regarded as paradise, in Hinduism, as *moksha*, in Buddhism, as *nirvana*, and in Taoism as 'immortality'.[470]

---

[468] Küng, *Global Responsibility*, p. 58.
[469] Küng, *Global Responsibility*, p. 59.
[470] Küng, *Global Responsibility*, p. 60.

The declaration of a global ethic requires the special commitment of major world religions with the moral authority to undertake such an important task. These global faiths have the moral power to address individuals' consciences and motivate them to create a better world. Religions can mobilize people towards formulating and presenting ethical goals so that these norms can be practical for living. Major world religions also have the authority and the wisdom to warn people about vices and sins and instil virtues and values that are universal.

The World Conference of the Religions for Peace met in Kyoto, Japan, in 1970. In spite of their differences, the representatives of various religions (Bahai, Buddhist, Confucian, Christian, Hindu, Jain, Jew, Muslim, Shintoist, Sikh, Zoroastrians, and others) shared the following values: convictions regarding the unity of the family; the equality and dignity of the human person; the sacredness of life and the value of human community; a recognition that 'might is not right'; a belief that love and compassion are stronger than hate and enmity; an obligation towards the poor and the oppressed as against the wealthy and powerful oppressors; and an unwavering hope that good will prevail in spite of all the evils in this world.[471] The underlying principle of all these values is the concept of *humanum* or what is truly human, a concept which puts the emphasis on human dignity.

Humanum can also be used to evaluate the authenticity of a religious tradition: a religion is good and true to the extent that it helps human beings flourish. The teachings, traditions, rites, and institutions of a particular religion must help to advance human dignity and rights. In other words, religion is false or bad when it hinders human progress and

---

[471.] Küng believes these statements can be made more concrete with specific contributions from Christianity, a religion that has suffered more from the onslaught of secularization. Here he stresses 'self-criticism by the church' and 'a new basic consensus on integrative human conviction', Küng, *Global Responsibility*, 63-6. Richard Fenn, however, maintains that Christianity is actually a secularizing force: 'By bequeathing to the world a mediator who was to end all mediation, Christianity stripped the world of any claims to embody the sacred. For Christianity, very little, if anything, is guaranteed to be sacred; it is and has been an iconoclastic religion. Certainly, Christianity itself can take much of the credit or blame for the process of secularization in Western societies.' Richard K. Fenn, 'Toward a Global Ethic: A Response to Hans Küng' *International Journal of Politics, Culture, and Society* 13, no. 1 (1999), p. 52.

meaningful existence. What is truly human has its source in the divine, for we are made in the image of God (Genesis 1:27). Küng assures us that *humanum* is not an external criterion used to evaluate the authenticity of religion, nor is it a Western construction influenced by Christianity.[472] It lies embedded within every authentic religious tradition. Besides the three Abrahamic religions, Hinduism and Buddhism also uphold the intrinsic value of the human person. Hinduism teaches the close relationship between morality and religion, Buddhism emphasizes compassion for all living things, and Confucianism possesses a strong humanistic tradition.

Rights and Responsibilities

Many people have a tendency to emphasize the rights of human beings at the expense of responsibilities, but Küng insists that 'all rights imply responsibilities'.[473] For example, while the journalist may enjoy the freedom of the press, he or she has the responsibility to report objectively and fairly. As we have seen over the last five years, with fake news so rampant, this emphasis on the reporter's responsibility is more urgent than ever. Further, the right to private property, guaranteed by the state, does not mean that the wealthy and influential should manipulate real estate through control of land distribution and speculation, leaving the poor without proper shelter. There must be 'some sense of proportion and moderation' when it comes to each person's right to property.[474] If not, private properties will be priced beyond the reach of the majority of people, as has happened in Hong Kong over the last two decades. Finally, the rights of individuals to decide according to their consciences also imply responsibilities and legal obligations.

Küng makes two essential points regarding rights and responsibilities: First, human beings have fundamental rights written in the Universal Declaration of Human Rights, and both the state and individuals also have the responsibility to respect and protect these rights. In other words, there are legal obligations incumbent upon the state and individuals. Second, there are also fundamental responsibilities coming from the

---

[472.] Küng, *Global Responsibility*, p. 92.
[473.] Küng, *A Global Ethic for Global Politics and Economics*, p. 100.
[474.] Küng, *A Global Ethic for Global Politics and Economics*, p. 101.

'heart', the 'conscience', or 'customs'[475] that the person must undertake as a human being. In other words, these responsibilities are not based on law but on ethical obligations. For example, a ceasefire treaty is only a piece of paper signed by two partners if there is no *ethical will* to make it work.[476] In the long run, neither law nor morality can assert itself without the ethical authority that comes from God, Küng believes.

Thus, the law is ineffective if it is not supported by moral inclination or obligation of conscience. In practice, a peace treaty must be backed by human heads and hearts determined to make it work. Justice and peace can be a reality only when clear-sighted human beings are ready to give law its validity: 'laws need a moral foundation'.[477] A better world cannot be created with laws and ordinances alone. It needs commitment to human rights and an awareness of responsibilities. Küng teaches that law cannot last without ethics, and a new world order can only be realized with a global ethic, which refers to fundamental moral attitudes of individuals as well as of societies.

Before a formal declaration of global ethics can be made, Küng insists that the following conditions must be satisfied: i. the global ethic must be related to human reality; ii. it must be able to penetrate to the deeper ethical levels beyond legal and political considerations; iii. it must avoid the use of technical jargon, as a global ethic must be comprehensible to the ordinary people; and iv. it must be capable of securing consensus.

Besides the fulfilment of these conditions, Küng also warns of three mistakes that we must avoid in order that the global ethic does not come to a dead end: i. the global ethic cannot be just a replication of the United Nation Declaration of Human Rights, but must provide ethical support to this promulgation; ii. this global ethic must avoid moralizing and judgmental and self-righteous attitudes, especially towards controversial issues such as divorce or euthanasia; iii. this global ethic must not be transformed into a religious enterprise, but must take into serious consideration economic and political realities.[478] Be that as it may, global ethics has its origin in the ancient wisdom of world religions, which themselves contain the minimum requirements to make life in society possible. For Küng, it begins with his faith in Jesus Christ.

[475.] Küng, *A Global Ethic for Global Politics and Economics*, p. 102.
[476.] Küng, *A Global Ethic for Global Politics and Economics*, p. 103.
[477.] Küng, *A Global Ethic for Global Politics and Economics*, p. 104.
[478.] Küng, *A Global Ethic for Global Politics and Economics*, pp. 106–7.

Küng's Reflection as a Christian

As a theologian, Küng has observed the trend that many people, especially in the West, turn away from Christianity towards Eastern religions or other forms of spirituality. He believes the Church hierarchy, which is authoritarian in faith and morals, is partly responsible for this unfortunate situation. Küng wonders if 'the light of Christianity is slowly being quenched?'[479] He himself was punished by the Church hierarchy (specifically, the Congregation for the Doctrine of the Faith), who revoked his license to teach in 1979 as a Catholic theologian. Nonetheless, Küng has not given up hope, for he truly believes that Jesus Christ is 'the light of the world' (John 8:12) that shines in the darkness. 'The darkness has not overcome it' (John 1:5). For Küng, the essence of Christianity is this living historical figure of Jesus Christ, whose name gives hope to millions of people. This faith in Christ has allowed Christians to establish a spiritual home where faith, hope and love prevail. The gospel ideals preached by Christ can be lived out in our daily lives, as we have witnessed in the lives of saints and martyrs in the Church.

Be that as it may, Küng also concedes that there are other lights besides Jesus Christ; there exist other words, besides this Word of God. This means that Jesus Christ is not to be confined within the covers of the Bible or the walls of Church. The Spirit of God is present everywhere, not just in Christian communities. In other words, people of different religions, such as Hindus, Buddhists and Muslims, have their own lights to follow. In fact, in the gospel, we find Jesus showing respect to people of other faiths, for example, the Syro-Phoenician woman and the Roman officer. Jesus welcomes the Greeks and teaches us the true meaning of love through the action of a Samaritan. We can discover our Christian responsibility to the world through our encounters with non-Christians.

In our mission as Christians, Küng insists that we should put more stress on giving testimony than seeking to convert others to our faith. We should also emphasize works rather than words, especially within our communities. He also promotes inculturation at the grassroots level and dialogue rather than confrontation. Moving beyond our Christian confessions or denominations, we should promote shared ecumenical testimony. Further, Küng believes that our Christian mission should be strengthened not solely by church authorities but also the solidarity

---

[479.] Küng, *A Global Ethic for Global Politics and Economics*, p. 152.

of the people. Acknowledging the ecumenical progress we have made in the twentieth century, he foresees that we will face new challenges in the third millennium, and invites Christians to work with adherents of other faiths for peace, justice, protection of the environment and a 'renewed ethic'.[480] This is Küng's foundation of a Global Ethic.

Küng's call for a global ethic is urgently needed, especially when tensions and conflicts between China and the United States are escalating daily. He says such an ethic must come before politics because political actions deal with 'values and choice'.[481] This means our political leaders must be guided by ethical concern, which has its basis in world religions. These spiritual resources provide support and solutions to ethical, national, social and economic concerns. Though there are fundamental doctrinal differences among the world religions, they are united by a common ethical standard. What unites them as religion is greater than what divides them. This global ethic needs the collaboration of non-believers, such as the communist leaders of China.

Vision for the Future

We lack a vision of the future, and as a result, hopelessness, anguish and despair pervade our lives, Küng laments. Ideologies such as communism or capitalism that serve as pseudo-religions have failed us miserably. In spite of scientific and technological progress, we are confronted with ecological, environmental and economic crises. The very survival of humankind is at stake. Thus, at present, we urgently need to have a 'basic orientation' based on our cultural and spiritual foundations so that humankind can continue to exist and flourish.[482] This basic orientation can be found in morality. Küng distinguishes morality, which is positive, from moralism, which absolutizes norms and values.

Through dialogue with politics and economics, Küng attempts to offer a realistic view of a peaceful and humane future. Dismissing interference by institutions such as the market or the Church, he presents a vision of the future that will not be constrained by an economic ideology that serves the party or the state. This vision represents an ethically oriented view: 'diachronic and synchronic', objective, constructive, rational, open

---

[480] Küng, *A Global Ethic for Global Politics and Economics*, p. 156.
[481] Küng, *A Global Ethic for Global Politics and Economics*, p. 109.
[482] Küng, A Global Ethic for Global Politics and Economics, p. xiv.

and long term.[483] It is in this vision that Küng formulates his world ethic, which would humanize our present economic and political systems; the challenge should be taken seriously by the younger generation.

In view of the religious conflicts and 'the clash of civilizations' of today, Küng believes that democracy will not survive without the solidarity of believers and non-believers. Further, he asserts that there is a clash of civilizations because of conflict between religions. Hence, dialogue between religions is necessary for peace to exist. Since differences of dogma, which hinder dialogue, are found in all religious traditions and political ideologies, Küng believes a new global ethic must be formulated so that we can have a new world order. This new global ethic is not a substitute for the moral teachings of Judaism, Christianity, Islam, Hinduism or Confucianism. It is the minimum common human value that believers and non-believers need to possess so that there can be peace on earth.[484]

Samuel Huntington, author of *The Clash of Civilizations*, also maintains that the basic moral values of Asia and the West are compatible. A universal civilization could be established based on these common values. Huntington writes, 'Peoples in all civilizations should search for and attempt to expand the values, institutions, and practices they have in common with peoples of other civilizations.'[485]

Science and technology cannot create this consensus for a global ethic; in fact, they need it, Küng argues. Our economic and technological problems have become political and moral issues. For example, the vaccine for Covid-19 to contain the pandemic has become a political tool for control and domination. The vaccine is also a moral problem because poor nations cannot afford it. Thus we need to have a basic ethical standard that is universal – applicable to all nations, cultures and religions. Küng knows well that it is impossible to have total ethical consensus in our pluralistic and postmodern world. However, since we all share the same humanity, a 'minimal ethical consensus'[486] is achievable. In other words, there are some fundamental values, norms or criteria that we can agree upon as human beings because there is a universal longing for justice and truth.

[483.] Küng, *A Global Ethic for Global Politics and Economics*, p. xv.

[484.] Küng, *A Global Ethic for Global Politics and Economics*, p. 92.

[485.] Samuel P. Huntington, *The Clash of Civilizations and the Remaking of World Order* (New York, NY: Simon & Schuster, 2011), p. 202.

[486.] Küng, *A Global Ethic for Global Politics and Economics*, p. 94.

A universal quest can be found when we look at political conflict, which the media has helped to expose, when masses of people take to the streets to protest against despotic regimes, such as we witnessed in Myanmar in February 2021, when television viewers from all over the world expressed their sympathy and solidarity with the people there. This shows that there are universal core values that people share: a 'core morality or 'elementary ethical standards' that transcend regional or religious differences,[487] including the fundamental right to life and human dignity, just treatment, and equality before the law. The terms ethics and morality are often used interchangeably. It is useful, however, to make some distinction: morality is regarded as something personal, while ethics is the standards of good and bad agreed upon by the community or society.[488]

Küng believes that this basic morality which contains the minimum requirements fundamental to human existence is acceptable worldwide. However, for issues such as democracy or euthanasia, which are culturally conditioned, a consensus is not required. Notwithstanding our differences in political, social or religious orientation, Küng maintains that a minimal consensus regarding core moral values can serve as a basis for human flourishing, as demonstrated by the existence of the Golden Rule in all the major religious traditions.

Hans Küng's Insight and Foresight

Morality and ethics are linked to the concept of the human person and reason. These concepts provide the basic foundation for a society to function smoothly and the necessary discipline for culture and tradition to flourish. In Chapter 4, we have examined how the Protestant work ethic is related to the spirit of capitalism, as Max Weber held. Morality and ethics help us to resolve specific issues in life so, as society evolves, we

---

[487] Küng, *A Global Ethic for Global Politics and Economics*, p. 95. 'We may call morality the inner dimension of humanity that one finds in individual persons and ethics the outer dimension of humanity that one finds in human societies.' See Chung-ying Cheng, 'Integrating the Onto-Ethics of Virtues (East) and the Meta-Ethics of Rights (West)', *Dao: A Journal of Comparative Philosophy* 1, no. 2 (June 2002), p. 158.

[488] 'What's the Difference Between Morality and Ethics?' https://www.britannica.com/story/whats-the-difference-between-morality-and-ethics.

need to update and revise them in response to new challenges brought by advancements in science and technology. We have seen that some basic rules and practices from the past are still with us, and sometimes they are incorporated into our current lifestyle. Contemporary ethics return to the past to formulate new norms to deal with our current problems. In fact, moral theories and practices have historical roots going back to Plato, Aristotle, Confucius, Mencius, etc. Classical authors are indispensable resources for the formulation of new rules and regulations for our modern-day society.

It is important to acknowledge the plurality of our society, and the diversity of moral and ethical traditions existing in our world. In the West, the emphasis is on the ethics of rights, which seems to be individualistic and might lose sight of the big picture. Hans Küng reminds us to think of our responsibilities before our rights, requiring us to have a broader understanding of humanity in view of the many complex moral issues we are now facing, such as the arms race, trade wars, pollution, violations of human rights, etc. The threat of globalization has pushed some people to return to their roots. This search for indigenous traditions has been transformed into 'an awareness and assertiveness of cultural values and religion as sources of self-respect and self-affirmation'.[489] In fact, globalization has led to a renewed interest in native cultures and indigenous traditions as a protection against the onslaught of Western domination and liberalism.

Given the above, Küng, with keen insight and foresight, has performed an important task for humanity in establishing a global ethic, one that is informed by Eastern and Western ethical and religious traditions. This combination of resources provides us with a point of reference in the search for solutions to our current crises. Küng's call for a world ethic has given us a new horizon and helped create dialogues informed by the perspectives of Eastern and Western ethical and cultural traditions. The Chinese philosopher Cheng Chung-ying calls it 'a fusion of perspectives in ethical traditions'.[490] Its common basis is *humanum*. As we gain greater awareness of our moral and religious values, we recognize that what unites us is greater than what divides us.

Hans Küng's passing on 6 April 2021 is a great loss for humanity.

---

[489] Cheng, 'Integrating the Onto-Ethics of Virtues (East) and the Meta-Ethics of Rights (West)', p. 159.

[490] Cheng, 'Integrating the Onto-Ethics of Virtues (East) and the Meta-Ethics of Rights (West)', p. 159.

Topics for discussion and reflection

- What do you think of the author's proposition on the barriers to formulating a global ethic?
- Riding on the shoulders of Küng, the author argues that our moral and religious values unite us rather than divide us. Do you agree? Please discuss.
- Several religious traditions are briefly discussed in this chapter. Pick one religion that you deem as having the highest chance of positively contributing to fostering trust and being a bridge to build a common global ethic.

Epilogue

Focusing on Christianity, this work aims to explore religious issues and controversies in our pluralistic society, including how religion shapes culture, and the role and value of religion in the modern world. Topics such as religious commitment and tolerance, attitudes towards other religions, sociological aspects of faith, interreligious dialogue, syncretism, and dual religious citizenship are examined critically. Over the past decade, many religions have shifted the focus of dialogue from doctrinal comparison to global or common issues, such as ecological problems, globalization, medical ethics, etc., attempting to see whether different religious resources can tackle these problems and contribute to a solution.

In the conclusion of this work, I would like to reflect on what Christianity, or, more precisely, what the Christian faith means to me. A few months ago, I visited an 87-year-old lady upon the request of her two daughters, who are devout Catholics. The daughters are keen to have their mother baptized. As their priest, they want me to convince their mother of the joy of being a Christian. However, the mother is rather reluctant, for good reasons. She said to me honestly that she has been praying to Guanyin (觀音), the bodhisattva of infinite compassion and mercy in Chinese Buddhism, and it has worked for her all these years. Besides, if she switches religion, Guanyin would feel betrayed and hurt, and it is not fair. I understand and respect her convictions. Why should she give up her faith in Guanyin, who is so much part of her Chinese upbringing, for a bearded Mediterranean deity nailed to a cross? So I told the daughters not to push for baptism or coerce the mother to be a Catholic. I am convinced of this: to the extent that the daughters show love and care for their mother, she will find God in their religion.

Our Christian faith is a vision of how a human being can live his or her life to the fullest. As St Irenaeus (130-c. 202) said, 'The glory of God is a person fully alive' (*Gloria Deo homo vivens*); this comes about when he or she is full of love. Unfortunately, 'love' in English is an ambiguous word. Influenced by the media, pop songs, and Korean movies, our understanding of love tends to be rather narrow or confined. Sometimes we use the word 'charity' in place of love. Unfortunately, 'charity' has been institutionalised, like dropping a coin into a tin can on a Saturday morning at the train station for some organization seeking funds. We need a stretch of imagination to connect this act with love. So *what is love?*

The ancient Greeks were more sophisticated in their understanding of love. The Greek word that John uses in his gospel is *agape*. C.S. Lewis (1898–1963), a well-known Christian writer, wrote a thin volume called *The Four Loves* based on Hellenistic philosophy. He discusses four different ways of loving: Storge (στοργή) or affection; *Philia* (φιλία) or friendship; Eros (ἔρως) or romantic love; and Agape (ἀγάπη) or divine love. Storge or affection is to love someone as the result of familiarity. We are fond of each other because we get along well, share some common interests or agree on many issues. It could be the love of a mother for her child. This kind of love is the most natural and covers a wide array of positive feelings about people and things. *Philia* is the love between friends, quite like the relationship between husband and wife in a healthy marriage. This strong and stable bond exists between people who share common values. Eros is the feeling between lovers, like Shakespeare's *Romeo and Juliet*, which suggests strong passion and physical attraction. The word 'erotic' is derived from eros. Finally, agape is the unconditional love of God: it is a love that remains faithful regardless of what happens. Such is the love the Father shows in the parable of the Prodigal Son.

John the Evangelist says that where there is love, there is God. He does not say where there are Christians, there is God, nor does he say where there is a church, there is God. However, if a person is filled with *agape*-love for others, God is there. This is the meaning of the Good Samaritan: he is called *good* not because he is religious but because he reaches out in compassion even to someone who is supposed to be his enemy. So we can find *agape* or God in people who may not be Christians or who may have no religious belief at all. When there is compassion, truth, justice and peace, God reigns.

Joseph Ratzinger's first encyclical as Pope Benedict XVI, *Deus caritas est*, is about love: God is love. The Pope makes it clear in this encyclical that *eros* cannot simply be reduced to human love, and *agape* is not simply God's love. Eros is not merely human love but is already touched by the divine, and thus, the world is never merely the world. In the light of the doctrine of creation, the world is a sign of God's love. Therefore the secularist's desire to remove all references to the Creator in order to liberate the world is misleading. It subverts the proper understanding of God as Creator and undermines a proper understanding of the world.[491] If secularism prevails and Christianity is removed from the public sphere, then religion will be privatized in our pluralistic society. However, Pope Benedict believes Christianity has something important and relevant to say to human beings that will stand the test of time – Christianity speaks of human love as both a universal and a uniquely individual experience.

Hence, we should not separate the spiritual from the secular because *agape* comes to heal human *eros*, not destroy it. Ratzinger deals with these two aspects in the context of the famous *Song of Songs*: 'Love now becomes concern and care for the other. No longer is it self-seeking, a sinking in the intoxication of happiness; instead it seeks the good of the beloved: it becomes renunciation and it is ready, and even willing, for sacrifice.'[492] *Agape* neither destroys *eros* nor leaves it to its own devices. In other words, we should not try to separate the spiritual from the temporal as if they were antithetical.

Ratzinger shows that Christianity is beneficial to human beings as human beings. Therefore, it has the right and duty to spread its influence as far as it can, while simultaneously acknowledging the independence of the secular order. *Agape* does not wish to impose itself on *eros*, for Jesus did not use force to establish his kingdom. Ratzinger affirms that human *eros* is already touched by *agape*. This means that 'insofar as *eros* is distinctively human, and insofar as human beings are created in God's image, human love finds its origin and true end in divine love.'[493] The connection between *eros* and *agape* made by Ratzinger is also an attempt to bridge the gap between nature and grace. Natural order is not destroyed by its closeness to the supernatural order but rather, is preserved by it.

Regarding secularism's fear of religion interfering in worldly affairs, Ratzinger proclaims true love does not wish to absorb the otherness of the other. God is love and he loved the world so much that he was willing to die for us: *Deus caritas est*. Christianity teaches that all human beings are free, and therefore Hegel considered it as superior

---

[491.] Rodney Howsare, 'Why Begin with Love? *Eros*, *Agape* and the Problem of Secularism', *Communio* 33, no. 3 (Fall 2006), p. 436.

[492.] *Deus caritas est*, http://www.vatican.va/holy_father/benedict_xvi/encyclicals/documents/hf_ben-xvi_enc_20051225_deus-caritas-est_en.html.

[493.] Howsare, 'Why Begin with Love?', p. 446.

to all other historical religions. Despite its decreasing influence in the West, Christianity continues to flourish in Asia, Africa, and Latin America. In whatever form it takes and wherever it flourishes, this faith has offered hope and inspiration to millions of people in their sufferings and struggles. Christianity is here to stay.

Bibliography

Abbott, Lyman. *The Evolution of Christianity*. Vol. 1. Cambridge Library Collection - Religion. Cambridge: Cambridge University Press, 2009. doi:10.1017/CBO9780511692741

Ad Gentes, On the Mission Activity of the Church. http://www.vatican.va/archive/hist_councils/ii_vatican_council/documents/vat-ii_decree_19651207_ad-gentes_en.html

Allen, John L., Jr. *Pope Benedict XVI*. New York, NY: Continuum, 2000

An-Na'im, Abdullah Ahmed. 'Qur'an, Shari'a and Human Rights: Foundations, Deficiencies and Prospects.' In *The Ethics of World Religions and Human Rights*, edited by Hans Küng and Jürgen Moltmann. *Concilium*. London; Philadelphia, PA: SCM Press; Trinity Press International, 1990: pp. 61–9

Apostolic Exhortation, *Evangelii Gaudium* of The Holy Father Francis to the Bishops, Clergy, Consecrated Persons and the Lay Faithful on the Proclamation of the Gospel in Today's World. https://www.vatican.va/content/francesco/en/apost_exhortations/documents/papa-francesco_esortazione-ap_20131124_evangelii-gaudium.html

Aquinas, Thomas. *Summa Theologiae*. 2nd and revised edition. London: Burns Oats & Washbourne, 1920. https://www.newadvent.org/summa/

Arens, Edmund. 'Religion as Ritual, Communicative, and Critical Praxis.' In *The Frankfurt School on Religion: Key Writings by the Major Thinkers* edited by Eduardo Mendieta. New York, NY: Routledge, 2005: pp. 373–96

Assmann, Jan. *Moses the Egyptian: The Memory of Egypt in Western Monotheism*. Cambridge, MA: Harvard University Press, 1998.

———. *Of God and Gods: Egypt, Israel, and the Rise of Monotheism*. George L. Mosse Series in Modern European Cultural and Intellectual History. Madison, WI: University of Wisconsin Press, 2008.

———. *The Price of Monotheism*. Stanford: Stanford University Press, 2009

Athanassiadi-Fowden, Polymnia, and Michael Frede. *Pagan Monotheism in Late Antiquity*. Oxford; New York, NY: Clarendon Press; Oxford University Press, 1999

Bates, M. Searle, and International Missionary Council. *Religious Liberty: An Inquiry*. New York, NY; London: International Missionary Council, 1945

Bautista, Julius. 'The Rebellion and the Icon: Holy Revolutions in the Philippines.' *Asian Journal of Social Science* 34, no. 2 (2006): pp. 291–310

Benedict XVI. 'The Church and the Challenge of Secularization.' *Christ to the World* 53 (September 2008): pp. 389–92

———. 'Healthy Secularism for a Peaceful Coexistence.' *Osservatore Romano* 2070 (Weekly edition in English), (19 November 2008), p. 6

———. 'Meeting with the Representatives of Science (Regensburg Lecture).' http://www.vatican.va/holy_father/benedict_xvi/speeches/2006/september/documents/hf_ben-xvi_spe_20060912_university-regensburg_en.html

———. Declaration *Dominus Iesus* on the Unicity and Salvific Universality of Jesus Christ and the Church. http://www.vatican.va/roman_curia/congregations/cfaith/documents/rc_con_cfaith_doc_20000806_dominus-iesus_en.html

Benjamin, Walter. 'Capitalism as Religion.' In *The Frankfurt School on Religion: Key Writings by the Major Thinkers*, edited by Eduardo Mendieta. New York, NY: Routledge, 2005: pp. 259–62

Berger, Peter L. *A Rumor of Angels: Modern Society and the Rediscovery of the Supernatural*. 1st edn. Garden City, NY: Doubleday, 1969.

———. *The Sacred Canopy: Elements of a Sociological Theory of Religion*. New York, NY: Anchor Books, 1990

Beyers, J. 'Obituaries and Predictions: A Sociological Perspective on the Future of Religion.' *Acta Theologica* 33, no. 1 (2013): pp. 1–28

Boer, Roland. 'Opium, Idols and Revolution: Marx and Engels on Religion.' *Religion Compass* 5, no. 11 (2011): pp. 698–707

Boff, Leonardo. *Church: Charism and Power – Liberation Theology and the Institutional Church*. London: SCM Press, 1984

———. *Trinity and Society*. Theology and Liberation Series. Maryknoll, NY: Orbis Books, 1988

Borgman, Erik, Maria Clara Bingemer, and Andrés Torres Queiruga, eds. *Monotheism: Divinity and Unity Reconsidered*. Concilium, 4. London: SCM Press, 2009

Borowitz, Eugene B. 'The Torah, Written and Oral, and Human Rights: Foundations and Deficiencies.' In *The Ethics of World Religions and Human Rights*, edited by Hans Küng and Jürgen Moltmann. *Concilium*. London; Philadelphia, PA: SCM Press; Trinity Press International, 1990: pp. 25–33

Bowman, Jonathan. 'Extending Habermas and Ratzinger's *Dialectics of Secularization*: Eastern Discursive Influences on Faith and Reason in a Postsecular Age.' *Forum Philosophicum* 14 (2009): 39–55

Brahm Levey, Geoffrey and Tariq Modood. *Secularism, Religion and Multicultural Citizenship*. Cambridge: Cambridge University Press, 2009

Callisen, Christian Thorsten. 'Georg Calixtus, Isaac Casaubon, and the Consensus of Antiquity.' *Journal of the History of Ideas* 73, no. 1 (2012): pp. 1–23

Casanova, José. 'The Secular and Secularisms.' *Social Research* 76 (Winter 2009): pp. 1049–66
———. 'The Secular, Secularizations, Secularisms.' In *Rethinking Secularism*, edited by Craig Calhoun, Mark Juergensmeyer and Jonathan VanAntwerpen, pp. 54–74. Oxford: Oxford University Press, 2011
Chadwick, Owen. *The Secularization of the European Mind in the Nineteenth Century*. Cambridge: Cambridge University Press, 1975
Cheetham, David. 'Inclusivisms: Honouring Faithfulness and Openness.' In *Christian Approaches to Other Faiths*, edited by Alan Race and Paul M. Hedges. London: SCM Press, 2008: pp. 63–84
Cheng, Chung-ying. 'Integrating the Onto-Ethics of Virtues (East) and the Meta-Ethics of Rights (West).' *Dao: A Journal of Comparative Philosophy* 1, no. 2 (June 2002): pp. 157–84
'Church in the World.' *The Tablet*. https://thetablet.co.uk/article/1866
Clooney, Francis Xavier. 'Dialogue Not Monologue: Benedict XVI & Religious Pluralism.' *Commonweal* (October 21, 2005) pp. 12–17
Collinson, Patrick. 'Religion, Society, and the Historian.' *Journal of Religious History* 23, no. 2 (1999): pp. 149–67
Congar, Yves. 'Classical Political Monotheism and the Trinity.' In *God as Father?*, edited by Johannes Baptist Metz, Edward Schillebeeckx and Marcus Lefébure. *Concilium*, 143. Edinburgh: T. & T. Clark; New York, NY: Seabury Press, 1981 pp. 31–6
Cornille, Catherine. 'Introduction.' In *Many Mansions? Multiple Religious Belonging and Christian Identity*, edited by Catherine Cornille. Maryknoll, NY: Orbis Books, 2002: pp. 1–6
———. 'Introduction: On Hermeneutics in Dialogue.' In *Interreligious Hermaneutics*, edited by Catherinec Cornille and Christopher Conway. Eugene, OR: Cascade Books, 2010: pp. ix-xxi
Coward, Harold. *Pluralism in the Word Religions*. Oxford: Oneworld Publications, 2000.
D'Costa, Gavin. *The Meeting of Religions and the Trinity*. Maryknoll, NY: Orbis Books, 2000
———. *Theology and Religious Pluralism*. Oxford: Basil Blackwell, 1986
Dallavalle, Nancy A. 'Cosmos and Ecclesia: A Response to Richard Lennan.' *Philosophy & Theology* 17 (1 January 2005) pp. 279–91
Dawkins, Richard. *The God Delusion*. New York, NY: Houghton, Mifflin, Harcourt, 2006
'Deus Caritas Est.' (25 December 2005) http://www.vatican.va/holy_father/benedict_xvi/encyclicals/documents/hf_ben-xvi_enc_20051225_deus-caritas-est_en.html
Dingayan, Luna. 'Popular Religion and Evangelization: A Philippine Experience.' *International Review of Mission* 82, no. 327 (1993): pp. 355–63
Droogers, André. 'Syncretism: The Problem of Definition, the Definition of the Problem.' In *Dialogue and Syncretism: An Interdisciplinary Approach*, edited by Jerald D. Gort, Hendrik M. Vroom, Rein Fernhout, and Anton

Wessels, pp. 7–25. Grand Rapids, MI: William B. Eerdmans Publishing Company, 1989

Dupuis, Jacques. 'The CDF Declaration *Dominus Iesus* and My Perspective on It.' In *Jacques Dupuis Faces the Inquisition: Two Essays by Jacques Dupuis on Dominus Iesus and the Roman Investigation of His Work*, edited by William R. Burrows. Eugene. OR: Pickwick Publications, 2012: pp. 26–73.

———. *Toward a Christian Theology of Religious Pluralism*. Maryknoll, NY: Orbis Books, 1997

Durkheim, Émile. *The Elementary Forms of Religious Life*. Translated by Carol Cosman. Edited by Mark Sydney Cladis. Oxford World's Classics. Oxford: Oxford University Press, 2008

El-Ojeili, Chamsy, and Patrick Hayden, eds. *Critical Theories of Globalization*. Basingstoke: Palgrave Macmillan, 2009

Erlewine, Robert. 'Samuel Hirsch, Hegel, and the Legacy of Ethical Monotheism.' *The Harvard Theological Review* 113, no. 1 (2020): pp. 89–110

Fenn, Richard K. 'Toward a Global Ethic: A Response to Hans Küng.' *International Journal of Politics, Culture, and Society* 13, no. 1 (1999): pp. 41–61

Forst, Rainer. *Toleration in Conflict: Past and Present*. Ideas in Context. Cambridge: Cambridge University Press, 2013

Fowden, Garth. *Empire to Commonwealth: Consequences of Monotheism in Late Antiquity*. Princeton, NJ: Princeton University Press, 1993

Fürst, Alfons. 'Monotheism between Cult and Politics: The Themes of the Ancient Debate between Pagan and Christian Monotheism.' In *One God: Pagan Monotheism in the Roman Empire*, edited by Stephen Mitchell and Peter Van Nuffelen. Cambridge: Cambridge University Press, 2010: pp. 82–99. doi:10.1017/CBO9780511730115.006

Garaudy, Roger. 'Human Rights, Islam: Foundation, Tradition, Violation.' In *The Ethics of World Religions and Human Rights*, edited by Hans Küng and Jürgen Moltmann. *Concilium (Glen Rock, NJ); 1990/2, London: Philadelphia, PA: SCM Press; Trinity Press International, 1990: pp. 46–60

Geffré, Claude. 'Double Belonging and the Originality of Christianity as a Religion.' In *Many Mansions? Multiple Religious Belonging and Christian Identity*, edited by Catherine Cornille. Maryknoll, NY: Orbis Books, 2002: pp. 93–105

Gibert, Pierre. 'Introduction.' In *Monotheism: Divinity and Unity Reconsidered*, edited by Erik Borgman, Maria Clara Bingemer, and Andrés Torres Queiruga. *Concilium*, 4. London: SCM Press, 2009

Glenn, Gary D. 'Is Secularism the End of Liberalism? Reflections on Europe's Demographic Decline Drawing on Pope Benedict, Habermas, Nietzsche and Strauss.' *Catholic Social Science Review* 13 (2008): pp. 91–116

Gnuse, Robert Karl. *No Other Gods: Emergent Monotheism in Israel*. London: Bloomsbury Publishing, 1997

Goldstein, Warren S. 'Patterns of Secularization and Religious Rationalization in Émile Durkheim and Max Weber.' *Implicit Religion* 12, no. 2 (2009): pp. 135–63

Gort, Jerald D. 'Syncretism and Dialogue: Christian Historical and Earlier Ecumenical Perceptions.' In *Dialogue and Syncretism: An Interdisciplinary Approach*, edited by Jerald D. Gort, Hendrik M. Vroom, Rein Fernhout, and Anton Wessels. Grand Rapids, MI: William B. Eerdmans Publishing Company, 1989: pp. 36–51

Gort, Jerald D., Hendrik M. Vroom, Rein Fernhout, and Anton Wessels, eds. *Dialogue and Syncretism: An Interdisciplinary Approach*. Grand Rapids, MI: William B. Eerdmans Publishing Company, 1989

Gregory XVI. *Mirari vos* (On Liberalism and Religious Indifferentism). https://www.papalencyclicals.net/greg16/g16mirar.htm, nos. 13, 14, 15

Griffiths, Paul J. *Problems of Religious Diversity*. Oxford: Blackwell Publishers, 2001

Habermas, Jürgen and Joseph Ratzinger. *The Dialectics of Secularization*. Translated by Brian McNeil, C.R.V. San Francisco, CA: Ignatius Press, 2006

Hastings, Adrian. *A History of English Christianity, 1920–1990*. London: SCM Press, 1991

'Healthy Secularism for a Peaceful Coexistence.' *L'Osservatore Romano*, (Wednesday, 19 November 19 2008), p. 6

Hedges, Paul. *Controversies in Interreligious Dialogue and the Theology of Religions*. London: SCM Press, 2010

———. 'A Reflection on Typologies: Negotiating a Fast-Moving Discussion.' In *Christian Approaches to Other Faiths*, edited by Alan Race and Paul M. Hedges. London: SCM Press, 2008: pp. 17–33

Hegel, Georg Wilhelm. *Lectures on the Philosophy of Religion, 1: Introduction and the Concept of Religion*, edited by Peter C. Hodgson. Oxford: Oxford University Press, 1963

Heim, S. Mark. *Salvations*. Maryknoll, NY: Orbis Books, 1995

Hick, John. *An Interpretation of Religion: Human Responses to the Transcendent*. 2nd edn. Basingstoke: Palgrave Macmillan, 2004

———. *Problems of Religious Pluralism*. London: Macmillan Press Ltd, 1985.

———. *The Rainbow of Faiths*. London: SCM, 1995

Hintze, Almut. 'Monotheism the Zoroastrian Way.' *Journal of the Royal Asiatic Society* 24, no. 2 (2014): pp. 225–49

Horii, Mitsutoshi. 'Historicizing the Category of "Religion" in Sociological Theories: Max Weber and Émile Durkheim.' *Critical Research on Religion* 7, no. 1 (2019): pp. 24–37

Howsare, Rodney. 'Why Begin with Love? *Eros, Agape* and the Problem of Secularism.' *Communio* 33, no. 3 (Fall 2006): pp. 423–48

Hoyer, Theodore. 'Religious Peace of Augsburg.' *Concordia Theological Monthly* 26, no. 11 (November 1955): pp. 820–30

Hudson, Clement Wayne. 'The Enlightenment Critique of "Religion".' *Australian E-Journal of Theology* 5, no. 1 (2005): pp. 1–12

Huntington, Samuel P. *The Clash of Civilizations and the Remaking of World Order*. New York, NY: Simon & Schuster, 2011

Hurtado, L.W. 'First-Century Jewish Monotheism.' *Journal for the Study of the New Testament* 21, no. 71 (1999): pp. 3–26

'In Spain, Pope Benedict XVI Lambasts "Aggressive Secularism".' *The Christian Science Monitor*. 7 November 2010http://www.csmonitor.com/World/Europe/2010/1107/In-Spain-Pope-Benedict-XVI-lambasts-aggressive-secularism

James, William. *The Varieties of Religious Experience*. N. p.: Philosophical Library/Open Road, 2015

John Paul II. Centesimus Annus, http://www.vatican.va/content/john-paul-ii/en/encyclicals/documents/hf_jp-ii_enc_01051991_centesimus-annus.pdf

———. Redemptoris Missio. http://www.vatican.va/holy_father/john_paul_ii/encyclicals/documents/hf_jp-ii_enc_07121990_redemptoris-missio_en.html

Keir, Jonathan. 'From Religion to Business.' *The Journal of Corporate Citizenship* 2016, no. 62 (2016): pp. 131–42

Kelly, Conor M. 'The Nature and Operation of Structural Sin: Additional Insights from Theology and Moral Psychology.' *Theological Studies* 80, no. 2 (June 2019): pp. 293–327

Knitter, Paul F. *Introducing Theologies of Religions*. Maryknoll, NY: Orbis Books, 2002

Komulainen, Jyri. 'Raimon Panikkar's Cosmotheandrism: Theologizing at the Meeting Point of Hinduism and Christianity.' *Exchange* 35, no. 3 (2006): pp. 278–303

Kraemer, Hendrik. 'Syncretism.' In *Syncretism in Religion: A Reader*, edited by Anita Maria Leopold and Jeppe Sinding Jensen. Sheffield: Taylor & Francis Group, 2004; pp. 39–47

Küng, Hans. *A Global Ethic for Global Politics and Economics*. New York, NY: Oxford University Press, 1998

———. *Global Responsibility: In Search of a New World Ethic*. New York, NY: Continuum, 2001

———. *The Incarnation of God: An Introduction to Hegel's Theological Thought as Prolegomena to a Future Christology*. New York, NY: Crossroad, 1987

———. *What I Believe*. London; New York, NY: Continuum, 2010

Küng, Hans, and Jürgen Moltmann. *The Ethics of World Religions and Human Rights. Concilium, 2*. London; Philadelphia, PA: SCM Press; Trinity Press International, 1990

Lai, Pan-chiu. 'Barth's Theology of Religion and the Asian Context of Religious Pluralism.' *Asia Journal of Theology* 15 (1 October 2001): pp. 247–67

Lang, Bernhard. 'No God but Yahweh! The Origin and Character of Biblical Monotheism.' In *Monotheism*, edited by Claude Geffré and Jean Pierre

Jossua. *Concilium: Religion in the Eighties*, 177. Edinburgh: T. & T. Clark, 1985: pp. 41–9

Laursen, John Christian, and Cary J. Nederman, eds. *Beyond the Persecuting Society: Religious Toleration Before the Enlightenment*. Philadelphia, PA: University of Pennsylvania Press, 1997

Laursen, John Christian, and Maria José Villaverde, eds. *Paradoxes of Religious Toleration in Early Modern Political Thought*. Lanham, MD: Lexington Books, 2012

Leopold, Anita Maria, and Jeppe Sinding Jensen. *Syncretism in Religion: A Reader*. Sheffield: Taylor & Francis Group, 2004

Levine, Baruch A. 'Tolerance in Ancient Israelite Monotheism.' In *Religious Tolerance in World Religions*, edited by Jacob Neusner and Bruce Chilton. West Conshohocken: Templeton Press, 2009: pp. 15–27

Luckmann, Thomas. *The Invisible Religion: The Problem of Religion in Modern Society*. New York, NY: Macmillan, 1967

Lumen Gentium. Dogmatic Constitution on the Church. http://www.vatican.va/archive/hist_councils/ii_vatican_council/documents/vat-ii_const_19641121_lumen-gentium_en.html

Luzbetak, Louis J. *The Church and Cultures: New Perspectives in Missiological Anthropology*. American Society of Missiology Series; No. 12. Maryknoll, NY: Orbis Books, 1988

Macdonald, Charles J-H. 'Folk Catholicism and Pre-Spanish Religions in the Philippines.' *Philippine Studies* 52, no. 1 (2004): pp. 78–93

Madsen, Richard. 'Secularism, Religious Change, and Social Conflict in Asia.' In *Rethinking Secularism*, edited by Craig Calhoun, et al.. Oxford: Oxford University Press, 2011; pp. 248–69

Marx, Karl and Friedrich Engels. *On Religion*. New York, NY: Schocken Books, 1964

McGovern, Arthur F. 'Atheism: Is It Essential to Marxism?' *Journal of Ecumenical Studies* 22, no. 3 (1985): pp. 487–500

McGrath, James F. *The Only True God: Early Christian Monotheism in Its Jewish Context*. Baltimore, MD: University of Illinois Press, 2009

McIlhenny, Ryan C., ed. *Render unto God: Christianity and Capitalism in Crisis*. Newcastle-upon-Tyne: Cambridge Scholars Publisher, 2015

McKenna, Mary Frances. 'A Consideration of Christianity's Role in a Pluralistic Society.' *The Way* 55, no. 4 (October 2016): pp. 31–47

McKim, Robert. *On Religious Diversity*. Oxford: Oxford University Press, 2012

Mendieta, Eduardo, ed. *The Frankfurt School on Religion: Key Writings by the Major Thinkers*. New York, NY: Routledge, 2005

Mensching, Gustav. *Tolerance and Truth in Religion*. Tuscaloosa, AL: University of Alabama Press, 1971

Metz, Johannes Baptist, Edward Schillebeeckx, and Marcus Lefébure, eds. *God as Father? Concilium*, 143. Edinburgh: T. & T. Clark; New York, NY: Seabury Press, 1981

Mitchell, Stephen, and Peter van Nuffelen. *One God: Pagan Monotheism in the Roman Empire*. Cambridge; New York: Cambridge University Press, 2010

Moltmann, Jürgen. 'The Inviting Unity of the Triune God.' In *Monotheism*, edited by Claude Geffré and Jean Pierre Jossua. Concilium: Religion in the Eighties. Edinburgh: T. & T. Clark, 1985: pp. 50–8

Mong, Ambrose Ih-Ren. *Accommodation and Acceptance: An Exploration in Interfaith Relations*. Cambridge: James Clarke & Co. 2015

———. *Are Non-Christians Saved?: Joseph Ratzinger's Thoughts on Religious Pluralism*. London: Oneworld Publications, 2015

———. 'Crossing the Ethical-Practical Bridge: Paul Knitter's Regnocentrism in Asian Perspective.' *The Ecumenical Review* 63 (July 2011): pp. 186–99

———. *Dialogue Derailed: Joseph Ratzinger's War Against Pluralist Theology*. Cambridge: James Clarke & Co., 2015

———. 'Is There Room for Christ in Asia?' *Toronto Journal of Theology* 31, no. 2 (Fall 2015): pp. 223–37

———. *Power of Popular Piety: A Critical Examination*. Eugene, OR: Cascade Books, 2019

Mukerji, Bithika. 'The Foundations of Unity and Equality: A Hindu Understanding of Human Rights.' In *The Ethics of World Religions and Human Rights*, edited by Hans Küng and Jürgen Moltmann. Concilium (Glen Rock, NJ); 1990/2, London; Philadelphia, PA: SCM Press; Trinity Press International, 1990: pp. 70–8

Murray, Donal. 'The Secular Versus Religion?' *Origins* 37 (6 December 2007): pp. 411–17

Nederman, Cary J. 'Introduction: Discourses and Contexts of Tolerance in Medieval Europe.' In *Beyond the Persecuting Society: Religious Toleration Before the Enlightenment*, edited by John Christian Laursen and Cary J. Nederman. Philadelphia, PA: University of Pennsylvania Press, 1997: pp. 13–24

Nemoianu, Virgil. 'The Church and the Secular Establishment: A Philosophical Dialog between Joseph Ratzinger and Jürgen Habermas.' *Logos* 9 (Spring 2006): pp. 17–42

Neusner, Jacob, and Bruce Chilton, eds. *Religious Tolerance in World Religions*. West Conshohocken, PA: Templeton Press, 2009

Newman, Jay. *Foundations of Religious Tolerance*. Toronto; Buffalo: University of Toronto Press, 1982

O'Collins, S.J., *The Second Vatican Council on Other Religions*. Oxford: Oxford University Press, 2013

O'Leary, Joseph Stephen. *Religious Pluralism and Christian Truth*. Edinburgh: Edinburgh University Press, 1996

———. 'Toward a Buddhist Interpretation of Christian Truth.' In *Many Mansions? Multiple Religious Belonging and Christian Identity*, edited by Catherine Cornille. Maryknoll, NY: Orbis Books, 2002: pp. 29–43

Panikkar, Raimon. *The Intrareligious Dialogue*. New York, NY: Paulist Press, 1999

———. *The Unknown Christ in Hinduism*. London: Darton, Longman & Todd, 1981

Paul VI. *Declaration of Religious Freedom: Dignitatis Humanae*. http://www.vatican.va/archive/hist_councils/ii_vatican_council/documents/vat-ii_decl_19651207_dignitatis-humanae_en.html

———. 'Nostra Aetate: Declaration on the Relations of the Church to Non-Christian Religion.' (28 October 1965):. Online: http://www.vatican.va/archive/hist_councils/ii_vatican_council/documents/vat-ii_decl_19651028_nostra-aetate_en.html: p. 2

Phan, Peter C. 'Doing Theology in the Context of Cultural and Religious Pluralism: An Asian Perspective.' *Louvain Studies* 27 (2002): pp. 39–68

———. 'Multiple Religious Belonging: Opportunities and Challenges for Theology and Church.' *Theological Studies* 64, no. 3 (2003): pp. 495–519

Plato. *Laws*. Trans. Benjamin Jowett. N. p.: Xist Publishing, 2016

———. *Timaeus*. Trans. Benjamin Jowett. Urbana, IL: Project Gutenberg, 1998. Accessed 20 January 2021

Pope Benedict XVI Warns against "Aggressive Secularism" in Britain.' *The Daily Telegraph*. 16 September 2010. http://www.telegraph.co.uk/news/newstopics/religion/the-pope/8006272/Pope-Benedict-XVI-warns-against-aggressive-secularism-in-Britain.html

Race, Alan. *Christians and Religious Pluralism*. Maryknoll, NY: Orbis Books, 1982

Race, Alan and Paul M. Hedges, eds. *Christian Approaches to Other Faiths*. London: SCM Press, 2008

Rahner, Karl. *Foundations of Christian Faith*. New York, NY: The Crossroad Publishing Company, 2010

Ramachandra, Vinoth. 'Learning from Modern European Secularism: A View from the Third World Church.' *European Journal of Theology* 12 (1 January 2003) pp. 35–48

Ratzinger, Joseph. *Christianity and the Crisis of Cultures*. Translated by Brian McNeil. San Francisco, CA: Ignatius Press, 2006

———. *Handing on the Faith in an Age of Disbelief*. Translated by Michael J. Miller. San Francisco, CA: Ignatius Press, 2006

———. *Introduction to Christianity*. Translated by J.R. Foster. San Francisco, CA: Ignatius Press, 2004

———. *Many Religions – One Covenant*. Translated by Graham Harrison. San Francisco, CA: Ignatius Press, 1999

———. *The Nature and Mission of Theology: Approaches to Understanding Its Role in the Light of Present Controversy*. Translated by Adrian Walker. San Francisco, CA: Ignatius Press, 1995

———. *Pilgrim Fellowship of Faith*. San Francisco, CA: Ignatius Press, 2005

———. *The Ratzinger Report*. Translated by Salvator Attanasio and Graham Harrison. San Francisco, CA: Ignatius Press, 1985

———. *Truth and Tolerance*. Translated by Henry Taylor. San Francisco, CA: Ignatius Press, 2004

Ratzinger, Joseph and Marcell Pera. *Without Roots*. Translated by Michael F. More. New York, NY: Basic Books, 2007
Rausch, Thomas P. *Pope Benedict XVI: An Introduction to His Theological Vision*. New York, NY: Paulist Press, 2009
Rhonheimer, Martin. 'Christian Secularity, Political Ethics and the Culture of Human Rights.' *Josephinum Journal of Theology* 16 (Summer-Fall 2009): pp. 320–38
Rodney Stark. 'SSSR Presidential Address, 2004: Putting an End to Ancestor Worship.' *Journal for the Scientific Study of Religion* 43, no. 4 (2004): pp. 465–75
Ruggieri, Giuseppe. 'God and Power: A Political Function of Monotheism?' In *Monotheism*, edited by Claude Geffré and Jean Pierre Jossua. *Concilium: Religion in the Eighties*, 177. Edinburgh: T. & T. Clark, 1985: pp. 16–27
Ruse, Michael. *Monotheism and Contemporary Atheism. Elements in Religion and Monotheism*. Cambridge: Cambridge University Press, 2019. doi:10.1017/978110875835
'Ryōbu Shintō.' *Encyclopedia Britannica*. 19 July 2017. https://www.britannica.com/topic/Ryobu-Shinto
Sacred Congregation for the Doctrine of the Faith. 'Declaration.' https://www.vatican.va/roman_curia/congregations/cfaith/documents/rc_con_cfaith_doc_19791215_christi-ecclesia_en.html
Saint Augustine. *The City of God*, Books VIII-XVI. The Fathers of the Church: A New Translation. Washington, DC: Catholic University of America Press, 2008
Sala-Boza, Astrid. 'Towards Filipino Christian Culture: Mysticism and Folk Catholicism in the Señor Sto. Niño de Cebu.' *Philippine Quarterly of Culture and Society* 36, no. 4 (2008): pp. 281–308
Schall, James V. 'The Regensburg Lecture: Thinking Rightly about God and Man.' (15 September 2006). http://www.ignatiusinsight.com/features2006/schall_regensburg_sept06.asp
Schillebeeckx, Edward. *Church: The Human Story of God*. New York, NY: Crossroad Publishing Company, 1990
Schmidt-Leukel. 'Pluralism: How to Appreciate Religious Diversity Theologically.' In *Christian Approaches to Other Faiths*, edited by Alan Race and Paul M. Hedges. London: SCM Press, 2008: pp. 85–110
Schreiter, Robert J. *Constructing Local Theologies*. 30th anniversary edition. Maryknoll, NY: Orbis Books, 2015
———. *The New Catholicity: Theology between the Global and the Local*. Maryknoll, NY: Orbis Books, 1997
Screech, M.A. *Ecstasy and the Praise of Folly*. London: Duckworth, 1980
Sheridan, Daniel P. 'Faith in Jesus Christ in the Presence of Hindu Theism.' In *The Intercultural Challenge of Raimon Panikkar*, edited by Joseph Prabhu,. Maryknoll, NY: Orbis Books, 1996: 145–61
Shorter, Aylward. *Toward a Theology of Inculturation*. Maryknoll, NY: Orbis Books, 1988

Sivaraksa, Sulak. 'Human Rights in the Context of Global Problem-Solving: A Buddhist Perspective.' In Hans Küng and Jürgen Moltmann, eds., *The Ethics of World Religions and Human Rights,*. Concilium (Glen Rock, NJ); 1990/2, London; Philadelphia, PA: SCM Press; Trinity Press International, 1990: pp. 79–91

Sloterdijk, Peter. *God's Zeal: The Battle of the Three Monotheisms.* English edn. Cambridge; Malden, MA: Polity, 2009

Soldan, F. Louis. 'God as the Eternally Begotten Son.' *The Journal of Speculative Philosophy* 16, no. 2 (1882): pp. 171–94

Sontag, Frederick E, and John K Roth. 'Is the Criticism of Religion the Premise of All Criticism?' *Philosophy of Religion and Theology: 1976 Proceedings*, edited by Peter Slater,. Missoula: Scholars Press of for the American Academy of Religion, 1976: pp. 104–14

Stanford Encyclopedia of Philosophy. *Seneca.* https://plato.stanford.edu/entries/seneca/

Stark, Rodney. *One True God: Historical Consequences of Monotheism.* Princeton, NJ: Princeton University Press, 2001

Stewart, Charles and Rosalind Shaw, eds. *Syncretism/Anti-syncretism: The Politics of Religious Synthesis.* European Association of Social Anthropologists. London; New York, NY: Routledge, 1994

Strauss, Leo. *Natural Right and History.* Chicago, IL: The University of Chicago, p. 195

Sullivan, Francis. *Salvation outside the Church? Tracing the History of the Catholic Response.* New York, NY: Paulist Press, 1992

Tanner, Kathryn. *Theories of Cultures.* Minneapolis, MN: Fortress Press, 1997.

Taylor, Charles. *A Secular Age.* Cambridge, MA: The Belknap Press of Harvard University Press, 2007

Tillich, Paul. *The Future of Religions.* Edited by Jerald C. Brauer. New York, NY: Harper & Row, 1966

Turchetti, Mario. 'Religious Concord and Political Tolerance in Sixteenth- and Seventeenth- Century France.' *The Sixteenth Century Journal* 22, no. 1 (1991): pp. 15–25

Van der Veer, Peter. 'Syncretism, Multiculturalism, and the Discourse of Tolerance.' In *Syncretism and Anti-Syncretism*, edited by Charles Stewart and Rosalind Shaw. London: Routledge, 1994: pp. 196–212

Vattimo, Gianni. *After Christianity.* Translated by Luca D'Isanto. New York, NY: Columbia, 2002

———. *Belief.* Translated by Luca D'Isanto and David Webb. Stanford, CA: Stanford University Press, 1999

———. 'A "Dictatorship of Relativism"? Symposium in Response to Cardinal Ratzinger's Last Homily.' *Common Knowledge* 13 (2007) pp. 214–18

———. *The Transparent Society.* Translated by David Webb. Cambridge: Polity Press, 1992

Venter, Rian. 'Reflections on Schleiermacher's God.' *Hervormde Teologiese Studies* 75, no. 4 (2019): pp. 1–6

Vernon, Richard. 'Locke: A Letter Concerning Toleration.' In *Locke on Toleration*, edited by Richard Vernon. Cambridge Texts in the History of Philosophy. Cambridge: Cambridge University Press, 2010: pp. 3–46

Wacker, Marie-Theres. 'Biblical Monotheism between Dispute and Re-vision: Christian and Old Testament Viewpoints.' In *Monotheism: Divinity and Unity Reconsidered*, edited by Erik Borgman, Maria Clara Bingemer, and Andrés Torres Queiruga, *Concilium*, 4. London: SCM Press, 2009

Walf, Knut. 'Gospel, Church, Law and Human Rights: Foundations and Deficiencies.' In Hans Küng and Jürgen Moltmann, eds, *The Ethics of World Religions and Human Rights*. *Concilium (Glen Rock, NJ); 1990/2, London: Philadelphia, PA: SCM Press; Trinity Press International, 1990: pp. 34–46

Walsh, Gerald G., and Grace. Monahan. *The City of God*. Books VIII-XVI, 2008

Ward, Keith. 'G. W. Friedrich Hegel.' Chapter in *Religion in the Modern World: Celebrating Pluralism and Diversity*. Cambridge: Cambridge University Press, 2019: pp. 103–11

Weber, Max. *Protestantische Ethik und der Geist des Kapitalismus*. Florence: Taylor & Francis Group, 2001

———. *The Sociology of Religion*. Beacon Series in the Sociology of Politics and Religion. Boston, MA: Beacon Press, 1964

Wen, Haiming, and William Keli'i Akina. 'A Naturalist Version of Confucian Morality for Human Rights.' *Asian Philosophy* 22, no. 1 (2012): pp. 1–14

'What's the Difference Between Morality and Ethics?' https://www.britannica.com/story/whats-the-difference-between-morality-and-ethics

Wildman, Wesley J. 'Reader's Guide to Schleiermacher's Christian Faith.' *Friedrich Schleiermacher Resources Site*, http://people.bu.edu/wwildman/schl/cfguide/cfguide_para01.htm. Accessed 6 June 2021

Wooden, Cindy. 'Bishops Recall Fr. Hans Küng as Theologian Who Loved Catholic Church.' *National Catholic Reporter*. https://www.ncronline.org/news/people/bishops-recall-fr-hans-k-ng-theologian-who-loved-catholic-church

Zagorin, Perez. *How the Idea of Religious Toleration Came to the West*. Princeton, NJ: Princeton University Press, 2005

Index

Ad Gentes, 60, 72-73
Adorno, Theodor, 82
Age of Discovery, 8
Ahab, 16
Ahura Mazdā, 17,
Akhenaten (Amenophis IV), 17
Albigensian heresy, 38
anthropology, 52-54
anti-Semitism, 50, 165
apostasy, 32
Aquinas, Thomas, 38, 42, 92
Arabic, 105
Aristotle, 4, 179
Arius, 130
Asherah, 16, 19
Asian Bishops' Conference (FABC), 59
Assyria, 19
Athanasius, 130
atheists, 23, 43, 127, 154
Athens, 29, 142
atman, 161-162
Augustine, St., 10, 12-13, 40

Baal, 16, 54
Babylonian Captivity, 20
Barth, Karl, 134-136
Benjamin, Walter, 93
Berger, Peter, 97-98, 104
blaspheme, 47
Boff, Leonardo, 25-26, 72
Brahman, 26, 161

Brazil, 73
Buddhism, 3, 50, 60-62, 86, 89, 92, 102, 128, 131, 143, 154, 162-163, 171, 173, 181

Calixtus, George, 56-57
Calvin, 7, 44, 46-47
Calvinism, 44, 47, 93-94
Canaan, 9, 11
capitalism, 75, 92-96, 99, 119-120, 176, 178
Catholicism, 17, 37, 44, 56, 67-69, 71-73, 78, 103-104
Cebu, 67-68, 70
Charles V, 45
Chemosh, 18
Christendom, 37-38, 105
Christocentrism, 140
Church Dogmatics, 134, 136
Colonization, 8
communion, 25-26, 55
Confucianism, 3, 61-62, 89, 102, 128, 131, 154, 165, 173, 177
Constantinople, 36, 166
Covid-19, 4, 177
Cuius regio, eius religio, 45
cult, 9, 11-13, 16-17, 19, 21, 23, 35, 47, 61, 69, 83-94, 90, 93

Dao, 26, 164
Daoism, 26
Dawkins, Richard, 23

Decalogue., 19
Decius, 34
Deus terrenus., 26
Deuteronomy, 17, 19, 32
Deutro-Isaiah, 17, 21
dharma, 133, 161, 170
Dialectic, 2-3, 14, 29-30, 45, 71, 76-78, 86, 120
Dialectics of Secularization, 3, 102, 113, 124
Dignitatis Humanae, 49
Diocletian, 34
discourse, 3, 23, 57, 123, 126, 139, 147
Dominus Iesus, 144-145
Duke of Saxony, 46
Durkheim, Émile, 76, 84-90, 96-98

ecclesia non sitit sanguinem, 38
ecclesiocentrism, 140
ecumenism, 140
Engels, Friedrich, 3, 76-81, 95
Enlightenment, 1, 4, 33, 47, 50, 55, 64, 80, 106-108, 120-122, 136, 140, 148, 158, 161
Erasmus, Desiderius, 41-43, 51, 55-56
Eusebius, 22
Exclusivism, 26, 129, 131-136, 140, 147
Ezra, 11

fanaticism, 8, 41, 166
Feuerbach, Ludwig, 76, 155
forgiveness, 26, 31, 36, 39
Fourth Lateran Council, 38
Francis, Pope, 144
Frankfurt School, 81-82, 121
fundamentalism, 8, 166-167

Geffré, Claude, 151-152
Geneva, 46-47
genocide, 34
Germany, 43, 46, 113, 155
Global Ethic, 5, 153-156, 165, 169, 170, 172, 174, 176-177, 179-180
Global Responsibility, 153-154

globalization, 114, 118, 121, 123, 179, 181
Greeks, 24, 29, 35, 78, 149, 159, 175, 182
Gregory XVI, 49

Habermas, Jürgen, 3, 102, 113-124
Hebrew, 9-11, 33, 150
Hedges, Paul, 58, 132
Hegel, Friedrich, 13-14
Hegelian dialectic, 2, 29
Henry the Navigator, 8
Heresy, 37-40, 42, 45-46, 94, 130
Hezekiah, King, 16
Hick, John, 139-141, 148
Hinduism, 24, 26, 50, 62-65, 89, 92, 131, 143, 154, 161-162, 171, 173, 177
Holy Office, 37-38, 45
Hong Kong, 10-11, 173
Horkheimer, Max, 82
Hosea, 16

immigrants, 3-4
Inclusivism, 129, 132-133, 137-138, 147
Innocent IV, Pope, 38
Inquisition, 29, 36-40, 45
Institutes of the Christian Religion, 44
interreligious dialogue, 3, 29, 83, 112, 126, 144-146
intolerance, 3, 9, 29-32, 36, 38, 40, 43, 45, 47-51, 106, 113, 117-118, 167
Isidore of Seville, 37

Jephthah, 18
Jeremiah, 16, 32
Jerusalem, 16, 18, 21, 33, 166
Jezebel, 16
jihad, 159
John XXIII, Pope, 158
Jonah, 32-33, 55
Judah, 15-16, 19

Index

Judaism, 8, 12, 14-15, 23, 25, 37, 54, 92, 129, 154-155, 157, 159, 166, 171, 177
Judeo-Christian tradition, 4, 86
Julian, Emperor, 36

Kilat, Leon, 70-71
Kingdom of God, 22, 47, 130
kinship, 19, 60, 91
Kraemer, Hendrik, 56
Küng, Hans, 4-5, 153-156, 165-170, 173-180

Lactantius, 39
Late Antiquity, 12, 23
Law of Ravenna, 39
Letters on Toleration, 47
Locke, John, 47-48, 51
Logos, 4, 22, 26, 63, 130, 138, 147,
love, 10, 25, 29, 34, 36, 39, 41-42, 51, 55, 74, 87, 93, 115-116, 125, 137-138, 140, 157, 163-164, 170, 172, 175, 181-183
Lumen Gentium, 142-143
Luther, Martin, 42-43, 46, 51, 92-93
Lutheranism, 44, 92

Magellan, 67-68
Magic, 36, 84, 87, 90-92, 97
Mahayana, 61
Marx, Karl, 2-3, 75-77, 79-81, 95, 155
McGovern, Arthur, 80
Metaphysics, 109, 111, 150
Minimal Basic Consensus, 169-170
Mirari vos, 49
Moltmann, Jürgen, 15, 23
money, 38, 84, 95
monotheism, 7-10, 12-15, 17-27, 31-32, 36, 56, 136
Moralia, 55
More, Thomas, 41-43, 51
Moses, 18-20, 32, 50, 159
Mount Sinai, 20

Nebuchadnezzar, King, 17
Neoplatonic Hellenism, 36

New Testament, 41, 74, 116, 134, 138, 150, 170
Newman, John Henry, 1, 104
Nicholas of Cusa, 41
Nietzsche, Friedrich, 116
Nostra Aetate, 49, 142-143
noumenal Real, 140

O'Leary, Joseph, 133,147
Old Testament, 10, 17-18, 21, 25, 29, 32, 54, 84, 88, 110, 115, 150, 170
ontology, 109, 111, 128

Pacem in Terris, 158
pagan, 16, 22-23, 43, 54-55, 57, 68, 92
Panikkar, Raimon, 62-65, 74
Paul III, Pope, 44-45
Paul IV, Pope, 45
Persia, 15, 17
pessach, 20
Philo of Alexandria, 22
Plato, 4, 12, 29-30, 179
Platonists, 12-13
Polytheism, 7-11, 14-15, 18-19, 22-25, 27, 29, 32, 36, 56, 69
Popper, Karl, 31
praxis, 83, 113
profane, 85-88, 127,
Protestant Ethic and the Spirit of Capitalism, 93-94

Qur'an, 160, 170

Rahner, Karl, 137-138
Ratzinger, Joseph, 50, 102-104, 106-111, 113, 115-121, 123-127, 129, 132-133, 136, 144-151, 182-183
Reformation, 7, 30, 40, 42-47, 54, 56, 93, 104, 150, 158
Religious pluralism, 3, 18, 61, 97, 101-102, 104, 109, 126, 128-129, 132, 139, 144, 147, 168,
Rhonheimer, Martin, 104, 107
Roman Empire, 12, 22-23, 30, 34-35, 53, 79

Rome, 9, 36, 59, 62, 79, 131
Ryōbu Shintō, 60

sacred, 16, 26, 38, 67, 75, 85-88, 91, 94, 98, 106, 112, 122, 127, 143, 155, 160, 161, 167, 169, 172
Sanskrit, 105
Santo Niño, 67-71
Schillebeeckx, Edward, 131
Schreiter, Robert, 58-59
Secularisation, 98, 128
Secularism, 3, 84, 98, 101-106, 109, 113, 115-116, 120, 123-128, 158, 183
Seneca, 12
Shangdi, 7
Shingon Shintō, 60
sinulug, 68
Sisebut, 37
slavery, 19, 78-80
Socrates, 29
solidarity, 4, 31, 51, 76-77, 113, 115, 120, 123, 169-170, 175, 177-178
Solomon, King, 21
sorcery, 90-91
Spain, 37, 62, 69-70, 103, 165
Strauss, Leo, 116-117
Summa Theologiae, 38
Supreme Being, 42, 55, 68
Syllabus of 1864, 49
Syncretism, 3, 29, 51, 53-55, 57-60, 62, 64-67, 69, 71-74, 181

Taiping Revolutionary, 7
Taoism, 3, 61, 89, 102, 128, 131, 154, 171
Tarshish, 32
theocentrism, 140
Theodosian Code, 36-37
Theodosius, 36
Thich Nhat Hanh, 162-163
Thirty-Year War (1618–1648), 7
tiandao, 164
tolerance, 3, 7, 18, 29-36, 41-51, 56, 116-117, 122-123, 133, 139, 145-146, 169, 181
totem, 88, 91
Tres de Abril, 70-71
Trinity, 10, 25-27

United Kingdom, 3, 103
United States, 4, 93-94, 176
Unknown Christ of Hinduism, 63, 65
Utopia, 42-43

Vattimo, Gianni, 111-112, 115
violence, 4, 9, 36-37, 40-43, 112, 117, 159, 167
Virgin Mary, 17

Weber, Max, 3, 76, 89-94, 97-98, 178
Wong Tai Sin (黃大仙), 10

Yahweh, 11, 15-21, 32-33, 54-55
yoruba, 73

Zoroastrianism, 15, 17, 92

You may also be interested in:

Theology and Society in Three Cities:
Berlin, Oxford and Chicago, 1800-1914
Mark D. Chapman

Berlin, Oxford and Chicago were extraordinarily dynamic centres of theology during the nineteenth and early twentieth centuries. However, significant differences in the political climate and culture of each location bred strikingly divergent theological approaches in the universities of each city. Mark Chapman offers a highly original exploration of the subjection of their theologies to the changes and developments of educational policy and national and international politics, shedding light upon the constraints that such external factors have imposed upon the evolution of the discipline.

Chapman highlights the efforts of theologians and churchmen to relate the true core of Christianity, a lived religion free of shibboleths, to their rapidly changing world. The opinions of conservative and liberal theologians are skilfully balanced to reveal the problems of critical history, of political authority, of increasing global awareness and of the need for social amelioration, which profoundly shaped the ways in which theology was conceived during the period.

New ground has been broken in this inter-disciplinary study of the social, political and ecclesiastical contexts of Western theology. This book will be invaluable to any reader interested in the use of theology as part of the wider quest for social integration and meaning in an increasingly fragmented society.

"Essential reading for students of modern theology as well as for intellectual and cultural historians."
Thomas Albert Howard, Director, Center for Faith and Inquiry, Gordon College, Wenham.

Mark D. Chapman is Vice Principal of Ripon College, Cuddesdon and Reader in Modern Theology in the University of Oxford. He has written widely on the history and theology of Anglicanism as well as in Church History and Political Theology. He is also assistant priest in three rural Church of England parishes. He is a member of the General Synod of the Church of England.

First published by James Clarke & Co., 30 October 2014

Paperback ISBN: 978 0 227 67989 0
PDF ISBN: 978 0 227 90246 2
ePub ISBN: 978 0 227 90247 9